The Mangaliks of Meerut and Lucknow:
A Century of Change

Dr. Aroop Mangalik

Copyright © 2013 Dr. Aroop Mangalik
All rights reserved.

ISBN: 1-4792-9514-0
ISBN-13: 9781479295142

DEDICATION

I dedicate this book to my son, Dr. Saurabh Mangalik, who is now the caretaker of this history. May he be as proud of his heritage as I am of him.

ACKNOWLEDGEMENTS

This book is a collection of memories. Memories from a long time ago. They were "notes" which I discussed at different times with my family who provided important additions, corrections, and different perspectives. My sister Meera, who died in September 2011, was the eldest of my siblings. She and her husband Kishin, who has known the family for over sixty-five years, encouraged me and provided a lot of information that has been incorporated in this book. My brother, Lt. Gen. Ashok Mangalik, Neetu as he is known to everyone, provided a major change in my perspective on Papa. Without him, this would have been a somewhat unbalanced picture. Mohini, technically a cousin's wife, has served as trusted confidant over the years. During the writing of this book her knowledge of the family and her training as a Professor of English made the information more coherent.

Aftab Ahmed Ali, brother of my best friend Salman, provided interesting insight into the life and history of his family and of Muslims in the part of India where I grew up.

I have always struggled with the English language; its formal rules do not always correspond to my own personal style. However, the writing in this book is mine, the style is mine. Cynthia Barber has done a great job of editing the book, getting all the details right and keeping me on track. She tried to improve on my writing style, but I felt it should be my style. Without her, this book would not have reached completion.

Nila Judd, over the years, typed and retyped what I wrote on used paper. She dealt with my poor handwriting and unclear instructions.

I thank you all for bringing this project to completion.

Aroop Mangalik

Table of Contents

Part One: From the *Galis* of Meerut to Rockefeller Center   1
    Chapter One: Early Life and Career   3
    Chapter Two: Papa the Person   11
    Chapter Three: Changes in the Medical World   27
       Medicine   27
       Medical Education   36
       Twenty Years at Lucknow   40

Part Two: The People and Their Ideas   47
    Chapter Four: Family   49
    Chapter Five: Ancestors   73
    Chapter Six: Politics   79
    Chapter Seven: Amma's Family   85
    Chapter Eight: Friends   91

Part Three: The City   97
    Chapter Nine: General Life in Lucknow   99
    Chapter Ten: Sociology and Religion   105
    Chapter Eleven: The Neighborhood   123
    Chapter Twelve: The Home - Nandinee   137

Part Four: The School and Education   167
    Chapter Thirteen: Colvin Taluquedar's College   169
    Chapter Fourteen: Education As I See It Now   205

Appendix - *Seven Gifts of Life*, Address to Final Year Students by Dr. V.S. Mangalik, King George's Medical College, Lucknow.
February 1950   207

PART ONE
FROM THE *GALIS* OF MEERUT TO ROCKEFELLER CENTER

Chapter One
Early Life and Career

This is the story of a man born at the beginning of a new century, who lived through changes in the world that are hard to relate to – some things that we take for granted today were just not there when the story begins. The beginning of the century to the freedom of India and the social changes it brought about are also a part of this story. From the life in a small town in western United Provinces to the creation of a center of excellence in a medical college in the renamed state of Uttar Pradesh was a part of the change seen by my father, who was also responsible for some of those changes.

Meerut as spelled by the British was really Mae ruth (u as in Rush) in Hindi. It was a small place but has been in the history books because some historians place the origins of the 1857 revolt against the British to this town's cantonment. Historians continue to debate what to call the events of 1857. Mutiny, revolt, war of independence, national war of independence are suggested by different historians as the true events of May of that year. The revolt they say was triggered by the introduction of a new cartridge for the Enfield rifle used at that time and which was "embalmed" in pig/cow fat. Pig fat, cow fat or not, the fact remains that a major part of this town's recognition comes from that year. After that it does not appear in any major historical context nor does it become prominent in other ways.

Ours was a family that traced its origins to the village of Dasna (Kasna) in Bullandshahar. Dasna is about 30 miles from Meerut and 20 miles from Delhi. The family did fairly well and in the 18th century is said to have had a *haveli* (mansion) near the Jama Masjid in Delhi. One of my ancestors was a magistrate. In the 1890s my grandfather was a deputy collector. He was promoted to that position by a *Saheb* (British Civilian Officer) who liked him. By all accounts that was a high position for an Indian to hold at that time. Apart from his position and that he owned a house in Meerut, little has been said about him. The house was in the old part of the city, reached by series of *galis* (lanes) winding through the city.

There was a large wooden gate into the property and in the gate was a door that was used for daily in and out activities. It led into an antechamber part of which was raised and then onto courtyards and rooms beyond. There was a well in one corner of the courtyard. There was little privacy, as most rooms did not have doors. There was no plumbing and no electricity.

In January of 1900, Papa was born in this house. He was the third son of Baba ji and Maa ji. Baba ji died the year Papa was born. With that, the family lost its income and probably some of its prestige and power. The eldest brother, Madan Mohan Saran, who was twelve, took on the responsibility of the family. He supported the younger ones' education. He joined the government service and continued in that role through World War II when he retired as a deputy collector's rank (assistant district rationing officer).

The two younger brothers pursued their education in Meerut, going to the well known Nanak Chand High School and Intermediate College. When Papa signed up for the high school board examination his name was registered as Vanmali Saran Mangalik. The Mangalik came from our gotra (sub-caste) Mangal with an emphasis on the first "a" to say manga lik. The name was chosen by the middle brother, Murari Saran, who was and remained, the most creative and artistic member of the family. The gotra and village name is how one tracks down the family history through the pandas at Haridwar. More on that later.

MS Mangalik, Chote Babujee, the second of the three brothers, studied Sanskrit and education and obtained a scholarship to go to England in the twenties. He got a diploma in education and returned to join the U.P. state education department, becoming head of Government Colleges, Teacher's Training Colleges, and Inspector of Schools. He had an encounter in England with a woman who claimed to photograph "spirits." He brought home photographs of the spirit of his sister-in-law who had died while he was in England. Many in the family seemed to accept the images as the real thing. However, a book published in 2005 exposed this Mrs. Deane as one of the great frauds of England.

The youngest brother, Vanmali Saran Mangalik (Papa), pursued a career in medicine. All this with the help of his eldest brother who himself earned very little. I recently read a biography of Madam Marie Curie and noted a remarkable similarity to my family. Marie's family in Poland was also poor. Her brothers and sisters sacrificed their own careers and sent her to Paris to study and she went on to be one of the greatest scientists in history and the only person to have won two Nobel Prizes in the same field. (Linus Pauling won two Nobel Prizes, one in chemistry and one for peace.) It is worth noting here that, as was common in those days, the wives of the two brothers, who excelled in their fields, had limited educational opportunities. The two younger brothers, once they completed their education, helped and supported the eldest all through their lives,.

Papa entered Lucknow Medical College, King George's Medical College, graduated in 1925, and got an M.D. in Pathology, also from Lucknow. He was interested in pursuing a career in academic medicine. Jobs in the medical college in those days were mostly given to British members of the Indian Medical Service. These IMS doctors were usually not specialists. By virtue of their position in the IMS they were given different assignments; they taught in the medical college and also went on other postings. The professor of pathology - or any field - was not necessarily a specialist in the field.

Since he could not find a job in the medical college in pathology, Papa went into the Provincial Medical Services and worked as a general practitioner in small towns in UP. He took care of cataracts, general day to day problems and some specialized problems as they were presented to him. He described how he operated on a few goat eyes and then did cataract surgery on people but I do not know what kinds of results he got. He even described how he did surgery for bladder stones with no training and had some complications. After a few years he saved enough money and received a scholarship to go to the London School of Postgraduate Medicine where he obtained a Diploma in Clinical Pathology. He had the privilege of working with professor E.J. King, a pioneer in the field.

On returning to India he taught at the Agra Medical School. This was one of the institutions in India that awarded a Licentiate in medicine - a degree more suited to providing medical care for common every day diseases. After a few years there he found an opening at Lucknow Medical College, which until then had only British professors but was now recruiting Indians. He became a reader in pathology and moved to Lucknow. His career and life seemed ready to take off. He rented a house in a relatively new and nice area near the University. There was a lot of land and the area was near but not at the end of town. Lucknow was small in those days, so the medical college was about a fifteen minute drive, Hazratgunj was about the same. The club was conveniently located so he could stop there for tennis on the way back from work or go back after returning home. His mentor and guru Dr. J.G. Mukherjee lived nearby, as did his friend and colleague from the medical college, Dr. Bir Bhan Bhatia.

The University was close by so many of the faculty lived on campus; others lived in his neighborhood of New Hyderabad. The old Hyderabad was primarily the campus of the Colvin Taluqedar's College, meant originally for the children of big landowners but which opened to non-taluqedars about that time. Papa had a wife and three children now, a garden, friends, and family in town.

Photograph of our family a few years before Amma's death, the only photograph of all five of us together. I am the one on my father's lap.

Then Amma got very ill. She developed an acute gallbladder infection that spread into the blood. Papa probably performed the blood culture test. His friends Dr. Bhatia and Dr. S.N. Mathur were the treating physicians. These were the days before antibiotics and a positive blood culture was a death sentence. Amma was ill for a while with nurses at home and was finally admitted to the hospital. She died in the hospital. My sister Meera, the eldest, did go to visit her, but could not go in to see her. We two younger boys stayed with Babujee, our uncle.

Things changed drastically with Papa now being left to take care of three children below the age of ten, while establishing a new life and a new job in a new place. Soon after Amma's death, the two boys developed diphtheria, another serious disease in the days before the availability of antibiotics. All this happened in quick succession. How he coped probably only he knew. He never talked about it. But the family pitched in. Our cousins came to stay with us to help run the house and to take care of us while they were getting their education; Papa supported their education. Also, Babujee's wife, Chachee, helped with our nursing when we were sick.

Life went on as it has to. His career was on track; he was teaching, mentoring students and was a part of the KGMC family. There were sports activities, hare and hounds races, picnics and gatherings at home. The college being small — 250 odd students and 30-40 faculty members — everyone knew everyone. We children participated in many of these activities and went to functions at the college and the department. Meera, the eldest, had gone away for her high school in Benaras, at the well known Annie Besant school.

The boys went to Colvin, which was in the neighborhood, and added to the feelings of the extended family. Many of the teachers from Colvin lived in the neighborhood and became a part of the family and Papa's friends. Papa's mentor, Dr. Mukherjee, was his guide in gardening and his overall advisor but did not get into medical college issues. He came to the house regularly for a morning cup of tea and to discuss improvements in the garden.

We were ahead of our times in many ways. Apart from being well to do (house, garden, servants, car), we were progressive and well known in the city. One cousin was a lecturer in Obstetrics and Gynecology, the first woman doctor in the extended Vaish, Gupta, Agarwal, Mithal clan. The other girls received postgraduate education and studied in Shanti Niketan, literally at the feet of Gurudev Rabinder Nath Tagore, India's first Noble Laureate.

A digression is in order regarding Papa's meeting with Gurudev. I do not know of the exact circumstances of the meeting but when Papa was introduced to Gurudev as "DOCTOR Mangalik" Tagore asked, "Are you a real doctor or a fake one like me?" An incident he did not forget and nor have I.

We were recognized in the shops in Hazartgunj and could buy provisions at Balujas or books at the Universal Book Depot by just going there with no signature apart from our name and face. In terms of creature comforts, we had a phone and could ask the operator to connect us to our friends by giving the name only. We had a Frigidaire, a car, a room for each of us.

Papa was well known for his interests in the broader aspects of medicine, science and life in general. He had a lot of books and so did we. We were encouraged, even forced, to read and write reports. This led to our being broad based in our education. He played tennis at the club and we were encouraged to participate in a variety of sporting activities. We (Papa, Neetu, and I) were enthusiastic and good but none of us excelled in any sports. Papa's interest and knowledge in science and literature and in gardening led to an invitation to give radio talks on All India Radio, and we were allowed to go to the studio and sit and watch.

At a personal level and socially, there were ups and downs. Whether because of his domestic situation or because of pressures or because of his inherent nature, Papa could be a difficult person. Along with his emphasis on education, progressive (even revolutionary) thinking, and excellence in work, he was prone to periods of moods. For days, sometimes more than a week, he would speak to no one or speak only to point out faults and problems. At work and home, we all felt the tension, the pressure, the fear. Elaborate strategies were planned by us at home and by people at work to avoid him or his wrath. When not in such moods, life was interesting, stimulating, even fun.

In 1946, when Papa was forty six, Dr. Abdul Hamid the head of pathology retired,, and Papa stepped into his position. In the subsequent 2-3 years he instituted a number of changes and improvements in the pathology department and the medical college that gained him recognition at the national level. India became independent in 1947, and major changes occurred in the country - including those in medicine and medical education.

The American establishment was looking for a foothold in the Indian subcontinent. In 1948, the Rockefeller Foundation sent a delegation of Indian physicians, including Papa, to the U.S.A. for six months. It was a deluxe tour - literally. They traveled first class, stayed in fancy hotels and met top people from first rate medical schools. They even traveled first class on the Queen Mary and met Paul Robeson, a famous black singer. This was the first step in the entry of American Medicine into India. The American influence led to changes in medical education, medical economics and general thinking in medical schools in India. The changes were incremental but the seeds were sown then. In the mid '50s the Rockefeller Foundation increased its presence even more. It funded many programs including the All India Institute of Medical Sciences in New Delhi and a residency program at K.G.M.C. in Lucknow.

Papa in the First Class Lounge of R.M.S. Queen Mary.

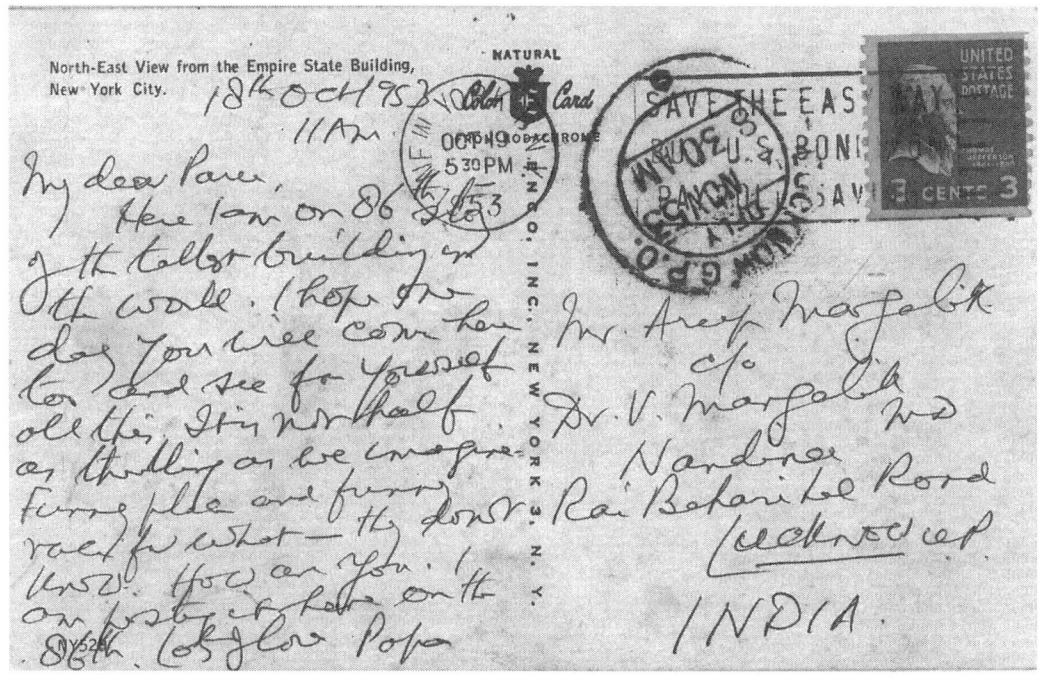

Postcard sent from the Empire State Building.

A number of top executives from Rockefeller visited Lucknow Medical College and Nandinee (our home). The upshot was that Rockefeller gave a large grant to K.G. Medical College with the condition that Mangalik be the head of the program. He had made his connection with the Rockefellers.

This is the brief story from the *Galis* of Meerut to Rockefeller Center. I would like to go further and expand on it. What was life like in Meerut, Lucknow? What was medicine like? What changes occurred in education, science and politics? How did the families change?

***

Chapter Two
Papa the Person

He was Papa to the three of us and, interestingly, a few others also called him that. Mostly he was Chacha ji to a wide circle of friends who were influenced by our cousins. I said "cousins," but that would not be acceptable to the family. When our grandfather died soon after Papa was born, Papa's brother, twelve years old at the time, took on the responsibility of raising and supporting the family. It could not have been an easy life, but they all worked hard and focused on education. In turn, Papa helped in the education of his nephew and five nieces. They were very much a part of the family, so "cousins" is not a term we used. Those six children called him Chacha ji, and so did a series of friends and their families; even the parents of the friends called him Chacha ji. So he became "Chacha ji" to a large circle in Lucknow. The emphasis on education, despite limited resources, culminated in Chote Babuji getting a doctorate in education and Papa becoming a doctor.

Papa did talk about some ways he economized. He had two pairs of trousers and he pressed them by putting them under his pillow at night. Beyond that no one talked about being poor. He had ambitions for academic medicine and got an M.D. in Pathology. However, for about ten years he had to work in the U.P. as a regular doctor posted to small towns. He described some medical experiences he had with cataract surgery and bladder stones in those years. He must have saved some money and ten years after medical college, with encouragement from one of his professors (Col. Stott), he went to England and obtained a Diploma in Clinical Pathology. Soon after he returned from England he became a Reader in Pathology at Lucknow Medical College. From then on his life changed and we grew up comfortably. He was able to help with the schooling of our cousins; we all had a good education and our generation has done well.

I remember Papa telling me, (when I was a teenager and he was in a good mood), how spoiled I was as a two year old. He had left for England for his DCP degree soon after I was born and I was brought up in the permissive environment of "Kothi," my mother's home in Meerut. I became part of a joint family with lots of kids and parents doing their own thing; discipline was a low priority. They did not follow the rules of British child rearing. When Papa returned, we moved. I had been spoiled. He told me that on a few occasions I got a spanking and then I was ok. Pasha, my own son, was never spanked but had a fairly strict upbringing. However, let me say that in 1973 when he was five and I was a single parent for a year I was criticized by some friends for being too lenient and by others for being too strict with him. So I followed Papa somewhat, but not fully.

The memories I have of Amma are limited: one of her being in the house and one of her at a party we had at Nandinee. It was during the monsoon, there was a real downpour, and there were a lot of goodies served. I remember Mrs. Bhatia being dropped off at the bougainvilla archway and running in. Like many of these memories, I have no greater context, perspective, or continuity.

I have patchy memories of Amma's illness and death. I remember her being brought back from the hospital by ambulance. The ambulance was driving very slowly because of the rutted, rough roads. She was brought on a stretcher through the front gallery door. Someone said they took an X-ray of the back and here and there because the night nurse or someone thought she had pain in some part of her body.

Nobody told me of her death. I think she must have died in the hospital. In school Neetu was informed by his classmates that his mother had died and Mr. Bharadwaj consoled him. I watched Neetu being consoled by Mr. Bharadwaj while I had no sense of personal loss. It was like "Neetu's mother had died." Years later, Hem ji ji told me that she had septicemia and she was pregnant.

Much later, when we were in our seventies, Meera described her experience of Amma's death. She recalls going to see her at the hospital but not being able to go into her room. Soon after that she was sent to boarding school. When she returned home, age eleven, she asked, "Where's Amma?" It was then she learned that Amma had died a few months earlier. Communication about death was limited then and remained so at the time of Papa's death twenty years later, and does so now.

My childhood was definitely a strictly controlled one. The explanation of why Papa was strict and serious is probably that he wanted us to do well in life. He came from a background of some property but because of his father's early death they had little money. By hard work (and of course help from his eldest brother) he came up in life. In his forties he had just become a reader in the only Medical College in the state and the second or third oldest in the country. He was ambitious, and he succeeded in becoming not only dean and principal, but a nationally recognized figure. He had the Edwardian colonists as his role model; these doctors and military men were his professors and had their rules about behavior and bringing up children. Discipline was certainly high on their priority list.

Then again he was a single parent. He had help from our cousins, who were eight to fifteen years older then I, but he was the one who had to set the tone and the rules. Last but not least he was straddling two worlds: the world of Meerut and a joint family system where few rules reigned, and the world run by disciplined, ambitious people.

Papa had a hard façade, an air of being unreachable, and was generally strict. One can focus on the sternness but it is also worthwhile to remember his background, his own ambitions and achievements, and what he wanted for us. His performance in Medical College, and his later building up of the department of Pathology and the Medical College are clear indications of his intelligence and capability. In order to achieve his goals, he worked hard and expected others to do the same. His early upbringing shaped his values of honesty and fairness. His interactions with his British professors and seniors probably modified his style and demeanor. He did follow the British mode of dress and style and he was "proper."

Unlike our friends Salman and Aftab and Ravi and Shashi, we needed to ask permission for anything out of the routine. They would tell their parents that they were going to a movie or to a friend's house. We had to ask permission for similar activities. As a result, I missed some perfectly legitimate and appropriate activities because I was afraid to ask for permission.

The strictness and discipline showed itself in a variety of ways. Timing and punctuality were one part of it. We went to bed, got up, went to school, went for sports, did our homework, and had dinner at pretty fixed times. We had to account for our time; deviations were questioned, as was a change in routine. We ate properly, dressed properly and talked properly. (None of this is wrong and has done me well in life. Yet, I can't help thinking if it would have been easier if it were not so.)

Papa continued to work hard, and the department was recognized and designated as an upgraded department of Pathology. It's MDs and DCPs seeded medical colleges all over the country with top professors. The same was true for the Medical College as a whole.

I now see the origin of his values as a boy from a landed family from Meerut who grew up with limited resources but retained a strong sense of the importance of hard work and education. These values fitted well with the British emphasis on ambition and achievement. Of course in the thirties and forties, the British style was also a necessary part of the culture. He acquired the British traits, but with a style different from the "Brown Saheb." He spoke Hindi with a standard U.P accent. He spoke English well but with an Indian accent (except for a few western U.P pronunciations like "eskool" — school). He had the best western clothes but wore *kurta* pajamas at home. He liked western classical music but occasionally played the harmonium and tabla. He attempted to teach my brother and sister some Hindustani music. Tension between the western and Indian culture must have been there. His attitudes about politics and being ingratiating to politicians, I think came from the simple life of Meerut and the values of the Indian Medical Services' British doctors. He fought for his cause but did not grovel before the Health Minister or other politicians for personal gain.

At a personal level it is difficult for me to reconstruct and interpret events of so long ago. Nevertheless, in some ways the personal is what is most meaningful. Papa was widowed at forty-one with three children. He had support from the family for taking care of us. He also had the means to have a good lifestyle.

How did he manage the issue of values and how did he balance his own life with that of the children? He had the rules, which we observed and that allowed him to feel comfortable that we would not stray. Yes, he admonished me on a few occasions — something I resented. But I think he was aware of where we were and what we were up to. I did a few naughty things but within the physical and emotional confines of a *Laxman Rekha* (defined limits). We had tea and dinner together on a regular basis; we did have conversations at meals, and we had company at meals. But we also had times when there was tension. In some ways those days stand out in our memory, but I am sure the reasons were complex and communication was insufficient to break the ice.

The regular meals did generate a sense of family and togetherness, and I think that he made a conscious effort to do this. (As a husband and father I have to accept that I did not follow that course well, but Pasha has done that with his family). We went to dinner to common friends or family and we went as a family. We even went out to restaurants. He obviously had adults-only events but we still regularly had proper meals at home. We saw movies and shows together and I was exposed to a lot of classic movies at an early age. I have recollections of <u>Rebecca</u>, <u>Gone With the Wind</u>, <u>Kalpana</u> and <u>Dharti ke Lal.</u>

Even when we had important guests, we ate with them. The earliest one I remember is Prof. E.J. King who was papa's mentor at the London Post Graduate Medical School and a VIP. We shared meals with him when we were around 10 or 12. Neetu noted that when Prof. King was asked if he would have more, he said, "I have had two helpings of the meat and the vegetables," as opposed to an Indian who would have said, "I have had two rotis."

We even went shopping in Hazratgunj together and had a close relationship with Balujas, Batas and Universal Book Depot. We were a family. Meera was in the hostel from age eleven onwards and participated in these outings only during the vacations. Neetu left at sixteen. I stayed home through Medical College. We went on family vacations during the summer and did a lot together. We were exposed to a variety of political views especially leftist ones; we subscribed to <u>Blitz</u>, an alternative paper with leftist leanings. The editors of two Lucknow newspapers were among Papa's friends and visited our house. We wrote book reports and had summer assignments.

Papa did not accept any organized religion and had socialist/leftist leanings (I realize that the terms are somewhat meaningless after the break up of the Soviet Union and China's transformation to a capitalist economy). As a result, he gave us all a sense of fairness and egalitarianism.

I remember his comments about marriage ceremonies. I think it was after Tara's wedding in Meerut. He commented on the ceremony of breaking the *chulha* – the kitchen hearth. He pointed out that many of the rituals were leftovers from the days when armed bands raided homes, stole women, and as a final insult destroyed the *chulha*. He tolerated the religious rituals at home but we were not brought up in a religious environment. Yet we were not anti-religious. A lot was tolerated and accepted. It took me a long time to call myself an atheist. I called myself an agnostic till I read Richard Dawkins' book, <u>The God Delusion</u>. Papa inculcated a sense of balance in us.

The main way the strictness showed and was enforced was through Papa's temper. We dealt with it, feared it and faced it time and again. It set up an atmosphere that dominated and controlled our life. It was the same for people at work and even for friends; it was a way of life for us. It lasted sometimes for days, if not the outburst then the sulking and the tension it generated. We did not have laughter in our house. We had the amenities, we were comfortable. We did laugh, but there was no laughter in the house.

One time, possibly at age fifteen, I went into his office at home. There had been an unusually long and intense period of sulking in the house. I thought I would tell him about how it was affecting us. I can't remember who all was at the house. I went and said I wanted to talk to him. All I can remember is that he went on a tirade about all the things we had done wrong. I don't think he heard me out, but the tension did break.

I promised myself I would not repeat that behavior, but this is difficult and a matter of perception. With my own family I feel I was mostly argumentative, and shouted and raised my voice off and on. But I did that for specific actions, events or disagreements with specific people. But how does the other person know? Pasha tells me he was afraid of me at times. He mentions the time when he and his friends would be at home in Denver and I was taking my naps. I was nasty. Was he really afraid? I have two instances that I remember about Pasha's fear. One was in Denver, at Bill Robinson's place in Eldorado Springs, when he was four and I was telling him to behave. He might have said or done something which I don't remember. What I remember is his running away and my chasing him. He was shouting, but not really crying. I caught up with and picked him up and calmed him down. The incident was painful but the details are blurred. Was it fear or just a 4 year old's antics and our reaction? Another instance was in Delhi when he was six. Again, all I remember is that for an instant he had a stunned look of fear as if I were going to punish him. I certainly never hit him. I used harsh words from time to time, but overall we have had a close and fun relationship.

Recently I was talking to our neighbor, Steve, about my childhood. I described the strict upbringing we had and that I did not remember much laughter in the house. He asked about gifts, did Papa give us gifts? The short simple response is no. Not like Pasha and Cary or lots of family and friends who do. I too do not like to give or receive gifts. I think I learned early that in shops it was not proper or appropriate to ask to buy this or that. But I was told later that at some phase of my early life when Papa came back from work I regularly asked him if he brought me anything. He would ask "Like what?" My response supposedly was, "You could have brought a car or a Frigidaire." Lo and behold one day a Frigidaire did appear in the back of a lorry. It was unloaded carefully and placed in the dining room just inside the gallery door. It was one of the earliest Frigidaires among our family and friends.

As I said, we did not get gifts. While talking to Steve, something came to mind. Tuku, who was just 2-3 years older than I, was the grandson of Dr. J.G. Mukharjee. Dr. Mukharjee was Papa's mentor and friend and lived in the neighborhood. One day probably when I was 6 or 8 Papa bought Tuku a sword. He wore it with pride; I have a visual image of him walking out on the side of the veranda with the sword hanging from his belt. Was I jealous? Did it mean anything?

Gifts have had somewhat prominent roles in my interactions. I don't remember gift exchanges on a regular basis within the family. I remember getting some gifts at birthday parties, and also taking gifts to others' birthdays. I remember the wedding of a neighbor where gifts were displayed. Papa was critical of that practice. It was quite a display: every gift, cash, cheque, or item was displayed with labels on well lit tables.

Later I became an active non-gift giver. In my early thirties I went to a friend's kid's birthday party without a gift and the kid asked me what I had brought for him. I think my response was, "I don't give gifts." I remained friendly with the kid and the parents with no problems. I still find gift giving onerous and an unnecessary pressure.

Joanie has found a great compromise by giving donations to the recipients' preferred charity.

In the late forties Papa was in the U.S. as a guest of some professor at Christmas time. The professor asked Papa what he thought of American Christmas. Papa's response was that businessmen had pressured him and his wife into buying things for each other which they did not need. I have adopted that attitude. When Pasha was ready for a bike I got him one. I did not wait for his birthday, which was just a few weeks later. That is the way I am.

When Papa went on trips he did bring home gifts. I remember the saris he bought for all the girls - Meera and the cousins. Those were days when certain types of saris were only available in the region where they were made; these gifts were exotic. I don't know if I was jealous or felt deprived. I wanted guns, swords and sports items. We had very few. Certainly no guns or swords (remember Tuku's sword). We had hockey sticks and "tennis shoes" which we used for all athletic activities.

Neetu once bought a cricket bat, presumably without prior permission. During the day he prepared it with a soaking in oil and making holes on the surface with the school compass. I remember the big furor it caused. Since it was already prepped and could not be returned, he got to keep it. I used to envy and marvel at some of the boys who had cricket boots like Ravi Mathur, or the "spikes" that Aftab had for running. While in eleventh class I bought myself a pair of spikes because I thought I was good in the 440 yard race. There was a fuss about those.

We were well to do, so money was not the issue. We had books, good food, a comfortable life with servants, rooms to ourselves, desks, a lawn and garden to enjoy. The lawns were beautiful with lots of flower beds. We, however, did not play in our yard. We did that in common grounds at school or in the neighborhood.

As a child I was overwhelmed by the rules and discipline I was subjected to. This was during the time when Papa was actively building up the department and the College. I saw the events in his career evolve and unfold. I remember his conversations with his friends about the medical politics when he was appointed Professor and Head of Pathology. As I reconstruct it, he wanted the job, felt he was the best candidate, but he did not play politics.

Papa was particular about proper attire. I had a shirt with a hole in it. I used to wear it for games and sports. He did not see it because we played right after school and came home to change before he came from the office. One time he saw me wearing that shirt, was upset and put his finger into the hole and pulled. The shirt obviously was not usable after that, not even for the servants.

We had plenty of clothes, daily ones, and more fancy ones. But there was some dispute about necessary versus not really essential. We did not get school blazers unless there was an absolute necessity and the old ones would not fit at all. At a later stage, some time in the early fifties, Papa's friend Dr. Trivedi was visiting. He usually came in the summer but one year he came in the winter. I must have looked cold because he asked Papa why I did not have a woolen dressing gown. I don't remember the answer but the next day Dr. Trivedi took me to Ramlal's and got me a nice warm dressing gown that I had for many years.

There was also a strange deprivation of essentials. We had very few socks. They were often stinky and had holes in them. They were washed but as there were only a few of them, often they had not dried when we needed them. We had to dry them in the kitchen fire. In the winter our hands were cold but we did not have gloves. It was not just us, many of our friends also had this problem. It also reminds me of some friends later in life in Delhi. My friends' parents came from the south of India where it is not so cold. They lived in Delhi for over 25 years but had very few woolen clothes. They always said, "What is the point? We will be going south soon."

I too have an (overly) utilitarian attitude about things. Old tee shirts, shoes, backpack, pens and pencils, scrap paper - I like to use them as long as they are usable. It even bothers me when I see people in movies throwing things away. With food it is even more important. I am obsessed with not wasting food and about recycling. Sometimes it bothers me and I do realize what my nature is, but I can let go at times. The gift thing also is a part of the utilitarian approach. I do not give things to Kadin and Kyra mainly because they have so much. I feel the same way about souvenirs and decorative pieces. Recently on a trip to San Diego, I bought a Scrabble set for Sam and Neela because they didn't have one.

Performance at school was by far the most important thing. Apart from repeating 2nd grade, I did fine. But in 7th grade I was ranked third in my class, probably after Shankh Banerjee and Nirpendra Chakravarti, the two most brilliant boys. I don't remember if I was punished but I certainly was chastised in the morning on the side lawn when I think there were other people around. Luckily, such an issue never came up with Pasha — he did not have rankings. I remembered the way I felt unnecessarily humiliated and I did not humiliate him.

The high school examination was the worst. I got a second division - something that was totally unacceptable. "Everyone" got first division! We were in Rani Khet with the Misra family, a family that also had high expectations and, in the case of their cousins, a very strict father. I cried for hours. I got consolation from Romi and Ravender, but was almost ostracized by Papa; he made a lot of snide remarks any time I asked permission to go out during the rest of the vacation. A few weeks later when the marks sheet became available, I asked Papa for permission to go to school to look at my grades in each subject. His answer: "What is the point if it will be a low second division?" As it turned out, I had 290 out of 500; a first division was 300 or higher (58% instead of 60%). So I did get a high second; my Hindi and English were not good enough. I was way up in my science, math and geography.

The next two years were tough. I <u>had</u> to do better. I got tutors to help me with the main subjects and worked very hard. I did participate in sports and some outings, but work was high priority. It paid off. I got first division and two distinctions. I also got into medical college on the first attempt. I was redeemed. I worked hard through medical college and remained on top; working hard formed life habits that have served me well. In my seventies, I am having a difficult time letting go of these habits. Hard to say if it is good or bad, but that is the way it is.

After I entered Medical College, my relationship with Papa became somewhat more equal. We had a lot of things to talk about because of medicine. But this was a time when I was focused on studies and did not have time for the outside world and socialization. He retired from the Medical College when I was 25, and left for Mandalay, Burma on a World Health Organization assignment. Soon after he returned from there, he became sick. He was in and out of hospitals and needed care and comfort. I was so involved with my career that I resented the time I had to spend with him. We did not talk about his illness or what I should be doing for him.

The one conversation I do recall pertains to my career. Earlier he had expressed the wish that I go into Pathology. I, however, wanted to be in a clinical field and chose medicine. During my post graduate training, when I was considering areas of sub-specialization, he suggested I take up hematology which could be the bridge between clinical medicine and the laboratory. That idea appealed to me and it was a good choice. Unfortunately, he died before I became a hematologist. The field kept me close to the laboratory and also gave me a chance to work with patients. In terms of habits and attitudes, I am reminded of a time when I did not know the meaning of the word "conscience" (I can't spell it even now). Meera asked me if I had one. After she explained its meaning to me I said, "Yes." She said, "Kill it." I had no idea what she meant or why she said that. I wonder, in retrospect, if it had anything to do with our family friend, Billoo, who was interested in marrying her, but whom she refused.

In the same vein, when Pasha was forming his values I debated whether I should teach him good values or let him discover the realities of life which I learnt only in my thirties and forties. As I see it, he has both good values and, at the same time, a realistic understanding of the world. He understood the real world much earlier in life than I did.

Our tutors and schoolteachers were involved with us and made us think for ourselves. Papa made us aware of politics, the war, and social struggles, and he gave us, especially me, a socialist bent. I was exposed to *Dharti-ke-Lal*, Indian Peoples' Theatre Association, Soviet calendars and other propaganda materials. As the sole leftist, my ideas were sharpened by discussions with many friends. Yet I feel I maintained an open mind. Despite my leftist thinking I do accept the problems of Stalin and Mao.

Talking of leftists, I remember Papa describing, with admiration, the story of Renu and Nikhil Chakravarty. In 1948 when the Communist Party was declared illegal they went underground. The Chakravartys had a small child. Her uncle, who was Chief Minister of Bengal, took the child into his custody expecting the parents to come back for her. The two were devoted to their cause and remained underground.

Papa provided us with a lot of intellectual stimulation. There was shelf after shelf of books in his office, the drawing room and the gallery. Their subjects included everything from standard English literature to contemporary authors, medicine, lay medicine, science and politics. We also had a good collection of encyclopedias and Soviet literature. We went to the Peoples Publishing House and got books there. We also had an account at the Universal Book Depot and could buy books there.

He had books on the Soviet Union and we subscribed to <u>Blitz</u>. Another time he displayed his socialism was in the late 1940's when he visited *Rashtrapati Bhavan*, the president's palace. While there, he remarked that the country's average worker earned four *annas* a day. This comment has stuck in my mind along with an alternative view of the Taj Mahal which focused on the poor workers and the people who suffered because of the emperor's ego. Neetu and I differ on our attitudes. We agree on the facts and the reality of disparity between rich and poor and society verses the individual. The difference is that I feel it is sad that Shah Jahan satisfied his ego while the people suffered. Neetu just accepts it. I am also saddened that today the Chinese and Indian leadership are favoring "progress" over the basic needs of the people.

Papa was focused on my performance in school. He did not have the patience to understand my needs as a boy. I was denied a lot of activities; and even those that were allowed were regulated and contained. "Girls are bad," so and so "is not a good friend because he is not good at studies," "excelling in sports is not good." We also heard a lot of negatives about people we associated with.

We did not have too many conversations about personal things. We talked about politics and history, we had discussions about science, medicine, and the history of medicine. Since I did not read much fiction I only remember discussions Papa had with Mohini, Mungo, Ramesh Bhyya and Ram Bhyya about books.

I have little memory of his interactions with Meera and Neetu. Meera was in boarding school and college from around '42 to '46, and then in medical college. I just don't recall how we interacted. Neetu in his younger years did get scoldings as I did. But then at age sixteen he went into the academy and was suddenly a big boy. Papa did not attend his graduation from Joint Services Wing or the Army Wing of the Military Academy. Nor do I remember him at the railway station when Neetu went for his first posting in Kashmir.

Papa gave a lot of importance to our education, but never came to our school - not even to the yearly events like the school play or sports day.

We had the rules, the strictness and even fear. But we had intellectual stimulation, opportunities to learn and an atmosphere that encouraged thinking. We had discipline, a word with multiple connotations: on the one hand we lived with control and regulation by others; but we also had good work habits and full utilization of our potential.

The opportunities we had were so much greater and so different from what our friends had. Yet we had all of them as friends: boys who were smart and some who were average; boys who were athletic and some who were nerds; boys with whom I interacted in school and discussed subjects, tests, and books; boys whom we did things with but had nothing to do with in school. They were all friends, and I don't think we had a superiority complex. Papa helped us in keeping a balance. We did criticize some people and things, but we accepted many types of people. I learned about values from the other boys having what we did not have: some had more board games and sports equipment; one had a lot of new clothes; and some had a degree of freedom we did envy. Yet it was envy not jealousy.

Papa was available to us much more than the other fathers were. Also the others had mothers, something we did not have. It was natural for us to have books all over the house. I poured over them, read and reread them. I read a few novels but I definitely liked the science books. I remember discussing Lysenko and Soviet genetics before going to Medical College. So much of life and its quality is relative. We missed out on some things, had more of some, and less of others. Papa did give us a balance.

Some of our friends' fathers (and my father's friends) had two families. They neglected their first family and had a second family and life. What did they miss? Papa had us as a primary family.

Papa met a teacher from Isbella Thoburne College, the local womens' college that had a country-wide reputation for the excellence of its students, curriculum, and faculty. Papa and Ms. Chandy were planning to get married. In 1945 he took the highly unusual, unconventional step of taking the three of us children and Ms. Chandy on vacation to Mukteshwar, a small town in the Kamaon hills. Papa had a friend in Mukteshwar (Dr. Ray) who worked at the Veterinary Research Center doing research on Sara, a disease of horses. Through his help, Papa rented a cottage in Mukteshwar where we all stayed for a month. Even though Ms. Chandy stayed in a separate wing of the house, the arrangement was quite a bold move. Thinking back, for Papa and Ms. Chandy to be under the same roof for a month must have created quite a sensation and been a ripe source of gossip. As it turned out, they did not get married.

I was close to her. She was a regular visitor to the house and then just stopped coming. He never discussed her or the situation with me but he did stay with us. I will never know whether for him it represented a sacrifice or realization of potential problems.

Communication about personal issues was not a strong feature of our lives. Nobody told me of my mother's death. She was sick and then she was gone. We had days of active conversation at the dining table involving explanations of the war, of the independence movement, of science and art. And then there were silent meals where even the knocking of spoons on the plate added to the tension. We never understood the genesis of the tension, but we felt it as overwhelming and pervasive. We went about our days in a subdued manner with a sense of fear and uncertainty over everything and everyone. Even friends and visitors felt it. Did it come from unhappiness? We did not and I still do not know. In my forties when I had an unhappy period I was short to Pasha and did sulk, but not for a protracted time.

Papa was asked to give radio talks on All India Radio. I remember him practicing, perfecting, pruning his words so they fit in the fourteen minutes allocated. He practiced and timed his talk as he did his lectures in Medical College. He was unlike many lecturers who come to the end of their allocated time with material left over and either skip information or hurry at the end. The topics I remember are "gardening in the plains" and "science for the citizen." The last talk ended with the phrase *Satyam Shivam Sunderam*. We were allowed to sit in the studio while he gave his talk because we were considered mature enough to stay quiet. Quiet was also ensured by having each sheet of paper clipped on to a cardboard to prevent rustling of papers. Neetu claims that on one of these occasions I said something after the red light in the studio came on. We argued about that for a while.

Papa was interested in music and had learned some basics. I remember him trying his hand at a tabla and a harmonium at some wedding. He played piano at the Feldmans who thought that the raga sounded like Chinese music. Recently I discovered that there is a connection between ragas and Chinese musical structure. We had a gramophone, followed by a 78 RPM record player and later a long playing record player (33 ½ RPM). Our collections and records were mostly of western classical music. We had musical gatherings. I was the keeper of the record player and worked with the repairman from Devi radiograms. Getting the exact speed from those early record players was not easy. An innovation before long playing records was starting capability and "automatic coupling". This allowed us to stack all 6 records of a symphony in such a way that they played side 1,2,3 in order, and needed to be turned over only once. Papa did arrange for music lessons for Neetu and Meera. He talked about the beauty, complexity and nearness to human voice of the *Sarangi* (a complex and old Indian string instrument).

I listened to a variety of styles of music including those he did not care about - Hindi filmi (movies) and Western pop. I once wanted to go to a music festival being held in Lucknow but was denied permission. I started listening to Indian classical music more regularly much later in life. Papa also arranged a special musical evening for Mrs. Blumgart with the help of Shanti Hira Nand.

Describing Papa's day will bring out some personality traits and priorities and gives an insight into our life. Papa was an early riser all his life, as were his two brothers. He woke up around five, did not take a break during the day, and was tired and ready to go to bed early, usually around nine. He woke up at five and read in bed. He made tea for himself. Sometimes he would call us to his bed to share the newspaper or some anecdotes. He then went on to a one or two hour round of the garden with Makka Mali (and in the earlier years with DakSaheb.) The morning also involved some medical reading or preparation for his lectures or administrative work.

He left for work around ten. During the winter months our school also started around ten; we did our homework in the morning. He returned from work around 5 or 6 and had tea with some snacks and also enjoyed the garden. He played tennis in the earlier years.

Evenings were devoted to homework and reading, music and visiting with friends or family. Dinner was around nine. After dinner Papa would sit in his office and take the accounts from the servant, plan the menu for the next day, and go to bed with a book. He went off to sleep very quickly. Summer evenings we spent on the lawn, which was much cooler than the house. Chairs, tables, lamps were all properly arranged outdoors. We also slept outdoors during the peak summer heat.

(July 8, 2006) Joanie's dad died yesterday. She (Joanie was my wife at that time.) was able to spend a lot of time with him in his last weeks. She went with him for medical visits. She was his advocate and sounding board. She was there when he said he was tired and decided to stop treatments except those for comfort. She spent time with him doing nothing and everything, talking about things. She visited with him the day before he died and the last thing he said was, "I love you Joanie," and then just lay quietly at peace until he died. She grieved in a positive way.

I never grieved for Papa. He was sick during the final days of my residency and M.D. examination. I was busy with my thesis, my residency plans for Chicago, etc. I was there because he was in the Institute hospital where I was working but. my involvement was service oriented, not emotional. The morning of his death he had a sudden drop in blood pressure, but for 6-8 hours was awake, alert, and without the shortness of breath that had bothered him for months. I was in and out of the room, talked about generalities but not about death or our life. The whole family was the same way. Neetu came from his camp, Bhyya and Babujee came from Lucknow. When he asked if his condition was serious we glossed over the question. He did not and we did not talk about death. I think we did not want to talk. This was the norm for most people. Blame it on the English or the times.

Bade Babujee, the eldest brother, was with him in Delhi and looked after him. I have a feeling he and Papa had talked to each other about his death. Late in the evening he had a cardiac arrest and they took him for CPR; of course it did not work. The concept of futility of treatment did not exist. They worked on him for an hour and did an autopsy. Then he was taken for cremation.

There were no good byes. We the family did not talk to each other during his illness or afterwards. He was just gone. The next day we went to Lucknow for a few days and went on with our lives. At that time I did not think any more of it. I replied to letters I got from his friends and students, I cried briefly at the funeral, and that was it. A few months later I finished my examinations and proceeded to Chicago for my residency.

Years later, having seen death in my patients and having read about medical futility, I became a major advocate for peaceful death. I think Papa's death had an influence in my thinking about death and the need for saying goodbyes. I hope I have helped my patients by allowing them to die with their family and friends.

I was not there for the deaths of Bade Babujee in his eighties, Chote Babujee in his late nineties, Chachee in her early nineties, and Mango Bhyya in his late seventies. Theirs were not lingering deaths. Pushkin's death in his early forties was a tragedy. Hem ji ji also, I understand, had a painful death. As we age I hope the family will plan to be together at the time of the deaths that will be taking place in the future.

This broad narration of the things and people I saw during my early years is based on smidgens in some cases, notes in others. Some memories are verbal, some are visual. I have focused on Papa because, obviously, he had the most influence on me, Meera and Neetu.

Because of the closeness of the relationship, my age during the period I am describing, and the more than fifty years that have elapsed since these events took place, it is not possible to have a totally accurate perspective on the past. As far as I can see, Papa had certain parts of his life unfulfilled. He was ambitious and was constrained in the way he could express himself. He had contradictory pressures on him; his coping mechanisms and his strong personality ended up in a vicious cycle of inner tension, fear, and more tension.

All in all Papa did a lot and achieved a lot; he was a visionary. Reflexively, those close to him focus on the strong personality, but going deeper, much more emerges. He straddled several cultures and times. He succeeded in some ways but did not do too well in others.

***

Chapter Three
Changes in the Medical World

Medicine

During Papa's medical career from the time he entered Medical College in the early 1920's to his joining the same College as a Reader in Pathology in 1940, the practice of medicine changed dramatically. Again during his 20 years on the faculty (1940-1960), public health, medical education, and the social aspects of medicine also underwent reform. I will describe some of these changes, not as history, but as personal observations.

Infectious diseases have been the dominant medical problem throughout history. Epidemics and sporadic infections were the major causes of death in peacetime; even during times of war a large number of deaths were related to infections, not injuries. Chachee, my aunt who was born in 1900, talked of plague epidemics sweeping the cities and towns during her childhood. People left their homes to camp in the open to avoid the pestilence carried by fleas and rats.

Even The Journal of the American Medical Association (1908) reported the following on a decline of the plague in India :

In 1907 the mortality from the Plague in India reached the appalling total of 1,204,194. But a rapid decline has now occurred and the number of deaths in the twelve months ending June 30, 1908, is only 252,781. The measures adopted for combating the disease include rat destruction, evacuation of infested quarters, improvement of insanitary areas and inoculation. Grants amounting to $1,000,000 have been made to local governments in this year's budget for expenditure on sanitary improvements for the prevention of Plague. During the time the epidemic prevailed the mortality amounted to 2.1 per 1,000 of the population.

Every summer we had cholera and typhoid epidemics. We were protected by eating mostly home cooked food, and washing our fruit and vegetables in antibacterial potassium permanganate solution. We were not allowed to eat the delicious foods sold by street vendors. We felt so deprived! We also got immunizations for typhoid, cholera and plague. We had to get so many shots that we went around with swollen arms in a sling. Later, when I was in Medical College, our professors told us that those vaccines, when properly tested, had been found to be useless. It turned out the protection came from the hygienic measures and not the vaccines; those who took the vaccines were also more likely to have a cleaner environment. The gap between theory and practice continues and many treatments turn out to be ineffective when their efficacy is tested in a proper manner.

At a personal level, Amma died of a blood infection. Neetu and I got diphtheria, I got malaria, and Meera and I got the mumps. A cousin died of tuberculosis just a few years before anti-TB drugs became available. Many of my classmates got typhoid. These boys were absent from school for weeks. And because In those days the adage was to "starve the fever," they came back emaciated, with their heads shaved, and took a long time to recover fully.

I remember hearing, as a child, about the wonder drug Penicillin, and how it changed the course of war wounds and pneumonia. Chloremphenicol became available in the late forties and became the favored treatment for typhoid fever. I also remember how it was considered scandalous that the drug companies were exploiting the public by making the drug so expensive. This kind of price gouging continues.

In the early years of Papa's life and career research was understandably focused on infectious diseases. I had access, through our library at home, to books about the early pioneers in this research. Sir John Ambrose Fleming had been working on the natural killing abilities of body fluids, especially tears and saliva. To me, this phase of his work was more interesting than the so-called "accidental" discovery of Penicillin.

The development of antibiotics and other drugs for the treatment of infectious agents changed human history in many ways. An immediate effect of the new drugs was a rapid decrease in death rates around the world without a concomitant decrease in birth rates. The rise of world population and its effects on the world's food supply, global warming, and natural resources are unanticipated and unintended consequences.

Nuclear energy and nuclear weapons had their seeds in the late 19th century, but the full scaled development of this technology and its impact on world politics all occurred in the lifetime of V.S. Mangalik. The work of Pasteur, Koch and Virchow in the 19th century also came to fruition in the early 20th century with the development of vaccines, antisera, and diagnostic techniques for a variety of infectious and non-infectious diseases. The seeds of genetics, chemistry, and the understanding of DNA structure took place in the early 1900's. The advances of the late 20th century really just tweak the findings of the earlier period. How exciting it must have been to be in a field of medicine during the first decades of the 20th century!

Politics and world history called into question what had been the norm since the beginnings of civilization. Marx and Engels wrote about the state of the world in the 19th century. But the creation of communist states and the freedom of countries from colonial rule happened in the first half of the 20th century. It must have been exciting as a twenty, thirty, or forty year old to read about these events in the newspaper.

Papa himself in those earlier years had a different career and life. He graduated from Medical College in 1925 and stayed on to get a postgraduate MD degree in Pathology and Bacteriology. He was unable to get a job in the Medical College and went into the Provincial Medical Service and worked in small town hospitals. The faculty of the Pathology Department, consisting of a Professor, a Reader and a Lecturer, were mostly Englishmen; they were from the Indian Medical Service, which was a part of the Army. They rotated through the Medical College as they did through other Army assignments. Opportunities for Indians in Medical Colleges were limited. As a medical officer Papa worked in small hospitals and was posted to several small towns over the next 10 years.

I never got a feel of what life was like in those years. I just remember two incidents he talked about. At one time he told us of a man with a cataract who came to the hospital asking for surgery on his eye. Papa had never done cataract surgery and said he could not do anything for the man. Papa's assistant explained that the man was blind and had nowhere to go. He made Papa practice on a few goat eyes, and then they operated on the man's eyes. He never told us how successful the surgery was or how the man did. How did he get the eyeglasses he would have needed after the surgery? Did he do more similar surgeries later?

The other medical story he told from those days was that of a patient with bladder stones. In those days, the treatment was to pass an instrument through the urethra, crush the stone, and remove it by flushing it out with water. Papa was doing this under the supervision of someone his senior. It appears that in this case, the bladder was ruptured. Again, I do not know what happened to the patient. Both these episodes were described to us when I was about 15. They were narrated in a social setting with no follow-up questions.

Papa also described how, during a cholera epidemic, they ran out of saline for infusion. In that case, they took tap water, estimated the amount of salt needed, and mixed them together as a makeshift infusion.

Undertaking procedures in situations where there were no other options reminds me of an incident I was involved in soon after graduating from Medical College. An uncle of mine had a small medical-surgical practice in Meerut, a relatively small place at that time. When he went on vacation he put two of my classmates in charge of the clinic. A patient came with a badly infected penis and scrotum with complete obstruction of urine flow. My classmates tried to put a catheter into the bladder through an abdominal incision. However, they got scared half way through the procedure and stopped. They tried to persuade the patient to go to the government hospital in town. He said he would rather die than go to the government hospital. I arrived in Meerut the following day. I tried the same procedure and was successful in draining the bladder. The patient, however, died a few days later from infection and dehydration.

Papa's anecdotes from his early years as a general medical officer posted in small towns were a reflection of the health care system in India at that time. The few Medical Colleges in the country provided medical education based on the British system. The doctors trained in this system were more suited to take care of the needs of urban, well to do people. They focused on the treatment of each patient and were proprietary about those patients. That thinking and approach to medical care is still largely the norm and is the way most doctors in India and the U.S. behave.

Public health certainly was a part of the medical structure and organization. In fact, on the premises of the Medical College was an Institute of Hygiene. As students we did not have any contact with it in a medical context. However, because it was located in front of the gate of the women students' hostel, the building was commonly used as a meeting place by boys and girls. It was the office of the State's Public Health Department.

We had courses on epidemics, latrines, and other public health measures. But these courses were neglected or ignored by most students because the professor was a learned but a simple man who did not command respect from the students. Although there was a lot of rowdiness in his classes, I liked going to them and remember many of the pearls he gave us. In general, the subject was presented from the perspective of a medical officer responsible for the care of a community and covered topics like water supply, garbage collection, malaria control, etc. Overall health policy was not discussed; we did not learn about what happened to the patient when discharged from the hospital, or what effect the illness had on the rest of the family. In the hospital teaching we learned about diseases; we viewed the patients as objects, not as whole people. We gave lip service to a more holistic approach, but mostly our attitude conveyed: "We are helping you out with your problem and you should be thankful."

The relationship of the doctor to the patient was one of dominance. The doctors, with few explanations and choices, told the patients what they were going to do. As a medical student, I saw (and even was party to) many such encounters; in retrospect I see them as appalling. The patients were desperate and depended on the doctors for whatever help or treatment they could get. The worst case I recall was a man who was on the operating table with spinal anesthesia in place. He was in no position to move but was conscious. The senior surgeon had an assistant who wanted to learn a more drastic type of surgery than what the patient had been told he would have. The poor man pleaded that the less drastic surgery be performed. His pleas were ignored and the doctor went on to do the drastic surgery.

In the past few years, I have had a little more exposure to and interaction with the medical system in India. Unfortunately, there has been no major change. Even middle class patients are very dependent on the doctor's goodwill and kindness as well as his expertise. Patients have to use personal contacts to be seen by the doctors, and even then do not get adequate information to make informed decisions. The doctors' power and superior position continue to be the norm in India, augmented now by greed that leads to unnecessary and expensive tests and treatments. The conditions in the government hospitals is also getting worse because of increasing workloads and limited funding. The poor have to go into debt to get services and drugs at teaching hospitals because the budget does not allow much by way of free treatments.

At home I did hear Papa talk about looking at the patient as a whole person in a family and community. I tried to maintain that perspective while in medical school. Papa shared his experiences and knowledge about new discoveries with us. The discovery of Rh factor and its effect on fetal death occurred in the mid forties. As a ten year old I can recall Papa explaining this phenomenon to the older members of the family. Medicine, along with discussions about literature, politics, and social issues, was a topic of discussion in our family on a regular basis.

As I said earlier, the medical system under the British was developed and structured primarily by them to support the *Raj* and those who worked for the *Raj*. The Indian Army, the railways and other government employees had special hospitals that served that population. Those hospitals had facilities that were better than those for the general public. In the overall administrative structure each district had a District Magistrate, a Superintendent of Police, and a Civil Surgeon. The Civil Surgeon was the doctor to the government employees and the main doctor for the civil hospital. The civil hospital did treat the general public, but the emphasis was on taking care of the government employees.

Despite the emphasis on hygiene, Professor Yajnik our head of what is now called Preventive and Social Medicine did talk about the broader aspects of medicine. He gave us historical perspective; he talked about the impact of disease on communities and people. Health policy was not discussed in detail, but he gave us some general ideas about that. When I combined his information with that from Papa at home and what I saw during my medical college years, I ended up with a perspective on medical care and health policy that was different from that of many of my classmates.

Our health system was based on the model of caring for the individual and those who were working with the rulers of the day. Those doctors and medical students who wanted to advance their careers followed the British model; they went to England to get their advanced degrees and received recognition from the Royal Colleges of London and Edinburgh.

In 1948, the Rockefeller and Ford Foundations started work in India; Rockefeller focused on medicine and Ford on agriculture and the social sciences. They provided funds for visiting professorships, invited prominent Indians to travel to the U.S. and also provided funds to develop laboratories and centers of excellence in different Medical Colleges. Papa was one of those invited to travel to the major universities and medical schools in the U.S.

American influence on the medical system in India grew gradually. The teaching and examination methods, and even the laboratory instruments became Americanized. Instead of getting equipment from England, we got more from the U.S. Some were gifts and grants; some came under the auspices of the food program. A complicated deal in which America sold its excess wheat to India involved the Indian government's buying medical supplies from American companies and paying for Indians to study in the U.S. (I remember our servants complained that the American wheat was of poor quality and did not make good *chapatis*. At that time I told them they were mistaken because wheat was wheat; I did not know that there were many varieties of wheat.)

More doctors (and engineers) went to the U.S. for further training. They provided coverage in the less desirable hospitals in America. Many stayed on to work in America, providing the host country with well-trained professionals whose training costs had been paid for by the Indian government. The U.S. received the net gain. The grants given to the Medical Colleges consisted of equipment from American companies - usually older models for which there was no demand in America. Again the Americans earned a good name and influence with little meaningful investment. The cycle continues.

During one of my visits to India in February 2011, I had a chance to talk to Dr. N.P. Gupta. I have kept in touch with him over the years and respect his views and largely agree with his perspective. He was considered to be a leftist. Even though he was never charged or arrested for his views or affiliations, he did have some problems because of them. His wife, Habib Bano, did go underground for a few years, resulting in a delay in her completing her medical school career. One of the points he made was related to the program to eradicate malaria in India, as opposed to controlling it. There was a fundamental difference between the two approaches. Eradication was based on the premise of killing all malaria parasites. The approach was to spray D.D.T. into every home, every pond, and every woodpile. It was assumed that the mosquito, after sucking blood from a patient with malaria, rests on a wall or in a woodpile. The D.D.T. saturated surface would kill the mosquito and, with time, all infected mosquitoes would die. That did not happen. What did happen was a lot of toxicity from the D.D.T. and mosquitoes becoming resistant to D.D.T. Dr. Gupta pointed out that this scenario was predicted by many experts, but they were overruled; It turns out that the United States had a lot of surplus D.D.T. The firms who had these wanted to sell this stock, and India and the World Health Organization were persuaded to buy the D.D.T.

Apart from the help given to Indian Medical Institutions and medical education, Rockefeller, in conjunction with the U.S. government, funded Virus Research Centers in India and around the world. Twelve such centers were funded, all in the tropics. It appears that this was to use the fundings for biological warfare.

Some of the funds came, not directly from the U.S., but via Japan and New Zealand. The beneficiaries included the Virus Research Center in Poona (now Pune) and the All India Institute of Medical Sciences. One of the projects was high altitude entomological research. Again, possibly related to biological warfare. Dr. Gupta is one of the men I admire very much. He has had views different from those of the main stream but I think this is because he can think deeper than most people and he does have a lot of skepticism.

At a later time, I saw another example of the dumping of American surplus on India. I visited the Central Food and Technological Research Institute in Bangalore as a part of an Indo-American study group. The Americans were promoting the use of lysine-fortified wheat in India. Their theory held that while wheat was a good source of protein it lacked the essential amino-acid lysine. Lysine fortified wheat would become a "complete" protein. As it turned out, there was a large surplus of lysine in America (it was a by product of some pharmaceutical manufacturing process). The Americans were trying to dump the lysine into the Indian market. During this same visit I also learned that there are many varieties of wheat and their characteristics varied in terms of pliability, stretchability, etc. The servants were right. Lysine fortification was a sham and as far as I know went nowhere.

Papa was involved in the increased influence of the American establishment on Indian medicine. He was not the initiator but had an important role in the implementation of policies at a crucial stage after India's independence. The Rockefellers praised him, used him, and profited from him.

The Russians also tried to influence Indian medicine. Papa was also invited on a tour of the Soviet Union in the fifties. He was impressed by the Soviet system's emphasis on public health as opposed to individual health. As far as I can judge, the

Soviet influence on Indian medicine was marginal. What is obvious, however, is that medicine in India has remained patient focused and public health has been neglected.

Broadly speaking, when Papa was born medicine was mainly a study of infections, epidemics and disease processes. In his early career, some drugs were developed for the treatment of infections. Gradually, as more diseases were studied in detail, understanding of the mechanisms of disease grew. By the end of his career, many previously untreatable diseases were treatable. In addition, antibiotics, steroids, oral hypoglycemic agents (to control blood sugar), and diuretics to remove excess fluids from the body were developed. The art of medicine had gained the science of understanding and treatment. The establishment, however, remained focused on the individual. Though some attention was paid to public problems in the fifties and sixties, the practice of medicine has not changed much; in fact, since the nineties public health has been neglected even more.

The early advisors to the government and those who shaped medical care in India were educated by and had bought into the high tech medicine of England and the United States. The emphasis by the government was on the new institutions of higher learning and the status of a doctor was based on how closely he was affiliated with those establishments. The specialist was the one who received recognition, awards and accolades. Those who worked on behalf of public health were sidelined and considered to be second-class; their voices were drowned by the triumphs of modern, scientific medicine. Papa was one of those whose voice was heard and who played a role in elevating the modern specialization. Today the system is even more focused on the new technology and the benefits it gives to the individual who is able to afford these new methods.

In the nineteen thirties the Congress Party's health care manifesto stated that they would change the British system and pay more attention to the common man! That never happened. This system was co-opted by the Indian doctors who were trained by and enamored of the western system.

Another clash of medical cultures occurred in the early years after India's independence. Some of the political leaders were interested in reviving the ancient Indian systems of medicine. They wanted the medical schools to teach Ayurvedic medicine. In Lucknow Medical College a special track of students were taught the regular medical courses, but were also given courses by Ayurvedic physicians. The experiment failed because of the conceptual and factual discrepancies between the two systems. The concept of humors was not compatible with studying visible changes in the organs of the body as a result of disease. The dual track was abandoned after 1 or 2 years.

Interestingly the Ayurvedic system has seen a resurgence in the U.S.A. since the 1980's. More recently, multiple studies have demonstrated the lack of efficacy of treatments based on what has been called Complimentary and Alternative Medicine in the United States. The enthusiasm for such an approach seems to be declining, but maybe not.

Ayurvedic Medicine reminds me of an anecdote in Papa's career. In the early years after independence, a prominent local politician developed a fever. A diagnosis of malaria was made by Papa who had examined the blood smear. The politician was opposed to taking quinine. The clinicians taking care of him suggested that the quinine be mixed with Ayurvedic Medicine. Papa was opposed to this idea. He felt that if Tandon was helped by that medicine, it would further strengthen his belief in Ayurvedic treatments and further reduce the support for scientific medicine. I do not know what was done ultimately. The program of combining Ayurvedic and modern medicine was abandoned. But Ayurvedic and other systems of indigenous medicine continue in India along side Western medicine.

This may be a good time to offer some of my personal observations and comments. While I was working at the All India Institute of Medical Sciences I had a number of patients with chronic myeloid leukemia, a type of leukemia that can be controlled easily for several years with 1-2 tablets of a cheap and fairly non-toxic drug. Unfortunately, in most cases the disease comes back, and at that point is refractory to treatment. There was an Ayurvedic physician in Meerut who claimed to treat this leukemia successfully with some medicine. Because we had a few patients in common, I sent a request to the physician to work with me; I had hoped to find some successful treatment and to understand each other. The meeting never took place.

I did learn from one of the pharmacologists that there is a drug used by Ayurvedic physicians called Argemone Mexicana which has the effect of reducing the white blood cells in mice. He did not know of any clinical trials with that drug. It is remarkable that this drug had been used in the Ayurvedic system long before we had modern drugs for this disease and even before the existence of blood cells was discovered. It would have been nice to do studies in collaboration.

Some family and friends claim that they have been helped by homeopathy and Ayurvedic medicine. It is difficult for me to comment on this in the absence of the details and specifics.

It is unfortunate that I did not get an in-depth understanding of Papa's medical education, and how patients were treated. I would have cherished first hand information from someone who practiced medicine before we understood autoimmune diseases, or the body's response to infections before antibiotics.

***

Medical Education

Medical education, like education in general, changes over time and place and has its own contradictions, disagreements, and limitations. When Papa was studying at Lucknow Medical College in the early twenties, there were three or four Medical Colleges in India. There were a few more institutions that provided limited basic training for medical practitioners who were roughly comparable to current Physician's Assistants in the U.S.

Graduates of the Medical Colleges received an M.B., B.S. (Bachelor in Medicine, Bachelor in Surgery). The degree was based on the British system, and the name remains unchanged. The teaching was done by members of the Indian Medical Service, a somewhat fluid organization that consisted mainly of doctors who were in the British Indian Army. They spent a few years of their careers teaching in the four Medical Colleges in Calcutta, Madras, Bombay and Lucknow. (Lucknow Medical College was the youngest of the four, founded in 1905; its first students graduated in 1911.}

By the nature of their careers and the short time spent in the Medical College, these teachers were not greatly experienced or specialists in their fields. Their research interest was limited, as was any specialized knowledge of what they taught. Unfortunately, I never got a feel for what or how students were taught in those days. Papa did give an example of postgraduate research from this period. A student took samples of blood from Hindus and Muslims. He found that the concentration of urea in the blood (a product of the breakdown of protein) was higher in Muslims. This observation was attributed to the fact that Muslims ate more meat than Hindus. Again, I do not know the details of the statistics or the methodology of the work. Obviously it was a simpler time.

The degree of specialization gradually increased in all areas of medicine. But well into the forties and early fifties, the fields of Anatomy, Medicine, Surgery or, say, Pharmacology remained the major disciplines. In the fifties, we saw the first plastic surgeon, cardiologist, and liver pathologist. The teaching, however, was still done under the umbrella of the department. The cardiologist took care of all types of patients with "medical" problems and taught "medicine." In the western world by the thirties there was more compartmentalization.

In the fifties, as the influence of the Rockefeller Foundation on medical education in India increased, so did specialization. Through the Rockefeller advisors at Lucknow Medical College and their links to the newly formed All India Institute of Medical Sciences in Delhi, specialization became the main theme in medical education and medical care in India. The Pathology department at Lucknow Medical College was upgraded and developed special centers for virology, liver diseases and others. The Institute in Delhi developed separate departments (as opposed to sections) of Cardiology, Neurology, Intestinal diseases, etc.

The process of specialization and sub-specialization continues as medicine gets more complex. As a result, the qualifications of those who teach medical students need to be re-examined. What and how much detail is taught to a beginning student is an issue of considerable debate and discussion - and raises some interesting questions for me. I have been in academic medicine all my life and have worked in many different environments and have seen a lot of changes. When I was in medical college in the mid fifties the teachers were all specialists in their respective but broad fields, and were good at what they did. However, most of them were not researchers; they maintained a generalist's point of view. We had fairly good opportunities to interact with them through their lectures, bedside rounds, and in our practical laboratories. What we learned from them was the way to approach a subject and the core knowledge on which we could build. This technique has served me well, as it has many of my contemporaries. Many have gone on to specialize; others have stayed in more general practices. The fundamentals ('funda' was what we called it) worked well for us. We could build on that foundation and go on to our respective fields without feeling inferior to others who came from other backgrounds.

At the All India Institute of Medical Sciences the structure was different. The faculty was recruited from medical schools in India, the U.S.A. and England; they came with a background of research in their respective, narrower fields. When they taught they emphasized details of their particular field, often neglecting the broad principals of the topic. Many of the students from the AIIMS have become prominent in their fields but it seems to me they have too narrow a base.

After the AIIMS, I had the opportunity to observe medical teaching in the U.S.A. There, even more than at AIIMS, the teaching is done by very specialized professors (called super-specialists in India and sub-specialists in the U.S.A.). They teach all they know or are working on in their fields. They teach piecemeal what that special field has to offer but with inadequate contextualizing of the information to the whole. The students end up knowing a lot of details of small pockets of information without a broad perspective on the problem. They cannot apply their knowledge effectively.

I have no influence on the curriculum. I feel that students lose a lot by this intensely focused approach. I find my opinion marginalized professionally. When dealing with students, usually in small groups, I try to put their knowledge into a broader context. I am not saying that specialization is wrong, but I do feel that broad principles are crucial for a medical student who is beginning a new career. The debate will continue and we will have to watch what develops.

I remember Papa recounting the teaching philosophy of a prominent anatomy professor in the 1950's. At that time a medical student spent 18 hours a week for 2 years just in anatomy. They learned of protuberances and holes and branches that no one else cared about. The professor was asked how much anatomy a medical student should be taught. The answer apparently was "as much as a professor remembers without preparation." Obviously this professor felt that too many details were not necessarily helpful.

The importance of devoting so much time to anatomy in medical college was never understood by me. Maybe it was, simply, a continuation of an old practice from the days when there was not that much to teach in medical colleges. Anatomy was the only subject in which there was a lot of factual knowledge that could be transmitted to students. In subsequent years the time devoted to teaching anatomy has decreased.

When I appeared for the admissions test for the Medical College, I was tested in Physics, Chemistry, Zoology, and Botany. I could not understand the relevance of botany as a subject for qualifying for medical college. Later it was explained to me that one of the professors of botany who had political power had added that subject to the entrance examination in order to gain even more power and money. He was paid to check the answer books. (In those exams, tests were answered in long hand in notebooks that were corrected and scored by an expert.) One of the reasons why certain subjects, even if they are not important or directly relevant, get a lot of time and attention is the power of an individual professor. Some professors with power impose their subject or area of research on students to the detriment of other more relevant fields and topics.

One striking and unfortunate feature of education in King George's Medical College was the relationship between the faculty and the students. The accepted relationship was that of a power play based on fear. It is true as a general Indian phenomenon that in schools the teacher was powerful and some degree of physical punishment was acceptable. In the medical school, the power differential was very great. Most students avoided encounters with the faculty outside the classroom. Papa was one of the most feared of the professors. The irony is that he probably recognized very few of the students.

The power differential between the professors and students still exists. I had an interesting and disappointing experience when I moved from Lucknow Medical College to the All India Institute of Medical Sciences for my post-graduation and residency. I had been given to understand that at the AIIMS the atmosphere was collegial;

the professors allowed free discussions and even encouraged different opinions. Soon after joining, I contradicted a professor about the definition of congestive heart failure. I was quoting from one of the major textbooks of cardiology. Rather than pointing out that the two definitions were looking at the problem in two different ways, he became angry and berated me for not understanding even the simplest aspects of medicine. It was sad that a young professor, who had been trained in the U.S., where open discussion was encouraged, could not accept or explain a point of view different from his. My subsequent experiences showed that the use of power, rather than logic and explanation, is still common in Indian Medical Colleges.

Whether that is good or bad is a matter of opinion and perspective, but Papa was a part of that change. He was not a pioneer or initiator but he was a channel for the change that has had a major impact on medicine in India. The passage from the Galis of Meerut to the Rockefeller Foundation covered huge changes. A man who grew up in a house with no electricity or plumbing, drawing water from a well, owning two pairs of pants, subsequently travelled first class on the Queen Mary, and had his suits made in London. He was part of the progress in the early Independent India.

***

Twenty Years at Lucknow Medical College

Apart from the changes in medicine and medical education, I saw a lot of interactions in the Medical College during my school days as a small child and later as a teenager. As a young boy I used to go to Papa's office. We also went to Medical College events and had people coming to the house. Chajjoo, a laboratory technician and a glass blower in pathology, used to make glass pens filled with an orange liquid and a little floating glass piece in it. We went to a body show once, held in one of the lecture halls where, ten or so years later, I sat for my lectures.

The Medical College, King George's Medical College (KG for short), had, like many institutions with tradition, some core people. Two stand out in my memory. Jungli was, by the time I met him, old and frail. He had been selling fruit at the boys hostel at KG from the time Papa was a student. He had the reputation of having the best quality, most tasty fruit. He did charge more for it. Papa said he would bring a selection to his office, even if Papa did not need any; he would just leave the fruit there and get paid later. I definitely remember eating a lot of good quality fruit. In later years, Jungli (the word means "savage" but without negative connotations) became blind but continued to sell fruit on an honor system. Papa said the students would steal fruit and not pay him for it - a reflection of the change from a small, family like institution to a larger impersonal organization.

The other person I remember was Munna (little one). He was the keeper of sports equipment, organizer of sporting events, and the most enthusiastic fan of the KG sports team. He was good at the sports himself but, of course, did not get to play with the students too often. I did play tennis with him a few times. As a cheerleader, he was full of energy but also criticized the home team- and not in very polite language - if they did something wrong.

We went to several sporting events. Papa was head of the athletic department and the annual sports meet was a big occasion. In those days the whole college seemed to participate. Of course the college was smaller, with only fifty students a year. The faculty was also small. The cricket matches and athletics were all very well attended, with large crowds and lots of peanuts and peanut shells. We were disciplined and kept our shells to put them in trashcans even when the grounds were covered in shells. We got little ribbons that allowed us to roam around the field like the officials. One time Neetu was given the ribbons for the two of us. He threw mine towards me and I did not realize what I was supposed to do with it or what it was for and I left it on the ground. Later I went back, found it on the ground, put it on my coat, and was an "official." From time to time a human chain used to be formed to clear crowds from the field; we of course, were "official" and stayed on the field.

The older faculty, Papa's bosses, came to the field. I remember Professor Swift wore a monocle, which was quite intriguing. Then there was the old Dr. C.P. Misra and Misraniji. They, especially she, sounded like they were institutions but I have no idea what it was all about. There was a strong man who came to show his prowess. He pulled cars, had people sit on his chest, and bent iron rods. One time bending the rods caused him to faint and he lay on the field being fanned by the servants.

Talking of strong men, in our community there was a Mr. Shukla who was an artist but also a strong man. He could, supposedly, eat a bucket of rice in one sitting. On one occasion he was able to put his shoulder under a car to allow the driver to change a flat tire because the jack was missing. The other strong men were Gama and Zabisko, a team of Europeans, probably Russians, who were on tour of India and came to Colvin. They did wrestling, bending rods and so on. I learned of the Nelson grip from their demonstrations. They were showmen and quite a hit. One time one of them got the other in a Nelson grip and walked him around like one would a dog or a pony. They stayed in Lucknow for a few days and we saw them in Hazratgunj. One of them got in to a cycle rickshaw and occupied the whole thing and was more than a full load. I was with Chote Babujee and he made some remark about the poor rickshaw and rickshaw wallah.

Anyway, back to the main theme of Papa and my recollections of him in the context of the Medical College. His friends and colleagues were topics of conversations. I have vague memories of some them. Many were my professors when I was in college. Some, like Dr. B.B. Bhatia and S.C. Misra were a significant part of my life; their kids have remained my friends.

Papa's boss was Professor Abdul Hamid who was later made a *Rai Bahadur*, an honorific given by the British. Hamid Saheb apparently did not work too hard. He also did not do much supervision or administration. He was from the first graduating class of KG. In some instance where the technicians mishandled the specimens and allowed them to boil for a long time, he did not care. The structure of the department of Pathology and Bacteriology in those days put the professor in charge of histopathology and the reader was in charge of bacteriology. It was interesting that after being head of bacteriology for seven or eight years, when Papa became professor he switched to histology as his field. Of course the field was smaller then and there was only so much one had to know or do. Papa was responsible for the serological tests. Thursday was the day when the Wasserman and Kahn tests were done. They were labor-intensive tests, and specimens from all over the state came to K.G. for testing. Periodically something went wrong and the whole test had to be repeated. Papa was in a bad mood on those days. We used to wait for the news whether the Wasserman *theek chala* (went well).

Two faculty members, Dr. Nigam and Dr. (General) Bhatia, had a reputation for being great surgeons but of also fleecing and blackmailing their patients. It was said that they paid Ekka Wallahs (a common mode of transportation) to go to the railway station and bring patients to their private clinic rather than to the government hospital.

Papa pointed out Dr. Hargovind Sahai, a retired professor of medicine, taking a walk. He had been a famous rich man in his heyday, but was now dressed shabbily. Dr. Nigam's son, general Bhatia's daughter and Dr. Sahai's son were ten to twenty years younger than Papa. Around Lucknow and Delhi we saw them as people who did not rise to the stature of the old stalwarts. In that category we can also place professor Bhal of Zoology or, for that matter, the sons of the next generation of stalwarts, Mathur, Bhatia and Mangalik!

One of Papa's professors was truly intriguing. Professor Alexander was an Englishman in the Indian Medical Service who sometime in the thirties or forties became a Sadhu. He gave up medicine, wore saffron robes, and became a nomad. Papa said when he came by from time to time he only spoke Hindi. Even if asked a question in English he responded in Hindi. I think he came to Lucknow after Dr. J.G. Mukherjee died.

Papa had interactions with V.I.P.s during his tenure as professor of pathology and as principal of Lucknow Medical College. He used to go to the Governor's house to collect blood and do tests on the family. At one time he described drawing blood from Padmaja Naidu, daughter of the Governor Sarojini Naidu. Padmaja was the daughter of a Bengali mother and Andhra father. So when Papa drew her dark blood she said, "What do you expect with a mixture of Bengali and South Indian blood?"

Another unrelated incident about Mrs. Naidu. She was in some way related to Dr. Ram of Lucknow University. Dr. Ram's two sons were at Colvin and knew Neetu who is the source of the story. In 1948 Hyderabad (now Andhra) was an independent state. Hyderabad was invaded by the Indian Army in a police action. In a strange paradoxical situation, Mrs. Naidu was a freedom fighter and a Governor of an Indian state, yet her staff was scared to tell her that the Indian army had successfully brought a "renegade" part of India under government control. Of Dr. Ram's sons, one joined the army with Neetu, and the other became something at the U.N. The latter son supposedly wrote 2-3 notebooks in the Inter exams when most people could barely fill half a notebook's worth of answers. Dr. Ram's daughter married President Giri's son.

Another V.I.P. incident was related to some Raja's son in the Ayodhya area. He was quite sick and many of the Lucknow Medical College doctors were involved in his treatment. I remember hearing how they could not decide on the diagnosis or how to treat him. I think Papa went to Ayodhya to draw samples or something. We all went there one time. On our way there we saw his funeral procession coming from the other direction. I guess that with difficulties in communications the doctors had not known the patient had died while they were proceeding there to save him. We stopped the car and let the funeral procession pass by. We went on to Ayodhya and visited some temples. I have a vague recollection of a devotee taking a liquid offering from the priest (charnamitra) and drinking some of it and putting the rest on his head. During that trip Hem jiji got engaged.

During his years on the faculty at the Medical College Papa had many students whom he mentored and guided either for their research or for their careers. He also had interactions with his colleagues, many times at the house. There is no reason why some of these stand out and have stayed in my memory. But that is the point of what I am writing.

Dr. Yajnik was a colleague of Papa's; they had been in Medical School together. He was one of my teachers and I thought his lectures were thought provoking. What he taught us has stayed with me and has helped me whenever I have looked at issues beyond those directly related to my career. Population issues, health planning, justice, and fairness all were covered by him, and this was in the fifties! Papa, however, told stories of him from earlier years. Yajnik apparently was a simple man. When he went to England he had to be given lessons in behavior and etiquette. At one time, he had lost the buttons on his fly and spent the evening adjusting the fly.

Papa told stories of Dr. T. Prasad, an ENT surgeon. This gentleman supposedly came late to a party still wearing his headlamp and operating gown claiming he was very busy. He also allowed his sweat to drip into the operating field, claiming it did no harm. Dr. Zaidi went on to found the Toxicology Research Center in Lucknow. I just remember him visiting Papa for long meetings. It sounded like Dr. Zaidi was being criticized or even scolded. The monologue seemed to go on and on, and we felt sorry for him.

Dr. N.N. Gupta has a long association with our whole family. He was one of the better-known faculty members in Medicine. I remember Papa telling someone that he sent Dr. Gupta a telegram to "ask, indeed order you" to return to India as soon as possible without completing the Royal College Examination. Apparently his job was in jeopardy if he did not return. Dr. Gupta did return early, got the job and rose to the top. I heard only recently that he did not like Papa and that Papa was afraid he would be vindictive towards me after Papa retired. Such hearsay is hard to corroborate.

Dr. K.G. Mittal was a practitioner in Meerut. He had always been very eager to have me at his house, so during the sixties I visited him. I did not know much about him. He was effusive in his welcome and talked a lot about Papa, who had died a few years earlier. He had a picture of Papa in his living room. I can only presume that at some point in his career Papa had helped him out.

Papa mentored many others during his career. Dr. R.M.L. Mehrotra was his special favorite. He was one of our best teachers and had an illustrious career. Dr. N.P. Gupta and Dr. Mahmud Shah also stand out in my memory as people Papa helped in their careers. He also mentored his brother-in-law, Amma's brother, who established a strong presence in Meerut.

Over the years, I met a lot of Papa's friends, some in Lucknow, some when we travelled. One time there was gathering of a few of the classmates from medical college at our home. These men in their fifties had not seen each other for some years. There was a lot of joking, reminiscing, and using of nicknames like "Mangaldin", "Pancho" for each other. We went to some party in Delhi where Papa met a General in the Medical Corps. The man was very proud that he could get into his twenty five year old tuxedo; he seemed unaware that it was frayed and too tight.

Papa had two women friends that we, as children, interacted with. As far as I can judge, these were not serious relationships. Auntie Sujata was a pathologist who had worked with Papa in Agra and went on to the Lady Hardings Medical College as head of pathology. There are a number of photographs of her at family picnics. She came to Lucknow a few times and we visited her in Delhi also. We got to know some of her family, especially her eldest brother's children who were good friends of Kishin and Meera. The elder Mrs. Choudhary made wonderful *paish* and *kheer*.

Dr. Mary Thomas was the gynecologist at Queen Mary's Hospital and a striking English or Anglo-Indian woman. She smoked cigarettes with a long holder. She had some kind of a game going on with Papa, Dr. Mathur and Dr. Bhatia. She had the three of them vying for her attention. Meera remembers all this as a big joke. Mary Thomas got married and left Lucknow. Her father was Justice Sir George Thomas. I recall going to their very fancy house.

A pathologist from Calcutta, Dr. B.P. Trivedi, was a good friend of Papa's. He came regularly as the external examiner for the postgraduate students. He was like Papa, a sahib. He said his wife was only into *pooja* (prayers). He was appointed head of pathology at Calcutta Medical College and talked about it while he was in Lucknow. He said that there was some opposition to his appointment because he was a non-Bengali. Yet Dr. Trivedi's ancestors moved to Bengal in the time of Akbar in the 16th century; he was a Bengali in every way. Dr. Trivedi was very fond of the delicate Lucknow Kakris (cucumbers). He was nervous about missing trains "just in case we have a puncture." He usually got to the station an hour early. He brought us ballpoint pens when they had just become available. We were not allowed to use them in school because teachers thought that they would spoil our handwriting.

Dr. B.B. Bhatia was one year senior to Papa and Dr. S.N. Mathur was one year junior to him. In the forties the three headed major departments of the Lucknow Medical College: Bhatia Medicine, Mathur Surgery and Mangalik Pathology. They were considered pillars of the college, were well respected, and were also feared by the students and even the faculty. They were aloof, well dressed, and English in their mannerisms. For a long time they were friends. They became deans of the college in succession. We were close to the Bhatias who lived in the neighborhood. Their sons were friends of ours. Our contact with the Mathurs was less close but cordial. In the early fifties there was some conflict between Papa and Dr. Mathur who left the medical college and was in private practice. The three of them died in the early sixties: Dr. Mathur of a rare type of sarcoma; Dr. Bhatia of coronary atherosclerosis; and Papa of primary amyloidosis. We all visited Mrs. Mathur after Papa's death and lamented the deaths of the 3 stalwarts over such a short period of time and the families having being estranged.

In the early years, the student body and faulty at KG was small and seemed like a family. Many of the students came to the house and were like older brothers to us. Two students were top-level tennis players; Muni Kaul and I. Chitamber reached national levels. N.S. Jain and Mahesh Gupta were like family. Dr. Jain became one of the most famous ophthalmologists of Delhi in the fifties. Unfortunately, he got involved with some woman who caused his downfall. It ended with the sordid murder of his wife. He spent many years in jail where he provided ophthalmic services to prisoners. Dr. Gupta was the brother-in-law of Papa's friend Dr. V.P. Gupta. Dr. Gupta's son Anil was in Medical College with me. He and I have remained close friends since the early fifties.

Students and faculty participated in many activities together, one of which was a Hare and Hounds race. Two teams had to find their way to an undisclosed destination where an elaborate picnic was held. This good-natured activity was a far cry from the later years when the relationship between the students and faculty became adversarial and had a strong element of fear and intimidation. Similar changes took place at the All India Institute of Medical Sciences. In my 10 year association with AIIMS, the family environment changed to one of "do your thing and do not worry about the other people or the Institution." Sporting activities, plays and social gatherings continued to take place but the collegial harmony gave way to piecemeal activities.

On a more serious note, one needs to look at changes that took place in the relationship between the Medical College and the Government. During the British days, the influence of the Government officers on the College was limited. When the new Congress Government came to power they gave more money to the Medical College. As a result, the Ministers got personally involved in the affairs of Lucknow University in general and the Medical College in particular. Power struggles between the Government Ministers ultimately reached to the faculty of the College. "Dirty politics" was used to unseat deans and professors. The Health Minister used his power and "his" money (money he allocated) to control and even humiliate the Medical College faculty.

The University of Lucknow and the Medical College were used by many of the state politicians for their own gain. They had support from different factions of the faculty. Mr. C.B. Gupta was the most notorious for his role in Lucknow and U.P politics. He was a powerful local politician. All those who wanted to get ahead sought his patronage. He had a special interest in Lucknow University and the Medical College where he controlled the budget, approved new projects, and helped his cronies get ahead in their careers. The way he ran the operation was to have morning *Baithak* (gathering). He sat in his living room, allegedly in his underwear, and all those who wanted favors just came in and waited for him to ask them to speak. It sounds like Lyndon Johnson giving interviews to reporters in his bathroom. Anyway, there was no privacy. You asked for your favors with everyone listening. When Papa became dean and was already head of Pathology and Bacteriology, he wanted to build a new building for the department. He had to go to "Guptaji's *Baithak*" to get approval for the project. There was a lot of discussion in the family about what was the right thing to do. Papa was a man of principles, opposed to this type of pleading - especially in the presence of all the hangers-on. However, he felt that his was a legitimate project for the advancement of the Medical College and the Department, and not a personal favor. Ultimately, he decided that he had to be practical and accept the reality of the situation. So he did go and pleaded his case in that "informal" setting. He felt demeaned but the project was approved; the new department building was built and inaugurated with great fanfare in 1956.

Unfortunately, politicians' involvement and interference in the affairs of universities and medical colleges has become more pervasive and noxious in recent years.

***

PART TWO
THE PEOPLE AND THEIR IDEAS

Chapter Four
Family

We are quite a family. Then, aren't all families special? Anyway, to us we are special. We were made to feel special - first, because we were the Mangaliks. Then we became the Mangaliks; we, only we, had the second 'a'. We were special. Mohini said the Mangalik men were special!

Who are we? Who can say? Who can know? Does it matter? Anyway, I have memories - my memories - very vivid in some cases, vague in others. There were gaps, there were questions, and I felt I wanted to straighten them out. My grandfather lala Munna Lal was a deputy collector. I was told that when he went into a *mohalla* (neighborhood) the streets were specially washed and *nalis* (gutters) were cleaned. The special cleaning of the gutters implies that they are normally dirty. That is all I know of him and that he died the year my father was born.

He had three sons. I have a vague recollection that my father had a sister who died a long time ago. Bade babujee, as he was known to our whole world, was very young when grandfather died. He took responsibility for the two brothers age 8 and a new born, and of their mother. I don't know how much formal schooling he had, but he was a man with many admirable qualities. He introduced me to the phrase "grow more, eat less, waste nothing" - so important in this day when we are laying waste lands and people, rivers and oceans. This thought also helped me to deal with many difficult personal and work situations. "Give more, take less, and expect nothing" (from others) has helped me accept many a raw deal from people. I wonder if that was his approach to interpersonal relations; certainly my memories of his later years suggest that it was. He was never a burden, always self-effacing, and yet always in control of the situation.

What about the earlier years? His earlier years only raise questions for me. How did he support the family as a teenager and yet go onto the life of a Government official with power and authority. Was there family money?

The house in Meerut was our only property. I do not know when it was built. It was a typical home of the period, built at the end of a lane, referred to as a *Sotion-ki-gali*. It was built, as was the norm, from *Lakhori* or *Lahori* bricks. These were bricks similar in size to the currently used bricks, but only half as thick. They were baked to a higher temperature than current bricks, and are stronger, but also more brittle. I remember in the early forties seeing a demonstration of strength using some of these bricks in an Indian version of the Karate chop. I wonder if this brittleness added more drama to the demonstration.

Anyway, in 1915, Murari was 23 and Bunno 15 when the name Mangalik was taken by the family. What an extraordinary move. I understand it was the product of Viakul Taoji's mind, an indicator of the creativity that showed up in later years. The name comes from our subcaste "Mangal".

Babujee's father-in-law was a *zamindar* but lost his money. Bade babujee's first child was born when he was 25; his wife died when he was around 40. How lonely was he? Forty more years without a wife - no steady and certainly no acknowledged female companionship. Dada Advani and Papa were in the same situation. How did they cope with that lifestyle?

The two younger brothers were supported by him; the brothers helped him out after they were settled in life. My own memories of him go back to Khurja where he was *Tehsildar* (in charge of a unit of a few villages) in the early 40's. The headquarters of the *tehsil* was a huge walled rectangular enclosure with a big gate in the middle of the long side. There was a guard. The far left corner after you entered the compound was Babujee's office, and above that his residence was reached by a single flight of straight steps. There was the *angan* (courtyard) on the right with iron girders on the outside, and then a big room. The rest of the house was probably to the left. There were quite a few trees in the *tehsil* compound, and also a lock-up of some kind.

One day an elephant was called in for us to ride on. I was all excited but scared, and refused to climb on. Neetu went and bragged about it. While the elephant went on its round with Neetu and some others, Ghanshyam, the family servant and caretaker, gave me a pep talk. When the elephant came back, bells clanging, I built up courage and was walking out to get on. Babujee was in his office and got really angry and told me I had missed my chance and could not get on. I guess I cried some, but do not recall too much.

I have no memories of Ghanshyam the person, but he was an institution unto himself - a part of the family and in overall control. He was the expert in *Gajar-ka-halwa* (carrot pudding), which I recall he made with eggs. One day I recall a big *gadda* (mattress) was brought in - it was huge and thick (one foot) and hauled up the long stairs by a lot of people under Ghanshyam's supervision. It was installed in the big room behind the *angan*.

Other memories of Khurja are sketchy, but I recall a prisoner in the *tehsil* (the memory still makes me feel bad). The poor man was sitting on the floor just inside the bars of the cell with half a *roti* and some *dal* on it. The policeman was shouting "*khao*" (eat) and the poor man was crying. He looked so pathetic. (Not quite the same but in the film <u>Gandhi</u> Om Puri shouts at Gandhi "*khao*" to make him break his fast.)

There was a patient with rabies (Neetu called it hydrophobia) who was tied to a *Bael Gari* (bullock cart) and was begging for water. At the same time he was spitting constantly and knew that he could not drink. Neetu's descriptions of these situations seem to stick in my mind very strongly. I recall him telling me how the body went into a spasm if the patient drank water. Did he also tell me that Dr. Mathur gave him an injection to euthanize him?

Khurja was where Vimla got married, I have some recollection of the daughter of Dr. Mathur or Munsif saheb named Ramesh who was discussed as a possible person for the rehearsal, since Vimla was to marry a man named Ramesh.

After Khurja came Barelli, I remember Sushma's wedding to some degree. The Halwai making *Chak* (big flat cake on which our names were written) and *Parwal ki Mithai* (a dessert) and a store room where all this was kept. I can even recall flies in one of the *degchis* (cooking utensils) in which the food was stored.

In Barelli I was unhappy. I thought Babujee was partial to Neetu. Papa, who was my only support, was not there. I remember the cantonment and the tanks and trucks. The house was cleaned and Dinesh, the bridegroom, was around one day. A sweet smelling Champa tree was being trimmed and Dinesh said "*Isme Saanp Devta to Nahni hain*" (I hope there are no snakes in here).

Babujee's stories of the *Raj* are rather interesting as a means of analyzing his and other middle level Indians' mind set. Here was an austere man who shaved with used razor blades and took pride in using a blade for 6 months. He kept his clothes very clean and proper but also took good care of them for years. Yet when he talked of the Raj it seemed that he was proud to have been a part of the glitter and glamour of those people. He lamented that the lawns of the circuit house were being cut with a *Talwar* (sword-like device) in post independence India when in the old days they were cut only by lawn mowers. He described (without criticism that I detected or remember) the 5 trunks of clothes that came with the viceroy Lord Linlithgow on a hunting trip. Yet, when the *Saheb* needed a khaki shirt a new one was made because the assistant did not feel like searching through the trunks (well maybe he was critical of the assistants). He also described the sport of pigsticking and how the *Sahebs* did it.

During the riots of 1947 Babujee objected to the use of the classification of "muslim" and "non-muslim" refugees. He thought that in India the terms should be "hindu" and "non-hindu". Babujee was posted in Deoband. It meant nothing to me except I recall Sushmadi telling us about the water there being dirty and full of worms. However, since 9\11 Deobandi School of Islam has been in the news and piqued my curiosity.

My memories of Babujee, which extend over a period of 30-35 years, are still very limited and anecdotal. I don't even remember when I heard these stories. What was my perspective? Was I capable of detecting tone and meaning about the situation? Certainly I did not ask him directly. He lived with Mungo, his only son, for the last 20 years of his life. In the Indian culture, that is the way it should be. He, however, made himself as unobtrusive as can be and was not a burden on Mungo or his wife, Mohini Bhabhi. His needs were few and demands minimal.

He was the brother least influenced by British manners and style. He was, however, very well read in English and Hindi. He had great insight into life and the world. One of the points he made to me was that Gandhi was an admirer of English work ethics (*Angreziat)*, while Nehru was enamored of the English (*Angrez*).

My uncle, Chote Babujee, age 94, seated at left with family members. Lucknow, 1987.

I recall another story Babujee told about the time of Sarla (his oldest daughter) and Prem Sunder's marriage. The *baratis* (groom's family) asked for 60 *Thalis* (food trays) serving. The order was written in Urdu. Since in Urdu zero is written as a dot it was misread as a 6. Prem Sunder's brother was very upset about it and was insulting towards Babujee. Babujee's apologies were to no avail so he put his cap on Prem Sunder's brother's feet. Then the tide changed; the brother was chided by Sir Sita Ram and other seniors for being so rude and petty.

I have a lot of memories of *Chote* (smaller) Babujee, my middle uncle. He was the artist and creative person in the family. Vimla, Hem, Sushma and Usha's weddings were all grand affairs arranged by him. I remember the music, the program, the careful planning for them. He composed the songs, set them to music, played the harmonium, and directed the singers. He also sang from time to time. Sushma was the only other artist in the family. She played the sitar and painted and sculpted.

Neetu and Meera had a music teacher for a while, but they hated music. I never had that chance. I don't know how I would have reacted or done as a music student, but as an adult I certainly feel it would be nice to have had some musical training. I do recall as a teenager wanting to learn music, but being turned down by Papa.

Chote Babujee's musical and creative talents were used again for the dedication ceremony of the new Pathology building in 1956-57 at the Lucknow Medical College. There too he had a very elegant ceremony that was dignified without being ostentatious.

As a result of the hard times they had had as children, Papa and his two brothers were very close. The respect and care for the eldest was apparent to all of us as we were growing up. However, I do recall some instances of criticism of Chote Babujee. He was somewhat of a rebel and treated Chachee (his wife) poorly.

In the early forties Chote Babujee lived in downtown Lucknow in a place called Halwasia Court. I have a number of memories of Halwasia Court. We were sent there when Amma was sick; we were being protected from the death experience. The 3rd floor house had a long narrow staircase going up from a car showroom. The house was just outside Hazratgunj and gave us the chance to visit the "big city." The big veranda had a colored tile floor and big balcony facing Mayfair and Lalbagh. From the balcony we used to watch the city, St. Joseph's school, also the Tommies (British soldiers) in Hazratgunj. We saw Mungo going to work and lighting up his cigarette after reaching the street.

Inside was a big room in the back and a smaller courtyard. I remember going there for many visits. At one time Neetu and I both had new glasses (black babu type).

They were identical and got mixed up. With many trials we decided which suited whom the best, and Babujee put a mark on the bridge using a blade.

The house in Halvasia court was connected to the house of a family in the Punjab National Bank Building next door with a *cheenka* (basket) slung on a rope. Food, messages, and other items went back and forth across that narrow road that lead to the Halwasia's garage and the cold storage. I remember going to the garage when our car, the Hillman (USJ 1413), was being fixed. Neetu asked why they used "soot" (discarded threads from cotton mills) to clean up rather than rags. I guess he thought it was tacky to use loose pieces of thread to clean car engines and hands.

The house was very important to Babujee. He had a transfer delayed because he did not want to leave the house. When he had to leave the house he was transferred out of Lucknow to Jhansi. The reason he had to leave Halvasia court was that the war effort required more office space; I presume Mr. Halvasia got more money from offices than he did from flats. Ironically Prem Sunder's (our widowed brother-in-law) office moved into Halvasia court at some time. (or am I totally confused?).

A few years after the posh Halvasia court became offices, the Halvasia market was built. It was a crowded market, and certainly not exclusive.

The years are fuzzy to me, but Chote Babujee lived in all these places and towns: Halwasia, Jhansi, Jublie College, Normal school and Akbarpur House. What is the time frame? He was in Mahanager in 1960, when I left Lucknow.

At one point he moved to the grounds of Normal School, 98.4 school as he called it, alluding to the normal body temperature. The teacher's training school was quite a place. It was closer to Nandinee and had a huge compound where we had lots of room to do things. In his style, Babujee remodeled the house extensively. By one description the house had lots of pottys, no plumbing, and no style.

When Babujee took over at Normal School he cleaned up the whole place. It had been a mental hospital at one time and from its store room Babujee unearthed many interesting items. I recall 2 microscopes that were at Nandinee for sometime and then donated to the pathology department museum. I have my eye on those microscopes, and will try to get them back with Dr. Mehrotra's help.

Babujee also made a garden and built a bridge over the *nala* (open drain.) Due to wartime shortages, he gave up his car and got a horse and buggy. Babujee's buggy with

Chapla (Lightning) pulling it used to go over the bridge, cutting a mile off the journey to Nandinee and the university area. Neetu and I did a bit of riding on Chapla as well. I remember falling off Chapla once.

For a while Babujee stayed at Nandinee, and I recall some events from that time.

Babujee was characterized by his rituals: the shave, the bath, the meals. The bath included a tub with a tall back on one side. I have seen pictures of those in American Westerns and recently saw one somewhere at an antique store. His shaving used to take a long time. It was his time for organizing, putting things together and for a number of rituals. One that I recall involved *Shahad* (honey) and *Amla Murabba* (preserves).

He ate his meals slowly, taking only small amounts of a number of things. He also chewed each mouthful 32 times! Somewhere in that time he also created the single *roti* when *dabal roti* (western style bread) was rationed. Babujee is the only one in the family who never had a weight problem. What a contrast to me who eats fast, eats a lot, and always complains about gaining weight.

At Normal School, they once had a scout troop's performance in which one of the babus was rude to the villagers who came for help. Later I remember many in the family saying that a scout troop should not depict such behavior. One of the comic skits was about a villager/servant who was sent to get some milk from the store. He used the rim of the *lota* (liquid container) to fill in the little extra milk while losing the bulk by inverting the *lota*. I guess some jokes are timeless! This skit was part of a campfire that was on the grounds. There was a good turnout.

One time Babujee lost his whole bunch of keys. Everyone was sure it happened in Nandinee, but an extensive search proved fruitless. For some reason, I was poking around in the joint of the big sofa and found them. I was a hero for a while. Afterwards Babujee tried to reenact the event and figured out how it happened.

Babujee wore his clothes for many years, a habit I am proud to follow. He also kept his shoes very well polished and even carried a cloth in his pocket for his them. Sadly, that is a habit I do not have. I polish my shoes about once a month or so.

Unrelated to his rituals is a vivid memory I have of Babujee during Ushadi's wedding. I know nothing of the background (but would like to find out), but I remember we were near the back entrance of the *angan* near the dressing room. There was a lot of bickering and shouting going on among the three brothers. Chote Babujee was acting as a mediator, and it was the only time I can recall his raising his voice. His words were *"Shadi ke Ghar me Klesh kyon ho raha hai"* (why is there conflict during a wedding?) I remember nothing more, and the wedding took place and all seemed well.

Another one of Babujee's houses was near Jublee College, fairly close to the Medical College. I remember very little about it except that I thought its being near the railway track was a big thrill. One of our bearers was there with me once. He explained to me how the engine driver had seen the signal down the track and was warning the level crossing guard about his approach. I took a *paisa* once and put it on the track of an approaching train. It was interesting to see it flatten out. I recall being scared even though I was standing at quite a distance from the track.

With Babujee, I once accompanied Mr. Sahni, Director of Public Instruction and a big shot in the education department, on an inspection tour. I remember the reception he got at each school with special gates and garlands and the children shouting slogans for his long life. Also I remember kids using the slates and the other modes of writing - like writing in the sand and using pencil shavings to write with their fingers. What the Director of Public Instruction did on tours like this I have no idea.

When Babujee moved to Jhansi for a while, he rode his bike all over the place. I think it was the green Raleigh. (I too am now a regular bike commuter). Once when we visited there, the Gupta family was also there and Shri took us on a picnic. But the car heated up. So we ate up all the *rasgoolas* and made some attempts at cooling the radiator using a towel to drain out the water. Another trip was to some fort that had a *bhool bhulian* (maze) where I was lost for a short time. I was impressed by the plaster which had become shiny from repeated touching in some places.

The Akbarpur house was one of Babujee's houses in Lucknow, and was the seat of a lot of activity for us. I remember spending many evenings there. Karua Chaut was observed there. There was always great food of course. Chachee would take the girls aside and tell them stories while waiting for the moon to come out. Babujee owned a new Vauxhall when he was at Akbarpur house, a grey car with a red trim. The license plate, USJ 5000, had a red line between the USJ and 5000. Babujee said it looked like the plate was made by the Vauxhall Company. I remember Papa asking Mungo if Babujee had enough money to buy the car. Mungo made a gesture indicating that he (Babujee) had to scrape up the money.

Babujee had two women friends, Deoki Pande and Justina Singh. Like so many things in India, particularly when it comes to males and females, nobody talked about the relationship. As a pre-teen, I recall only some murmurings but no discussion. I remember one time in the Normal School house, Deoki's midriff was showing and Babujee tucked it in. Justina, who was a nutritionist, talked about some doctor's recommendations for Vitamin C being too low. I don't remember the amounts, but I can say the American nutritional establishment in those days had very high recommendations. I think Justina said "Tissu" instead of "Tishu". In later years, Rama was another person who said Tissu, imitating the so-called Oxford accent.

Babujee and his *pandan* (a container for beetle leaves and beetle nuts) were inseparable. He has had the same pandan since I was a kid. The pans were made with care; they were *sada* pans (plain) but were good. Eating from them was a special treat for all of us.

Babujee was a founding member of the International Club in Lucknow. I don't know what they did, but they had periodic meetings where Chachee's cooking was featured. I seem to recall some murmurings about how Chachee was being used. The International Club sponsored a group of Pacifists to Lucknow, including Vera Britain.

Chachee's cooking, of course, was the standard by which all cooking in the family was judged. We all craved it and were always amazed and thrilled by it. It was innovative and tasty. Still, when he came to Nandinee at meal times, Babujee often used to say *"Dekha Viddya, aloo kitne achche hain"* (see how good the potatoes are) comparing her cooking to our servant's fare. It was a way to humiliate chachee. Chachee said *"Hanji"* (yes, you are right). Our meals were cooked by servants.

Babujee had a dog named Jolly, a short haired, medium sized brown dog. I remember Babujee was very strict with him. Chachee loved the dog. I wonder if he was humiliating her by beating the dog.

Chachee nursed Neetu and me through our diphtheria and its complications. Thinking back, it must have been hard for the family with Amma dead and both boys with serious illnesses. I remember Chachee asking for *"seel utra pani"* (warm water - literally water without dampness) for our sponge baths. During our diphtheria, we got large doses of anti-diphtheria serum that made me sick with swollen joints. I had a splint put on me. The first splint papa brought was small so he went back and had a custom splint made. I could not move for some days. I remember after a few days being able to turn in bed with the splint on.

While Chachee was staying with us I bought a whistle from a passing vendor. I always wanted a whistle and from somewhere I got a rupee. I got a lot of change back, so I had the problem of walking past her with the change. I was afraid it would jingle in my pocket, so I devised a strategy and placed the coins inside my socks. I must have been walking in a funny way. Chachiee, without fanfare, just asked me to take off my shoes in her presence and the game was up. I don't remember any repercussions, but I do remember the coins distributed all over my feet!

Chachee talked about the riots in the 1920's in Agra. She described a Muslim man all bloody and hurt coming to the house. She helped him with new bandages and gave him milk; then she allowed him to leave.

Babujee's experiences in England were quite interesting. One involved his landlady, Mrs. Harlan, and her friend who photographed spirits. Mrs. Harlan claimed that Mrs. Deane could take photographs of dead people and communicate with them. Babujee did not believe in this and said so. Mrs. Deane said that she had learned this skill from India. One day Babujee felt restless for no reason. He did not know of Tai ji's (his sister-in-law) death. Somehow he ended up at Mrs. Deane's who claimed to bring the spirits in and photograph them. She took a lot of photographs and in them somewhere was a picture of "Tai ji" with her Sari pulled near her face. After he learned about Tai ji's death he got the picture in the mail and fainted. He said he never said "impossible" after that.

At first, when he brought the pictures back to India, he did not show them to anyone. Later, when the family saw them, some people thought they resembled Tai ji. Remember, Mrs. Deane took a lot of photographs and Babujee eliminated many of them as not resembling his sister-in-law. Did Mrs. Deane get from Babujee the facial features of Tai ji and put them in the photographs that matched his descriptions of her? The New York Review of Books had an article in its February 23, 2006 issue about photography and the occult. Here are some quotes from the article. Mrs. Ada Emma Deane features prominently in the article.

The Perfect Medium: Photography and the Occult exhibition at the Metropolitan Museum of Art, New York, September 27— December 31, 2005
That the manifestation of spirits would eventually be recorded by photographic means was inevitable, especially since spiritualism and photography had experienced coincidentally synchronous careers through the nineteenth century...The pictures are, for the most part, grossly and transparently fake...Great Britain never experienced that sort of preemptive court case, although controversies arose regularly... ...Ada Emma Deane produced nearly two thousand pictures before becoming a professional dog breeder in 1933. She was notorious for the pictures she made at several war memorial ceremonies in the early 1920s, in which a nebulous swirl of faces, apparently of dead soldiers, hovered above the crowd. Newspapers gleefully pointed out that the spirit faces included those of living athletes, but the exposure had no effect on Deane or her clientele...Deane's most prominent champion - in fact the world's leading proponent of spirit photography in the twentieth century - was Arthur Conan Doyle.

It is interesting that Babujee went to the most famous of the spirit photographers of England. I made my notes about this when I talked to Babujee in 1985; he was ninety two at that time. By my next trip he was too frail to give me much information. During the interview he said something about the postman rang twice for a letter and three times for a telegram. I think he was referring to the fact that when the photographs were delivered the postman rang three times and this added to the significance of the "photographs of the spirit of his sister-in-law".

In England he worked hard the first year and got his degree. He said the second year was more pleasant. He took a trip to the north of England and Scotland. He was taken to the slums of Glasgow and recalled the stories of slum children being beaten. He went to some islands in N.W. Scotland and remembered it being very cold. At some school in Scotland he attended a conference on plans to revive the Gaelic language.

His trip to Scotland was hosted by Dr. Watty, Director of Education for Scotland. Dr. Watty asked him to move from the YMCA to his house on 24 Burbank Road. Mrs. Watty took him around Glasgow and insisted on paying the bus fare. (Babujee said he had a good memory for details.) The Wattys' house had a maid, Nora, who apparently was very nice. He spent one evening with the maid, Nora, and her friends. He had tea with them. She had tears in her eyes when he left and he got a warm send off.

Babujee went to school and college in Meerut. He then went to Allahbad to get his licentiate in teaching. Following this he went to Calcutta and got a Madhyama in Sanskrit Literature that was equivalent to an M.A. After a few years of teaching he got a state scholarship to go to England; from 1923 to 1925 he studied Western teaching methods for teaching in India. He specialized in Vedic Sanskrit and "regular" Sanskrit. I did not know about all this to ask him more details about his work and how he applied it to his career. Around age 15 Babujee studied music with his cousin Viakul Taoji. He explained that in Western music the emphasis is on harmony while in Indian music the emphasis is on melody. He said he went to a concert by Paderewski and it "fell flat on my ears."

He said he got married when he was twenty and Chachee was thirteen. She was the daughter of a family friend. He talked to her for five minutes and agreed to marry her. He also clarified and gave more details about some of the family.

He was a defender of India and Hindi. Some English woman said to him: "What a funny language you have when 'kal' stands for both yesterday and tomorrow". Babujee immediately wrote 'read' on a paper and asked her to read it. She had to acknowledge that English also had ambiguities.

Babujee was very methodical and kept a diary starting in 1937. I never read the dairy. I wonder if anyone did or where it is now. He also bought a lottery ticket every month for years - he never won.

When Babujee came back from England he also brought back with him a British family he had befriended there. Apparently, this family was not very educated or sophisticated and their presence caused some tension and problems in the family. They did not stay for long, but their being with him hurt his career. It appears that Babujee's association with this uneducated family was an embarrassment to his superiors who were upper class Englishmen. They somehow felt that Babujee was demeaning the English and it caused him to lose some promotions. After their departure, his career did progress, but the stigma remained and he was not able to reach the high levels that he had been considered capable of achieving.

Questions have been asked by the younger generation: why did one brother excel in life to become a well known Professor in the Medical College, while Chote Babujee, who had a Master's in Sanskrit and degrees from England in education, did not become as well known? A young nephew who had heard about the two but had relatively little contact with either asked me this question in 2009, many years after both brothers had died. It is a difficult question and I certainly do not have answers. I can conjecture and make some generalizations.

Babujee was more of a humanist. He did his studies and got his degrees but he was interested in people rather than his career. He also had a lot of interest in the arts, especially music. He had poor judgment in choosing friends. He let go of promotions because he liked the flat he lived in. He wanted that flat and the lifestyle there. He composed music, performed plays, and worked on aesthetics in his life. Maybe he was focused on himself (he was self indulgent) and did not pay attention to the necessary career moves. Maybe he did not indulge his bosses. From my perspective, he seemed satisfied with his situation. Maybe he felt that ambition leads to conflict and tension. Maybe. And creativity itself is associated with different priorities and behavior.

The two brothers were born in a well to do family, with a large house. The family was prominent in their small town. Their father died when they were very young. A brother not much older than them gave up his studies and took jobs to support the two brothers and their mother. The eldest sacrificed a lot but in the end had the satisfaction of having a successful and happy family. He died knowing that his brothers loved and respected him and they were happy and able to reciprocate some of what he had done for them.

But what of the brothers? How were their lives? How did they fare and how did the world see them? What did they achieve? Were they "successful"? The older of the two went into literature, music and education. He got his higher education in England in the 1920s, worked with some pioneers in educational innovation and had a career in the Education Department of the largest province in British India and subsequently the largest state in Independent India. He was a man with many talents. He could sing, compose and he wrote, but he did not rise to the highest levels in the hierarchy of the educational bureaucracy of the state. The younger of the two went into medicine. He too went to England for further education and training and returned to pursue a career in academic medicine in one of the oldest Medical Colleges in India, his alma mater. He was broadly educated, had an interest in literature, gardening and music. He reached the top levels of authority in the medical school.

Two brothers with difficult beginnings who, as Indians, did well under the British. They had their early education in a small town. They got their college and professional education in good colleges and did well. In the twenties, the elder brother went to England. He was to get further degrees but apparently did not complete them. He did get good training and education. He returned with ideas and joined the Government Education Department. He made changes in the colleges he worked in. But, despite his brilliance and intelligence, he did not reach the higher levels of the administration. He was friends with the top people like the Director of Public Instruction (DPI) but did not get that position.

But we should remember that in every bureaucracy there is a pyramid and only one person can get to the top. Who reaches that position? What are their qualifications and qualities? Was it just a matter of luck and circumstance? Was it his lifestyle, which included a lot of attention to his personal comfort, food, clothing and housing? Did he not do the right thing to please the bosses? Who can say? We will never know.

Did his younger brother have better luck? Was his ambition, his drive greater and that is what gave him the opportunities to rise? Then there is the field of each of their careers. Education has been the neglected field in all societies; medicine was much glorified and received a lot of attention and resources. At the time of India's independence, emphasis was given to post graduate education and medicine. There was help from foreign institutions like the British Council, which funded University education, and Rockefeller that funded Medical Colleges. Early education, which was Babujee's field, did not get that kind of support.

Also, Papa was more ambitious - more methodical and focused on his work and career. As best as I can judge, he did not "play the game" but still did work with some of the powers that be. His job allowed him to have a better home, better clothes, and the opportunity to impress more people. He was organized and had long term plans that led to the development of a better organized and modern department of pathology and medical school. He caught the attention of the Rockefellers, which further helped. One can only speculate.

Papa had a cousin, I just know him as Viakul Tao Ji. He wrote, sang, composed and was an overall creative person. *Harishchandra* is one of his plays. I remember a play on *Harishchandra* in school. I have a picture album which shows Viakul Tao ji - a man in a big but trimmed beard, tall, and wearing a *dhoti*. I was told once when the great V.D. Paluskar visited Meerut, Viakul was pitted against him and did well.

My uncle, Viakul. He was the poet, singer and playwright

Viakul died under tragic circumstances. He neglected a small ulcer that had developed on his tongue. Although Papa arranged for surgery when it was relatively small, Viakul would not have it removed; ultimately it lead to a slow, painful death from cancer. There was a discussion of trying to do his surgery without telling him. For a long time before he died he was unable to talk because of the tumor. He finally bled to death.

He had said he would not have his tongue cut out, because with that tongue he had charmed hundreds. He acknowledged his imminent death and told Babujee, "I will not be there to receive you when you return from England."

What was his family's connection with ours? How far removed a cousin was he? When was he born? I place his death in the mid to late twenties. Chandrahas Bhai saheb was Tao Ji's son. He would have been born around 1910.

All I remember is that Bhai saheb was very tall and lanky. I don't think I have met him in years. Usha's wedding? Mungo's wedding? But I did have the chance to talk to Chitto (Chandrahas Bhai's son) in the mid nineties, and he gave me some information that helped to put some of these facts together. My grandfather had two brothers, one whose name Chitto did not recall. The other, Badri Prasad, owned a bank and had no children. There was some mishap, the bank failed, and B.P. essentially disappeared. I do recall Chachi or Papa telling us about a failed bank from which we received some money over the years. Anyway, Chitto's great grandfather had a son Bishambar Sahai who died in 1925 at age 52. Viakul, the other son, was very upset by his uncle B.P.'s disappearance and became somewhat of a recluse, thus the name Viakul. He was a teacher and was also called Ustad Saheb, revered teacher. As I said earlier, he was talented and brilliant. He had 5 children: 3 died early; Padamhans died in 1936 from cirrhosis, and Chanderhas died in 1961 of a stroke. Chitto is Chanderhas' only living child, born in 1932.

Chitto had some rather interesting anecdotes about Viakul Tao Ji - who was something of a rebel and a pioneer. Apparently there was a *shradh* (death ceremony) for Lalaji (Chitto's great grandfather) and Lalaji did not like heavy foods. Viakul Tao Ji said there should be *dal-chawal* (simple foods) and not *puri Kachauri* (fancy foods). This of course upset the *pandit* (priest). However, since Viakul was "eating on behalf of his father" the pandits could not insist on *puris*. He was also responsible for some of our breaks from orthodoxy.

He may also have been an anarchist. Apparently he was arrested when a bomb exploded near Lord Hardinge, even though he was not directly involved. Ravi Pratap's (our classmate in medical college) grandfather was also involved in some way.

He founded a *Natak* (theatre) company, which did the plays Harishchandra and Gautama Buddha. Gandhiji is said to have seen Harishchandra and was influenced by it. Ustad saheb was not a worldly man. As a result, the Seths, his sponsors, made a lot of money off those plays and Tao Ji made nothing. Later the Seths tried to pay him and help him, but he refused. He also was the first man to write Hindi prose. Quite a set of achievements for a teacher from a small town who enjoyed chess and was rather casual about his teaching responsibilities!

Going back to some of my own memories, I remember Maa ji, my paternal grandmother, a little. I remember her in Halwasia court. She was very old and wrinkled. I recall her climbing the stairs slowly on all fours, one by one. I remember talking to her at Babujee's in a big room behind the veranda. All I recall is her referring to "babu" which of course was appalling to me since everyone else said "Babujee". The stories that I recall paint her as a tyrant in some ways, but being benevolent in other ways.

She was very progressive too. Apparently one of the neighboring mothers-in-law was very conservative and the daughters-in-law were only allowed to wear very thick materials. At night when they came to their husbands they were provided with cotton dhotis by Maji, and they were washed and dried at our house. The mother-in-law never found out.

She controlled the young women of her own household very strictly. The wives of her 3 sons lived with her for extended periods. They were under her control and had to perform demeaning tasks and be obsequious to her. The phrase used by her sons in later years was that they 'rescued' their wives as soon as they could. I am not sure when Papa was married and when he 'rescued' Amma, presumably after he graduated from medical college. But when he went to England, soon after I was born, Amma did live in Meerut. She managed to divide her time between living with Maa ji and living in the new house that her eldest brother had built outside the old city. An extended family lived there including: my eldest uncle (Bade Mama ji Sri Brij Nath Mithal); my Nana and Nani (grandfather and grandmother); several brothers, and the eldest of Mama ji's children from his first wife. After her death, he had several children from his second wife. I was brought up for the first two years in the permissive atmosphere of Ram Batika, commonly referred to as "Kothi." I was brought there to live with a host of my cousins. The environment, I imagine, was similar to a lion's pride where a number of cubs roam around among the lionesses of the pride, seeking solace with whichever mother happened to be around. Discipline was a low priority. I was spoiled - at least in comparison with the British norms that Papa followed on his return from England when I was two years old.

Bade Babu ji's wife died in the 1920s. He had five daughters and one son. Because of his circumstances they were sent to Meerut, and were under Maaji's supervision. She displayed some of her worst attitudes to those children. All the children did go to school, at least that was not denied by Maa ji. On returning from school, the girls were given leftover rotis and vegetables and had to fend for themselves. On the other hand, Mungo bhyya, the only boy was fed fresh cooked food of his choice by Maa ji herself. If the girls, in their envy and curiosity, peeked while Bhyya was eating, they were rebuked for spoiling his peace of mind. Such differences in her treatment of the children based on gender were presumably ingrained in society and were the norm of the day. Yet the discrimination did not prevent them from getting a good education. And the next generation also made every effort to "rescue" the girls from Meerut and provide them with the best of education.

Sarla ji ji, the eldest, was married early to a man about twelve years her senior. Hem ji ji was given a good education, doing her science in Naini Tal. She went on to enter Lady Hardinge Medical College in Delhi, and was one of the early women doctors in India. Vimla di came to Lucknow to do her Bachelor's and education training. She taught for some years and married one of the University lecturers. She stayed with us for a while when she was in college after our mother died. She got support for her education while at the same time helping Papa with the running of the household and taking care of us. Hem ji ji's medical education was also supported by Papa.

Sushma di and Usha di were educated at Shantiniketan, at that time a revolutionary institution directly supervised by the great Rabindra Nath Tagore. Their education was supported by Chote Babujee.

After the mid thirties we had minimal contact with Meerut. Maa ji did visit Lucknow and was revered and feared. None of her sons or their children lived with her. She died in the mid forties. Apart from the physical inconveniences of living in a 'primitive' environment, I can only generally speculate about the social aspects of the conservative or old fashioned life. We were not exposed to it, but continued to hear about and feel it in our lives outside of Meerut. The children of my generation were born between 1913 (Sarla ji ji my eldest cousin) and 1935 (me). We had varying numbers of years in Meerut, but lived outside Meerut for most of our lives. Education of girls and boys was a high priority. The two younger brothers supported their nieces' and nephews' education just as the eldest had supported theirs. Their love and respect for him never lessened and he, the least educated, remained the head of the family.

Weddings did bring the clan together. One of our chapters in school was an excerpt from Nehru's <u>Discovery of India</u>. He defended the celebrations because they provided a break from the "drudgery and prosaic life" that poor people have.

Another gentleman was Lachmiji, son of a female cousin of papa's. He was a simple man from the village. The story of him drinking a whole cup of pure ghee stands out from Usha di's wedding.

Amongst the closer relatives was Sarla ji ji who was Bade Babujee's eldest daughter. She was born in 1913. That makes Babujee 25 when she was born - a rather late age for those times. She was married to Mr. Prem Sunder, and died in the early thirties. Prem Sunder married twice after that and remained a part of our lives till the 1950s. The second wife ran away, but his third wife, also named Meera, was closely associated with the family. Prem Sunder Jija was very much a part of our life. He was close to papa's age and a good friend of Mungo Bhyyas. I remember him because he entertained us kids and played with us. He took us to Tarzan movies (Johnny Weissmuller) and afterwards would play Tarzan and made us play the part of the chimp. He did a trick with a pith helmet - made it lift up when he blew hard and pretended he had a hole in his head.

He had a series of jobs. One was with the Maharaja of Gwalior. Apparently he was a confidant of the Maharaja and had a good life. Papa warned him that such jobs are tenuous. And indeed he was fired with no warning. He then became a Government servant and at one time was in the Directorate General of Supplies and Disposal after the war. I seem to recall some remarks that he made a lot of money and was subsequently fired. He retired to Ghaziabad to his family home. His brother Anup was in the next house. Anup's son Ramesh then came to do his premedical test in Lucknow and stayed with us. We were classmates through Medical College and have remained close friends. At one time Papa called Prem Sunder a "*Binapendi ka Lota*" (a vessel with no base which could go every which way). Prem Sunder had no children. In his later years he adopted a boy. After the boy's marriage his new daughter-in-law and her family gave Prem Sunder and Meera di a hard time.

Hem Jiji was Bade Babujee's second daughter and was born in 1915. She was the one who spent the least amount of time in Meerut, thus escaping the wrath and harsh treatment of our grandmother. She got her Medical degree from Lady Hardinge Medical College in the late 1930s. I remember being at Charbagh Lucknow railway station to receive her after her graduation. I have memories of seeing the train at a distance as it negotiated a turn. The train was more important to me than a cousin returning home with a medical degree.

Jiji did her house jobs and subsequently worked at Queen Mary's Hospital and was a lecturer there. She drove a car. She needed a pillow behind her back to be able to drive comfortably. She was quite a hit in Lucknow.

In the mid-forties one of our uncles, Prem Sarup Mausaji, was posted in Fyzabad. There was an Indian Civil Service officer posted there. The family went to Fyzabad to meet him. It was during World War II and some luxuries were not easily available. Mausaji got a large can of cheese, which he opened with great excitement. It turned out that it was not cheese but salted butter. We struggled and dutifully, slowly, consumed it.

Mr. Bhairav Dutt Sanwal met the family. One encounter was on a pontoon bridge in Ayodhya when jiji and Dada met. I was standing next to them. Chaperone! A group of men were pushing a cart across the pontoon bridge and it got stuck in a rut. Dada Sanwal immediately went over and helped them pull the cart out. Anyway Dada was approved based on his intelligence and broad based reading (he had been in England for his studies). Jiji and Dada got married in Lucknow at Nandinee. It was quite a grand affair, with a carefully choreographed ceremony - orchestrated by Chote Babujee, the creative one in the family. The day after the wedding there was a reception at the Mayfair Ballroom. The outstanding thing about that event is that Jiji was late for her own wedding reception. Meera remembers that after the reception jiji sat in papa's lap and cried.

As I said, Jiji was quite a sensation in Lucknow. She was pretty, she was a lecturer at one of the best-known Medical colleges in the country, and she was married to the city Magistrate. She also caused consternation in the family when she wanted to use the name "Mangalik-Sanwal". Jiji and Dada lived in a large, elegant house on Park Road where they entertained in style. She was forced to resign her job when Dada was posted to different parts of UP in his job. She maintained her professional activities when she was associated with the All India Family Planning Association.

Dada Sanwal came from a family in Almora. They had limited resources. However, Dada's potential was recognized by the family, which put together everything they could and sent him to England to take the Indian Civil Service examinations. This previously British-only service had only recently been opened to Indians; it carried considerable prestige and power. Dada was successful and had an illustrious career.

Apart from being a civil servant, he was a scholar. He wrote a book on Nepal and the East India Company. In the late fifties and early sixties, while he was posted in Agra as Commissioner, he was the chief liaison and guide to a host of visiting dignitaries including: Bulganin, Kosygin, Khrushchev, Brezhnev, Queen Elizabeth and Prince Phillip, Eisenhower, and Jackie Kennedy. He wrote a book on "Agra and its Monuments," and one can see what a great guide he must have been to all those world figures.

In his earlier years I remember him talking to us kids about all kinds of things. His brother was an associate of the geographer Dudley Stamp (whose text book we used in our school). Mr. Stamp had a plane and we got to ride in it and went over Lucknow. He showed me Rai Behari Lal Road, which had recently been resurfaced with a red gravel. The repair of R.B.L. Road caused some stir. There were accusations that the road was repaired because his *sasural* (in-law's house) was on that road. The work allegedly then stopped prematurely.

Later, during another posting in Lucknow, Dada was city Administrator. One of his achievements increased the amount of water available in the taps in Lucknow. He did this based on his observation of large numbers of leaky taps all over the city that caused a lot of waste. I remember a communal tap in our neighborhood that leaked constantly. It was at the main intersection in New Hydrabad near the barbershop. It was designed to work with a lever which had to be pressed to make the water flow. Theoretically it was supposed to shut off as soon as the person using it left. However, it didn't, and continued to leak. Dada sent out a whole team of repairman all over the city to fix leaking taps free of charge. One of those people came to our house and did fix our one leaking tap where the pots and pairs were scrubbed. The interesting thing was that this worker had poor equipment and he had to borrow a razor blade from us in order to trim the leather washer to make it fit properly. But the strategy worked. There was more water in Lucknow than had been available for a long time. The Advani family, who lived on an upper floor, had been plagued with water shortages for a long time. They were thrilled to have a regular supply of water. Dada Advani, nick-named Dada Sanwal, was seen as "*Jal Daatta*" (giver of water).

Dada has been involved in a large number of intellectual activities. He is a pleasure to visit on our trips. He has interesting anecdotes from his career and his life. It is said that he was not a good civil servant. This may mean many things to many people. To me one of the meanings of this characterizations is that he chose to do what he felt was the right thing and not what would please his bosses or the politicians. He does not seem to be bitter. He has a lot of admirers now that he is ninety. He retains an interest in a variety of activities. He can provide relevant perspectives and insights into a variety of issues under discussion. He does not proselytize, but has his ideas and opinions. Recently he made an interesting comment about the population issue. Noting that the birth rate amongst the poor remains high and that of the well to do is lower and declining, he said: "Christ said: the poor shall inherit the earth." He was not being callous, just commenting on the sad reality that there are more and more poor in the world.

Mungo Bhyya was a part of my life for extended periods. Since he lived in Lucknow for most of his life, I remained in close contact with him until he died. His wife, Mohini was a mother figure for me for a long time - at least since my teenage years. She helped me with conflicts with Papa and helped me adjust to the problems of that difficult period. She and Sonoo, their son, have remained a big part of my life.

Mungo Bhyya is best remembered for his dapper style. He was the one who took us to the fancy tailors - Ramlal and Sons, and Draper and Company - and made sure we had the correct style, length, and cut to our winter coats and pants. He used to have the master tailor shave off a quarter inch or half inch to create the correct fall and feel of the clothes. I just cannot imagine how that worked; I have worn ready made clothes almost exclusively as an adult. I failed to appreciate the significance of those small changes until I read an article in the January 3, 2011 issue of the New Yorker magazine that described the finickiness of Claude Brouet, the creative director of Hermes, the high fashion house. It is said…"she could pick out the slightest imperfection in fit or proportion. 'She would say, 'A hair makes a difference,' he recalls. 'The precision of her eye! And I would learn. Why did she like a certain length in a skirt? Eccchhh, it was awful. But then I would really look, and she would be right." Mungo himself was always properly dressed. He and Papa had similar tastes and both were just as particular.

Bhyya lived in Nandinee for some years. He had the guest room and kept late hours. He had a motorcycle. He had been a tennis player in college, but I do not recall watching him play tennis. Later he was associated with the All India Lawn Tennis Association, and provided me with used Davis Cup balls of good quality. The tennis playing students appreciated those balls because the ones available to us while I was at the Institute were of poor quality. Bhayya did go the club regularly and remained well known through his life in Lucknow as being among the better bridge players.

From the family I heard stories of him being spoiled by our grandmother, and the contrast in the way he and his sisters were treated. I also remember his job in the railways and his signing up for the army during the war. The railway job did give me a chance to see the activities of the station master (blowing the whistle which had to be loud) and also a chance to go close to the railway engine which was a big thrill. Later, during our scouting trip to Nainital, I went around the Railway yard at Kthgodam on my own and climbed onto a railway engine. I talked to no one but recall that the fireman was chided for letting me on board. I, as I said, do not have too many childhood memories of Bhayya, but a lot of interaction starting from my days in medical college until a few days before he died.

I remember Khurja and Vimla di's marriage, the singing and rehearsals and the family. Ramesh bhayya was in Lucknow University and they lived for a while on the other end of Rai Behari Lal Road, an easy bike ride for us. She had an Ayah who had worked with the British and she took care of Rakesh while Vimla di was completing her B.Ed. degree. Before her final examination she asked me to bring some of my friends to her house so she could practice her lesson with us. She taught us a lesson on Tibet. She had a map and she began with the river that started in the mountains. I remember a description of one of their habits. Because they used butter and did not change their clothes, their clothes became like leather.

Rakesh was sick a lot during childhood. He had ear infections and needed surgery. At one time it was suggested to Vimla di that she use some kind of amulet, tie it on Rakesh and then leave it at a crossroad. Whoever touched the amulet first would have the curse transferred to them. Vimla di thought that was unethical and did not follow the advice. She told us that she was in a school play and was playing Abhimannyu. After Abhimanyu's death his mother said: "*Mera Abhimannyu tu Kaha hai* (My Abhimannyu where are you) Vimla di chirped "I am right here." Whether in rehearsal or in the real play I am not sure.

Vimla di was involved in our care after Amma's death and helped to take care of the household. She also remarked that the gifts that Rakesh received were mostly of a practical nature. I remember her going around on a bicycle. I also remember her house when she moved to Lucknow University campus. We played cricket there, and many of the traditional teeka and other events were held there.

Sushma di also stayed in Nandinee off and on. I remember her being the artist in the family. She did leather work, sculpting in soapstone, and painting. One of her pieces, a MiraBai. is with us. I remember her describing how, in the finishing stages of a

soapstone sculpture, the artist uses a silk cloth to give a sheen. I presented her with one of my paintings that I did when I was in school.

Sushma di was married to the younger brother of Vimla di's husband. (Two brothers marrying two sisters is an accepted practice in our culture.) The marriage did not last long; in fact, it was never consummated. Her husband remarried after a few years. I recall her making a comment to the effect that DInesh is a good man. I remained ignorant of the background and real reason for the unconsummated marriage. Sushma di is a lesbian. Imagine the implications of this in India in the 1940's.

She had a career in the education department. She rose to responsible positions in the system. Her strong personality led to some conflicts during her career; she did not rise to levels she should have. There was mention in the family of personal issues too.

Usha di lived with us in the late forties. She did Diploma in Foreign Affairs and Diplomacy-DFAD-which was quite a mouthful, and was new to most people. My most striking memory of her is her describing the multiple injuries she sustained and how she was afraid of being scolded. One time she fell from some ledge and immediately got up and said: "*Ladi Nahni, Ladi Nahni*" (I am not hurt). She was striking because of her height and her large *bindi*-which most people called a *binda* (a mark on the forehead). She also wore very few woolens and was never cold.

While Usha di was living with us, Meera was in college. Earlier I recall young men coming to the house to be interviewed for their suitability to marry Usha di. One was a salesman for Singer sewing machines. He was rejected ostensibly because he wore black shoes and brown socks. Obviously there was more, but even to this day I will not wear mismatched shoes and socks.

Usha di married a nice man, an engineer; they spent many years in the hill regions of the state supervising major construction projects in the heyday of Nehru's 5 year plans. Their postings gave us the opportunity to have some great trips. He and I had different political views but we had some good discussions.

I have written about the Mangaliks as I remember them and as I reconstructed some stories after talking to some of my distant relatives in Meerut who still live in and around our ancestral house. I was able to reconstruct some of the family tree after a visit to a panda in Haridwar in the early nineties. While this account may be patchy, it is interesting to me to have gone through this exercise. And those in the family who have read it find it interesting.

Are we special, who can say? Some have achieved excellence in their fields. Some have dealt successfully with problems, others not. That is not the point. I wrote what I remembered and was of interest to me.

***

Chapter Five
Ancestors

When I was growing up, we did not sit down and talk about our family. On and off there was mention of some family member from the time before I was born. I did not have a coherent story or narrative. Later in life, in my forties, I developed an interest in tracking the family down. With the help of some family members, I got some names and relationships. I learned the name of my village of origin and my sub-caste (*Gotra*) and used this to try to get more information. Armed with some of this background, I went to Haridwar, a holy place, to meet with the priests (*Pandas*) who specialize in genealogy. My observations and experience of that trip - which I wrote down soon after the visit in January 1988 - follow.

Well I can go back much further than I thought - to Samwat 1807 in fact, when Kishan Chand of Delhi was in Haridwar and visited the family of Pandit Mangat Ram.

Samwat 1807 is 1752 A.D. The current year (1988) is Samwat 2044. In Samwat 2044 I visited with Mr. Rameshwar Prasad, son of Mr. Mangat Ram. Others in my family have met with Mr. Rameshwar Prasad's family on previous occasions. The last visitor was my grandfather Mr. Munnalal who was in Haridwar in Samwat 1947 (97 years ago). Mr. Munnalal was Tehsildar of Dehra Doon, and came with his eldest son Madan Mohan and some servants. Chote Babujee was about 1 year old then. We just celebrated his 95th birthday.

What an experience! This process was something I had heard of and even tried once. But the *Pandas* I met in 1975 did not have much to go by because I did not know much about my family then. Well this time I came in with more information about the family - enough to be able to go further. We got to *Har-ki-Pauri* (the ghats) in a state of confusion.

Nobody seemed to know much. The place was teeming with lunchtime crowds of beggars and we were all bewildered, confused, and on short fuses. We took off our shoes and walked towards the ghat. I wanted to just walk around and get a feel for things, and then go step by step. Instead the *Pandas*, young, immature, pushy types came after me. You must do this, you must do that. I kept my cool and told them this was a free country and I didn't have to do anything. That did not go down too well and they kept talking. In any case, I did want to do something. I kept letting them know about my interest in checking on my family who had visited the place. Five, seven more people asked me caste — *Bania*, subcaste (*Gotra*) — *Mangal*, village — *Kasna* (Dasna) and district Bullandshahar.

Through a system of their own, people kept coming back asking the same questions and also telling me the network was working and "my man" was being located. One young fellow came by, opened the book, searched the index, but had no luck. Then came Mr. Rameshwar Prasad. He looked mature and I felt confident with him. Caste; Gotra; village, name — Munnalal grandfather. Wait he says, "I think I have it." So he is gone for a short time. He comes back with a cloth bound bundle of papers, loose leaf except for a string going through to tie it all together. He opens a page, putting the book on the Puja shop. He says, "I found it." He proceeds to narrate the names of grandfather, his brothers and some kids. They also make sense. The work I had done on my genealogy helped; I knew he was on the right track. Yes, 1947 (*samwat*) - 97 years ago they had been there. With my grandfather was his son Maden Mohan. No mention of the other kids. Murari was either unborn or a newborn, and Vanmali of course was nowhere in the picture. Now this man is my man. He tells me so.

Now that we have found the names and the family I get to do all the rituals. I was not interested in the ritual but Joanie (the woman I was married to at that time) said I should, so we begin. I like to know what I am getting into so, "How much?" I ask him. He is a pro: "5p to 5 Lac Rupee" he says. I say, "Ok. Let's go." He puts a damp gunny bag on the wet steps and asks me to sit. He comes back with a *Thali* (tray) with *Atta* (flour) *chandan* (sandalwood paste) *lal tika* (vermillion) and 2 rings of straw. He puts incense sticks on the step. The photographers take their places, Saurabh, Joanie and Matt and we get going. He asks me to hold my hands: right hand supinated with a cup being formed by the palm; the left hand holding the right wrist. The straw rings are on each hand's ring fingers. Name of father, mother, grandfather, grandmother. The prayer starts for the blessing of each of them. Then how much donation and offering, then how much for the poor and how much for the cows and how many Brahmins to be fed Rs 101 each. I mumble some numbers not knowing how they will be totaled. I decided it was educational and interesting and worth spending some money on. The ritual goes on to making balls of dough. He gives me each ball as he says the name and groups them in couples. He then asks me to put *chandan* on each, sprinkle rice and wheat grain (in husk) on them. Then I toss them all into the river. I get my *tika* at the puja stall, Pasha gets one too and then onto the Rameshwar Prasad house. Five rupees for the man at the stall.

We put on our shoes and go off to the bazaar and to the back of a tobacco shop. The tube light is turned on to reveal bundles of books tied together. Questioning reveals that the system is based on geography, and yet our family had moved and the record was together! In the shop we read the whole file. There is another entry that goes back to 1807 (A.D. 1752).

Mr. Kishan Chand was *kanoongo* in Delhi and he had been there with his family. In all the excitement and confusion and because I did not understand the system I did not find out if there were other entries or did it go from s-1807-1947, a 140 year gap and then a 97 year gap. That would be amazing!

The books in which the genealogy records are kept.

He asks me about the family since that last visit: my uncle, my father, my cousins, my brother and sister - no, not the sister, only the males, my cousin's son, not his wife, my son and those who were present that day, my American girlfriend and my son's American friend. We are all entered. The list is complete. My sister's children are not recorded.

I hope I get a chance to go there again to get more details and record them fully.

वरीये मंगल

वासी कासरो के रहे अमेरीका मे
वालषनऊ मे मो० केन्ट गे लीo
अरुप वा असोक वेटा बनमाली
सरसा पोता मुनालाल के: अरुपका
वेटा सोहरव: ताऊ भद्न मोहनका
वेटा मनोरजन का वेटा मुकुल रहे
दील्ली वालषनऊ मे: ताऊ सुरारी स
रसा: अरुप श्री गंगाजी आये
स्नान की साथ धर्मपत्नी जोनी बेटी
रनी की अमेरीका वाले की साथ वेटा
सोहरव आया वा सोहरव का मित्र
भिष्णीव आभा   प्राप्त

Entries made by the panda.

Our entries in the genealogy records

***

But I do have a family tree going back to the 18th century. It looks like the following:

MY ANCESTORS

Kishan Chand – Kanoongo (Magistrate) in Delhi around Samvat 1807 = 1751 A.D.
    Budh Singh
        Harbans Rai
            Janki Das
                MunnaLal d. 1900 (Grandfather)
                    Madan Mohan Saran (Mangalik added later)
                    Murari Saran
                    Vanmali Saran
            Unknown
                Viakul
                    Chandrahas
                    Tilak
                        Chitto
Rajan Singh
Shilapat

MY RECENT FAMILY'S TREE

MunnaLal and Maji (I did not know her name) Grandfather and Grandmother
    Madan Mohan Saran Mangalik (Bade Babujee uncle)
        Sarla
        Hem
            Harshvardhan (Pushkin)
            Mukul (Linu)
        Manoranjan (Mungo)
            Mukul (Sonoo)
        Vimla
            Rakesh
            Saket
            Raju
        Sushma
        Usha
            Mamta
    Murari Saran Mangalik (Chote Babujee uncle)
    Vanmali Saran Mangalik (Father)
        Meera
            Sameer (Bunu)
            Bhavna (Minnie)
        Ashok (Neetu)
        Aroop (Paroo)
            Saurabh (Pasha)

***

Chapter Six
Politics

We were not a political family. No one stood for elections. No one participated in the marches and procession during the 1942 Quit India Movement. Possibly one distant relative was in a march near the University in a mob that was tear-gassed.

We did hear stories of freedom fighters who sacrificed themselves. One story I remember went something like this: a man had loosened almost all the screws of a railway bridge but left a crucial screw intact. He stayed on the bridge until the troop train was almost at the bridge. He loosened the last screw at the last moment and died as the bridge collapsed, taking the troop train down with it. Highly romantic, but not a very likely story.

Some of my cousins wore *Khadi*, homespun cloth advocated by Gandhi ji. I am not even sure if Papa supported the idea of the British being forced to leave India.

However, Gandhi ji's death had a major impact on us. Apart from the fact that the country was mourning and we were all affected, Papa (a non-believer) went on a fast on the day of his funeral and actually joined the masses and walked with a procession of mourners.

We supported Nehru and talked a little about the local politicians. We did not get involved with the elections to any significant degree.

The major political exposure we had were the discussions on communism and the evils of capitalism. From very early in my life, I remember hearing about the positive aspects of the egalitarianism offered by communism. We had literature about the Soviet Union and read a lot of it. We also went to movies about the Soviet Union and World War II - mainly about the German atrocities in the U.S.S.R. I remember one in which a Soviet civilian killed a Nazi soldier and the Germans rounded up fifty civilians to be shot in retaliation. The civilians in the Soviet film managed to over-power the Nazi soldiers and killed many of them.

Such actions of collective punishment continue, as in Israel and Palestine and other parts of the world. We saw a documentary on Israel in the early forties. An Indian gentleman, a friend of Papa's, was married to a Jewish woman. I do not know which country she came from. The documentary, what I remember of it, showed how the great Jewish people had "made the desert bloom." They had learned to desalinate the soil, and had done this despite the hostile neighbors, the Arabs. It was a propaganda film and it was not until the late sixties that I learned the truth about the manner of Israeli occupation of Palestine. I do remember Papa's point that Jew was a religious term and Mrs. Kashyap's talking about "my people" was inappropriate.

Then there were the movies of the May Day parades with dancers, children and soldiers. We got the communist party newspapers. Peoples War (later named "Peoples Age"), and later, Blitz, provided us with an alternative view of the world.

There was a book entitled "The Terror of Birla House." It was an expose written by a man fired by the Birlas. Papa said the Birlas managed to have the book banned. I did see a copy - its cover showed a poor man's tears turning to money for the Birlas.

At the Indian People's Theatre Association we saw a show they put up at Mayfair and the movie about the Bengal Famine of 1943 called "*Dharti-ke-lal*" (jewels of the soil). This film made a great impression on me. I still remember many of the scenes. I have tried many times to find a video/CD of this movie without success. Even Udai Shankar's movie Kalpana had a leftist theme for me.

The influence at home was reinforced by Mr. Abid Ali, one of our teachers. He described how Karl Marx sat in the British Library for years documenting the atrocities of the rich on the poor. He also said that Marx was so busy that he did not have time to get a haircut or shave; for that reason communists kept long hair and beards. I did and still believe in the principle of communism, but have also accepted that there were many negatives. There was a real life story from Lucknow that also reinforced the views that we grew up with.

There were two brothers who had opened a successful bookstore in the posh Hazratgunj market. They started as newspaper vendors and gradually rose to open this bookstore - Universal Book Depot - that was successful. I once asked Papa how something like that could happen under a communist system. He pointed out that the way in which the brothers had succeeded was in making money. They did not have intellectual success. This made a lot of sense to me.

But of course the reality is that nowadays money is increasingly the main criterion for success. We never looked upon money made from sources other than salary to be of any worth, but we lived well. We were leftist, but had a comfortable life with a nice house and garden, servants, etc. But we did sympathize with and supported the peoples' movements. In our social circle I only knew of Dr. N.P. Gupta, Dr. Habib Bano, and Mr. Yashpal who were classified as "communists."

After the election of Eisenhower, Papa predicted that the Americans would be even more strongly in favor of business and against the peoples' governments. He was right. John Foster Dulles and the C.I.A. toppled the Iranian prime minister who dared to nationalize the oil industry of Iran. The U.S. got involved in Vietnam after the French were defeated at Dien Bien Phu. Eisenhower did do an amazing thing at his farewell speech when he warned of the rising power of the "Military-Industrial Complex". (Now we have a "Medical-Industrial Complex," and only Arnold Relman has had the courage to write about it.)

The Korean War also had a different reason for me. Based on the writings of Kwaja Ahmad Abbas in the Blitz, I believed (and still believe) that the Americans provoked the North Koreans and then started the "Police Action" despite a veto by the Soviet Union in the U.N. Security Council. From his 1948 trip to the U.S. Papa brought back reports of the conditions of the Negros living in Washington. That made quite an impression on me.

As time has gone on and as the Soviet Union has collapsed and China has become the world's greatest "Capitalist" nation, I have had to modify my thinking. Meera, Neetu and Kishin's points of view were and are different from mine. Most in my generation did not buy the communist model. They do, however, remain supporters of social services for the poor and agree that government in India has not done enough for the people. Even with my recognition of the terrible times of Stalin and Mao, I remain much to the left of my family and friends. The debate goes on every time we get together.

I saw and heard of some of the evils of the power of money in those early years after independence. The flat that Babujee lived in was called Halwasia Court. It was owned by a rich man, Mr. Halwasia. He had plenty of money, but made much more as a contractor supplying goods to the British Army during the war. He consolidated his gains by becoming a member of the Lucknow Municipal Committee. On the day of his nomination, when he was congratulated by his people, he threw baskets of coins to the crowd. We saw, from Babujee's balcony, how people went crazy picking up the coins that were thrown at them. One did read of such largesse being given out by kings of the old order. Some things don't change.

I also heard about the Chief Minister of U.P, Mr. Pant, who helped the Industrialists Modi and Dalmia by giving them large amounts of land and building a hydroelectric dam near a factory. These giveaways were presumably in return for donations to the party.

In our social position, we had the opportunity of interacting with rich people. On one occasion we visited a small town near Lucknow where there was a plywood factory and a sugar mill. The owner was a friend of a friend of Papa's. We got to see the two factories, which were very interesting. At the plywood factory, they took logs of wood and "shaved" them like one shaves a pencil in a pencil sharpener; straight and large sheets of wood were produced from the logs. These sheets were placed in 3 plys going at right angles to each other to produce strong 3 ply plywood. At another part of the factory they made the veneer that went on the outside. For this, they took thin sheets of the shavings with pretty patterns on them; these were matched and "sewn" together using heat and glue. All the pieces were put together to make attractive plywood sheets. The man who matched the patterns of the veneer and sewed them together was a wizened old man. On him depended the beauty (and presumably the salability) of the plywood that was used for high - end furniture - sofas, doors, wardrobes.

The other factory was a sugar mill. Here we saw all the stages following the piles of sugar cane brought in by the poor farmers in bullock carts. The cane was weighed and put into a conveyer belt. The farmers were paid the going rate - negotiated at a high level by the Government officials, the farmer's cooperative and factory owners. A lot of politics went into the process of fixing the price. The sugar cane was chopped, crushed, and pulverized. The residue was dry to touch and was used as fuel to run the boilers that ran the factory. The sugar cane juice was boiled, refined, and crystallized to provide the pure sugar crystals for our tables. Thousands of pounds were produced daily. I seem to recall that each day the production yielded more money for the factory owner than Papa made in a month. The owner complained that he could keep the production going with many fewer workers but the unions did not allow a reduction in the number of workers. I do remember there were workers just standing around watching the largely automated processing, Papa talked to the factory owner and just listened to his complaints. Later he analyzed the numbers and we were appalled by the high profits the factory owners made.

Papa's friend who arranged for the tours of the factory was an eye surgeon. He had established a large eye hospital in that small town of Sitapur. That hospital was amazing and made quite an impression on me. The focus of the eye hospital was cataract surgery. Cataracts affect a large number of older people and are the leading cause of blindness. The patients were provided the surgery at no or low cost. The costs of other facilities and services were kept to a minimum. The patients came from nearby villages in their bullock carts - often whole families came. They camped out on the grounds of the hospital. The post-operative care required seven or so days and was the responsibility of the family. The patient needed strict bed rest for the period. The family cooked their meals on open fires on the hospital grounds. I had seen the movie <u>Gone with the Wind</u> sometime before that trip and the scene reminded me of the camps of confederate soldiers after their defeat. The reality is, though, that these people got eye surgery that gave them the gift of sight. It was not perfect, not "first class," but much better than a life without vision.

The eye hospital was set up as an assembly line. There were four operating tables in a row. Papa's friend did all the surgeries, removing the cataracts and putting stitches in the eye. He moved on to the next table and the next. The first patient had the eye bandaged and moved out. By the time the fourth table was done, there was a new patient ready on the first table and so the cycle went. Dr. Mehra provided sight to many people and was a revered figure in the community and deservedly so.

Charity is a form of politics. Politicians use charities to get exposure. Also, people who run the charities get involved with politics. The eye surgeon was well known and did have influence.

***

Chapter Seven
Amma's Family

*My mother's house, designed for an extended joint family under one roof.
I spent the first two years of my life in this house.*

Amma died when we were very young. I had lived in Meerut for the first two years of my life when Papa was in England for his training in London. And we visited Meerut before she died, but my memories are fleeting and mixed with recollections of visits later in life. My contacts with the Mithal family, especially those who lived in Meerut, were sporadic. I do not recall Amma's father ever coming to Lucknow. He was born in 1871 and died in 1953 at age 82.

I am grateful to my cousin Nippoo, Nrapendra Nath, for compiling a lot of information on the family. Nippoo and I met a few times but never discussed the details of our family - one of the many regrets I have as Nippoo died in early 2010. (More on Nippoo at the end of this chapter).

Amma had six brothers and one sister. My contact with them was limited. Some I did interact with. Her eldest brother Brij Nath Mithal was born in 1890. He was a forward thinking man who broke many bad traditions. Especially important was reducing waste at weddings and funerals and, more importantly, not asking for dowry when his sons got married. At that time asking for dowry was the norm; he took quite a radical step. He had a lucrative law practice in Meerut. He probably had the biggest house in Meerut through the thirties, forties and fifties. It was a joint family house with many generations living in "apartments" around a central courtyard and sharing a common kitchen. He was an advisor to many big name political figures including ministers and ambassadors. My personal memory of him is of a rather obese man, but one who had dignity and a presence. He died at age 63, the same year as his father.

Of his five brothers, my other *mamas* (maternal uncles), I had contact with only two. One was a police officer who came by to visit us in Lucknow from time to time probably during my teens. One time when he was posted in Benaras (Varansi) he sent us *Langra* mangoes. Those were the days when each region had its special foods, especially mangoes. I cannot say I remember the flavor of those mangoes, but I do remember how special they were.

Amma's youngest brother was a doctor, a graduate of the old Agra Medical School that awarded a Licentiate degree. This was a program more suited to the needs of the common patient with common illnesses. Raja mamaji served in World War II and then set up a practice in Meerut. He was regarded as the best. He worked hard and provided treatments to a lot of patients. Patients preferred his clinic to the Government hospital. He was Papa's favorite brother-in-law and the only relative with whom Papa wanted to maintain a relationship. In 1953 his eldest daughter got married in Meerut. This was the only Mithal wedding that Papa ever went to. It was also my first visit to Meerut after Amma's death.

Raja mamaji had five daughters and one son. My contact with them remained infrequent until I started spending some of my vacations in Meerut when I was dating Asha, my first wife. In the fourth and fifth year of Medical College I visited Meerut several times. I got to know many of my cousins, not just Raja mamaji's children, but also the families that lived in the big family home (*Kothi*) which had been built by my eldest mama. It was a rewarding experience. They were all so warm, welcoming, and intelligent, well read people. I learned about the family, and about life in a world I had not seen before. Thinking back though, my focus was on my studies and work, and I did not develop a lasting relationship with them.

I visited Narendra Bhyya in Allahabad when he was a justice at the U.P. High Court. I met Navin and his wife from time to time in Bombay and in the U.S. The cousin with whom I have had the longest relationship is Raja mamaji's daughter, Manju. She was widowed early in life and remarried a few years later. Since OP Vaish and Manju live in Delhi, I have maintained close ties with them and their children. OP, Manju and some of the kids have visited us in the U.S.A. also.

The only other people I had continuing contacts with were Deoki Bhyya and his family. He was my eldest mama ji's second son. He had lived in Lucknow since the early forties. His wife, Rukmani Bhabhi, was a great cook and we enjoyed many a meal there. His older children were just a few years younger than I. Annu (Anirudh) and Nilu were three to four years younger and we played together. Deoki Bhyya lived in a house with a courtyard covered by an iron grill. It was, I think, to keep the monkeys out of the house, especially the kitchen. The grill was a sturdy structure but scary to me. Annu and Nilu walked across it without any fear. Despite my fear, I did try walking on it a few times.

Deoki Bhyya was a lawyer and worked for the State Legislature and was the Secretary of the Legislature for many years. I recall some conversations about how he had to deal with ministers and legislatures who wanted to bend the rules while his responsibility was to maintain the rules. A classic case of responsibility without authority. I think his biggest strength was his honesty; he was able to hold his ground because he was not beholden to any politician. He probably knew a lot of secrets about many powerful people in the state. He retired in the sixties and was a part of a select group of intelligent, well read people in Lucknow.

He was my first cousin but twenty years my senior so our relationship was like uncle-nephew rather than of cousins. I remember him as a pleasant, gentle person who did not throw his weight around. It was because of him that the family from Meerut visited Lucknow and allowed us to maintain some contact with them.

The children in Deoki Bhyya's house were not subject to the strict disciple that we were. As children we noted the difference between our upbringing and theirs. I remember being scared because Annu and Neelu behaved in a more free - spirited manner, and I was afraid Papa would scold me for what they did. They were all very smart and all did well in life. We have maintained a good relationship even though our lives have intersected in a sporadic fashion.

Annu, who retired from top jobs in the Indian Railways, lives in Lucknow. He has been invaluable in helping my paternal cousins Sushmadi and Mohini Bhabhi. These are cousins of mine from Papa's side and thus no relation of Deoki Bhyya's family. However, Annu continues to help them in multiple important ways. He says that Deoki

Bhyya asked him to help them, and he sees it as his duty. Annu and I have had some interesting discussions about politics and railways.

Recently another side of Amma's family opened up to me. Over the past few years I have had some very good times at Arvind (Deoki Bhyya's 3rd son) and Geeta's house in Boston. Arvind has been a professor at the Massachusetts Institute of Technology for many years. I have grown close to him and Geeta and their sons Divakar and Prabhakar. I have visited them many times and stayed with them in their very warm home. Prabhakar and Divakar have both chosen medicine as a career and that adds to my closeness to them.

One time Arvind was visiting Los Alamos National Laboratory. He and his friends dropped in and we had a very pleasant evening. It was informal and casual, as is common in India.

The Arvind connection opened up another part of Amma's family to me. On my visits to Meerut in the fifties and sixties I had occasional brief contacts with Deoki Bhyya's younger brother, Avadh Bhyya, who was also much older than I. After that I had no contact with him or his family. Then, during Arvind's sixtieth birthday celebrations in 2007, I met Avadh Bhyya's grandson, Abhinav, and granddaughter, Pragati. Abhinav was working in Boston for an electronics company. His sister Pragati and her husband were visiting from Connecticut. After due introductions, I gradually got oriented to our relationship, and then got immersed in the delightful company and conversation of these two groups of people. I also found myself as a "grandfather" to these adults. It was quite a shock. They continue to call me Baba ji, but my relationship to them is warm and close, not grandfather-like. Pragati's husband, Manish, is a delightful, intelligent caring man.

As a surprise, their father, Praveen, who is my nephew but about fifteen years my junior, also flew in from India. I got to visit with him and plan to spend time with him in Meerut on my next visit.

The most special of all these cousins was Nippoo, my eldest uncle's son from his second wife, who was five years younger than I. I do not remember meeting him earlier in life. When I was working at the All India Institute of Medical Sciences in the mid-sixties, he was doing his Ph.D in Microbiology. Nippoo immigrated to Canada and then the U.S. I visited him in Maryland when he was working for the American Red Cross. We again lost touch but knew of each other's whereabouts. About nine years ago he sent me his family's history that he had compiled. I read it, but not very closely. It did, however, inspire me to start writing my own story and that of my father's family. Only recently did I read Nippoo's writing in detail and realized how much we had in common. As I said, I feel sorry that we did not sit down and talk about all this in detail.

About three years ago he was diagnosed with a low grade type of leukemia. He was being treated by a good hematologist and he did have some control of his disease. Two years ago I spent an afternoon with him at his home outside Chicago. We talked about his disease openly; Margret was very much a part of the discussion. Nippoo was realistic and aware of the nature of his illness. We communicated from time to time about the treatments and their side effects. The disease progressed and he died in early 2010. Judging from the emails that were exchanged between the families it was clear how much he was loved and admired by all.

I started this sharing of memories and anecdotes by talking about "From the Galis of Meerut to Rockefeller Center". The same could be said for Amma's family. They went from Ram Batika to Massachusetts Institute of Technology or the High Court or high technology institutions in the U.S. and China. They all reflect change, adaptability, and progress in the conventional use of the word. It is not my place to pass judgment on what is better - Westernization, old Indian values, or a combination of both.

***

Chapter Eight
Friends

Papa had a lot of friends. Some I met and interacted with; others I just heard about. Some were doctors from the Medical College. Others were family friends or distant relatives.

Sir Sitaram was an older gentleman and a family friend whom I saw several times in my early years in medical college. He was the speaker of the U.P. Assembly and later High Commissioner to Pakistan, an important man in U.P. politics. Once we were invited to his house for dinner, probably in the late forties. After dinner he asked Papa if he smoked. Papa said he did, but he would not smoke in Sir Sitaram's presence. Papa was close to fifty years old. But not smoking in their presence was the normal way to demonstrate respect for elders.

Mungo used to smoke but only outside the house. When Babujee was at Halwasia court we used to watch him after he left the house and walked towards Gunj. As soon as he got to the street he used to light up, and we almost cheered when we saw him do that. I, too, was known to smoke by the time I finished medical college, but never in front of Papa. One time when I was doing my post graduation at AIIMS I came home for vacation and, in some kind of nervous action, pulled out a packet of Panamas from my pocket. Brinda and the other servants were aghast to see me do that. Papa commented that I had started buying packets rather than the more acceptable single cigarettes.

Papa had a unique way of smoking; he kept his cigarettes in his mouth all the time except to flick the ash once in a while. He could roll his cigarettes from one side of his mouth to the other without stopping his conversation, and could keep a pretty long piece of ash hanging from his cigarette without dropping it. It was quite an intriguing sight for many people.

A friend of Papa's with whom we had, and still have, a long association was Dr. Ram Surnan Lal. He had two children, Ravi and Sudha, so we called him "Ravi Sudha Lal". Papa and he were in Medical College together and spent many years together in Agra. Dr. Lal sported a mustache, which we called a Hitler mustache. However, looking at his photographs now, I don't think that was accurate. His was much wider than Hitler's mustache and he had a very pleasant, happy face. I do not have memories of Agra but Neetu and Meera do. Actually, that is not quite true; we did stay with them for a few days in the early fifties when he was head of the mental hospital.

Dr. Lal and family were in Lucknow at the Balrampur Hospital in the forties when I was 8-10 years old. We used to spend a lot of time with Ravi and Sudha and we ate at their house often. They were big meat eaters and it was at their house that we learnt to eat the marrow from goats. It was disgusting at first, especially when it came out as a tubular blob. Mrs. Lal was a strong character, but also very caring.

In those days Sudha used to sing and people said she looked like Shirley Temple. I was her "boyfriend" and we used to play "*Raja-Rani*" (King-Queen). One time Sudha and I saw a funeral go by their house. There was a band playing, and I seem to recall the body being in some form of an open frame. I was informed later that it was the funeral of an old lady and they were celebrating her life.

Ravi had an air gun and we shot that a few times. He used to say "by jove" a lot. The movie "A Matter of Life and Death" came out during that time. Ravi's hero was the doctor who rode a motorcycle. Ravi got hold of some pilot's goggles and pretended to be the doctor. Dr. Lal got posted out of Balrampur and we lost touch with each other for some years. When I was in the first year of Medical College, Sudha got engaged to Krishan whose family was from Lucknow. She came and stayed with us for a few days. She was quite scared by the human bones that I had in my room.

Sudha went home to Agra to be with her parents when her first child, Gita, was born in 1955. Dr. Lal had just picked her up from the railway station when he had a massive heart attack and died in the car. He was 55 years old. Papa was understandably upset and did go to Agra for the funeral. Ironically, Ravi also died at the age of 55.

We have kept in touch. While they were in Delhi (on different postings) we met regularly. When Krishan was posted to Gangtok we had a wonderful vacation there and then we spent several days with them in Goa in the early eighties. Both times we got VIP treatment. Krishan was posted to the Northeast border area during the 1962 invasion. Those were bad times. But he did go to Lhasa and met Nehru who had direct responsibility for that region in those days. Sudha and Krishan gave us an antique *tankha* -Tibetan tapestry. They now live outside Delhi; I see them whenever I can.

Papa and his close friend Dr. R.S. Lal in the 1930s.

Talking of Balrampur Hospital, around 1945 Papa had all his teeth extracted at the hospital by his dentist, Dr. Mahmood Shah. I presume Dr. Shah did not have privileges at the Medical College. Bade babujee, Neetu and I visited him. Babujee was sure that everyone would know where his "famous" brother was admitted.

I remember Papa spitting blood while we were there.

Two other friends of whom I have patchy but vivid memories are S.P. Sharma and Lt. Col. Asthana. Sharma ji and Mrs. Sharma were from Agra, where he was professor of English. The association with the family was longstanding. He visited Lucknow a few times and stayed with us. He had slick, black hair, which he brushed straight back. He smoked non-filtered cigarettes and removed small flakes of tobacco from his lips.

The Asthana family was present at some weddings. He was retired military. He was once describing how he had seen bulldozers make roads in Assam during the war.

For some reason Mrs. Asthana was in Nandinee at one time and she was boiling and purifying ghee.

Another friend was Mr. P.N. Katju whom Papa knew from the Agra days. He had the reputation of being a big talker and came by a few times. He happened to be Nehru's *Saru* (brother-in-law) and talked a lot about *Jawhar Bhai*. In 1948 Papa, Neetu, and Meera went on summer vacation while I still had my finals. I was staying with Vimla di. Katju Saheb came to visit and was eager to visit Indira Gandhi, his niece, who lived in Lucknow then. He designated me his friend, philosopher, and guide and we visited Indira Gandhi. Oddly, we were received at the gate where they talked for a while. And then we left. We were never invited inside the house!

Other friends were the Munnawar family. We went there for a Christmas party once complete with Santa, tree, and all. A group of Hindi carolers same by singing lustily, and using the *Dhapli* (tambourine) with gusto. Everybody got gifts. Neetu and I got a pencil set.

Dr. C.B. Singh was a friend from Papa's college days. I heard a lot about him, but had very little interaction with him. Dr. Singh married an English woman who made him live like an English man. Papa said one time he visited us while Amma was cooking Indian food. Dr. Singh became ecstatic and thoroughly enjoyed himself.

Dr. Khazanchand was another classmate of Papa's. He lived in a small town in the hills north of Lucknow. He had a general practice in Almora, a full day's drive from the rail-head, which was an overnight train journey from Lucknow. Later he became the head of the Tuberculosis Sanitarium in Bhowali and was much closer to the rail-head. His three daughters studied in Lucknow and we have been close family friends. We visited them in Bhowali many times. The Bhowali Sanitarium was in a picturesque setting in the hills, with cottages for the patients and a hospital building for the more seriously ill patients. This was the period before there was a drug treatment for tuberculosis. Surgical treatment was the main procedure.

Based on the understanding of the disease in those days, patients were treated with different methods to cause the lung to collapse. I don't think there was any real proof that the treatment worked. The other part of the treatment was the fresh air and good nutrition in the mountains.

One of my visits was after I had completed my preclinical years but before I had actually worked with patients. I was able to see one of the surgeries done by Dr. Khazanchand's assistants. It was a procedure called thoracoplasty in which half of the ribs were removed and led to the collapse of the lung. When I saw it, the surgery was done under local anesthesia. The patient was awake and sitting up leaning on a rest. The doctor was using scalpels, chisels and bone cutters. If the patient was in pain, he did not show it. It made quite an impression on me, and made me realize I was not cut out (pardon the pun) to be a surgeon.

Dr. Khazanchand had a 1928 car that he drove up and down the steep hills on unpaved roads. Their house was large, and there were guests coming in and out all the time. The meals were also large, with lots of people eating the delicious varieties of food. Dr. Khazanchand was lean and had a hearty appetite. One of his favorites was mango with *roti* (Indian bread) that he often ate on the run as a dessert.

Of the guests that came, the most memorable was Mr. Udai Shankar. He was a pioneer of movies and created a new style of Indian dance - classical but still with an appeal to the general audience. He was the elder brother of Ravi Shankar who is much better known in the Western world. Udai Shankar had a base in Almora when Dr. Khazanchand lived there, and they were friends.

While writing about Dr. Khazanchand, I was reminded of a picnic we went to while on that trip. We went by bus to a nearby lake that was relatively quiet. On the bus, there were some young men who started singing popular songs in English. I did not know those songs and I was quite impressed. I also felt inferior because I did not know those songs. I did not know Hindi songs either, but never felt inferior about not knowing them.

When I had a tonsillectomy a friend of Papa's was there with Papa during my post-operative period. Dr. Feldman did my surgery. I guess I did well and recovered quickly. I remember a friend of Papa praised Dr. Feldman's work by saying that the previous patients he had seen were in pain for several days. Somewhere down the road I looked up "several" in the dictionary and wondered if he had used the term correctly. In the post operative period Dr. Feldman let me handle his *Khukhri* - large Nepali Gurkha knife. I also got to eat ice cream.

Dr. Feldman treated Meera for her sinusitis. They used argyrole, a silver compound that was dark brown liquid. For a long time after that she was draining this brown liquid from her nose. She was using wads of cotton to wipe the argyrole because it could not be washed out from her handkerchiefs. Mrs. Feldman treated me with diathermy when I developed scrum sickness from my diphtheria serum treatments. She also treated me with ultraviolet light when I was considered to be weak and sickly. These treatments were used commonly in those days, but were later abandoned when they were found to be non-efficacious.

The Feldmans had an elegant home, and we had a few formal meals there. They had a piano and one time Papa tried his hand at it. I think he played some Indian Raga. Paul said that it sounded like a Chinese piece. Papa had learned some music; he also played the tabla a few times. Neither of us children had any musical sense.

The Feldmans came to Nandinee regularly. Some of those visits were related to my post tonsillectomy check up. He used to bring his head mirror to check my throat. He used the morning sunlight to reflect the light into my throat. To the great admiration and astonishment of the kids, he also used the concave mirror to concentrate the heat onto a match until it lighted. He also entertained us with the veins in his forehead. He used to put his head down and bring it up showing huge bulging veins.

Paul (Feldman) was also our swimming coach. We used the pool at Krishna Motors near the Feldman's house. He had a refrain for Jiji "Gooth, gooth the legs must touch" - the "t" being the soft European sound, like the Hindi "Tha".

About the time of Independence the Feldmans moved to London. He became a Harley Street consultant. Many years later Mrs. Feldman read one of my papers and wrote me a nice letter. Then in 1971 when I was in London, I saw their name at a clinic but for some reason I did not go in. I was scared, shy, or what?

***

PART THREE
THE CITY

Chapter Nine
General Life in Lucknow

When we moved to Lucknow there was electricity in the city, but its grid was primitive - probably on a par with other technological systems. We and our friends had fully electrified houses, but many other houses in the neighborhood did not have any electricity. Our servants' quarters also had no electricity.

There were just a few street lights. In those days a man went around on a bicycle with a hook on the end of a pole. Every morning he would turn off the street lights and every evening he turned them on.

We had several levels of fuses. Some were for parts of the house we called local fuse because we could repair them ourselves. There was a major fuse for the whole house that was fixed by one or two servants who had special expertise. Regularly, for reasons I did not understand, a fuse blew at the main transmission line. When that happened a group of workers came from the headquarters, which was 2-3 miles away. They walked to the electric pole, which was across the street from us, pushing a ladder mounted on a cart. The time it took for them to get to our house varied from 1-2 hours. If they were out to fix another fuse, they needed to return to the central office to get instructions for the next assignment. The men came and fixed the fuse and stopped by the house for a while. They were nice and we gave them tea and snacks. They spent their day walking from one trouble spot to another. In order to be efficient, they would ask us to call the central office to find out if there was another place they needed to go. This saved them some walking and also saved time.

Transport was mostly by horse drawn tongas and ekkas. Tongas were for us, the elite, and ekkas for the poor. The tonga and ekka wallas were proud of their vehicles; they did them up in colors, with feather decorations and shining bells for the horses. Cycle rickshaws and then buses were later introductions.

Papa's trip to England in 1935 was by ship. Even in the fifties many of my friends went to England by ship. In 1948 Papa did fly to the U.S., but that was quite an event. By the time he retired there were flights to most state capitals in India, but it was still an event to fly. Cars were around but so few in number that we recognized the ones owned by our friends and prominent people in town. We could track their social life by seeing their cars in front of shops or cinema theaters.

Phones and refrigerators could be called curiosities - so few of them existed. We had radios and we dabbled with crystal sets. Radios were found in only a few homes and in some shops where they were used to draw customers. We even had grapefruit that was developed in the Botanical Gardens (later research laboratories) in Lucknow.

The nuclear age began in this period and blossomed into the awesome arsenals of the cold war. Peaceful nuclear energy was touted by the powers that be as a solution to the world's problems. There was hype about being able to dig the Suez or Panama canals in a matter of weeks with one bomb, or powering a large ship around the world with a spoon of tea leaves. This too we discussed at the dinner table.

Plastic was another major change. We Mangaliks were ahead on that too. We bought a set of plastic dishes around 1948 that caused quite a sensation. They were said to be unbreakable. Unfortunately, I found out during a scouting trip that they did break. I had to be rescued from a "cupless" state by a kind scoutmaster. A family friend - and later brother-in-law - was a big hit because he made new and advanced plastic letter openers for us.

The city was very different when we first got to Lucknow compared to 1960, the time when Papa retired and we abandoned the city as our home. When we were small we could go from our place to shopping, visiting friends, and movies without much difficulty. We were, however, constrained by our own small town mind set. The two miles to Hazratgunj we considered to be a great distance. Four miles to the railway station was a big thing. We were also restrained by our attitudes about the city. We went to the other shopping areas like Aminabad, where we bought utilitarian things, only when it was really necessary.

We never went to the old city because it was just not up to our standards; we believed it was for the locals. In Aminabad we usually went to one store, that of Mr. Tandon. We went there infrequently, but the owner seemed to have a cordial relationship with Papa that went back to the days when Papa was a medical student. The things we bought there were special, not needed daily but still important. They were items not available in the posh places in Hazratgunj. For example, we bought our hats at Tandon's. The "right" kind of hat in those days was the *sola topi*. Police officers wore them for hunting, riding, and other outdoor activities. The scouts and cubs also wore them regularly. They were made from the pith - the soft core - of certain reeds. The material was fluffy, white, and light. It was in many ways like Styrofoam, being light and a good insulator. The pith was shaped into the form of the hat then covered with old newspapers. Over that was stretched a cover of cloth. The cloth was usually khaki, but some were white and a few even a darker brown. The inside was lined with a soft cloth and a leather band. They had a chin strap which could be taken over the brim to provide a smart look. There were also small holes to allow the warm air from inside the hat to escape. We had the hats fitted to our head shape and size, and then the salesman pulled them into shape by hooking them over his knee.

We also bought thermos flasks there. The thermos flask was quite an invention! In those days before Fiberglas or Styrofoam, insulation in the thermos flask was provided by blocking the three ways in which heat is dissipated - by conduction, convection, and radiation. We studied these actions in our physics class. The thermos consisted of an outer metal case inside of which was suspended the insulating part of the device - which was made of shining, reflective, smooth glass that reflected back a lot of the heat. This was the second mechanism of the thermos - containing radiant heat. The glass itself, being a poor conductor of heat, helped to produce insulation. The third method of heat loss - convection - was minimized by the clever construction of the glass container; it was double walled, and the space between the walls was devoid of air. The vacuum prevented heat transfer by convection. The glass was fragile and its most fragile part was the nozzle through which the air was sucked out in the factory. We checked it carefully before we bought the thermos flask. The glass container was suspended inside the metal container at the lip and there was some soft material around it. Despite all these safeguards, the whole contraption was quite fragile and had to be handled carefully. The top was closed with a cork lid. Thermos flasks came in many shapes and sizes. I remember one that was about 4" in diameter and 18 or so inches high. There were many smaller ones including I cup versions for coffee and tea.

A Thermos flask or *sola topi* may be quaint now and some may say, "What is the big deal?" The point to remember is that the materials available in those days were limited. Plastic, polyurethanes, Fiberglas, and Styrofoam were either not available, or in the early stages of laboratory development. In my opinion, developing an effective insulating container from the available materials was quite an achievement. The use of natural materials like pith is also significant. It shows the ingenuity of the manufacturers. They collected the pith from reeds, each one providing probably a cubic inch or two of the material. I am sorry that I never got to see factories where pith was processed. I did see a small factory where the *sola topis* were put together.

Another thought that came to me as I started writing this was: now that we have so many good insulating materials, how come no one makes *sola topis*? Styrofoam or Fiberglas hats would be good insulators. My guess is that it was a British fear of the hot tropical sun that led them to devise that type of hat. After the British left, that phobia disappeared; the need was gone. This, however, does not fit with the saying "Only mad dogs and Englishmen go out in the midday sun," (a phrase coined by Noel Coward). Maybe the Englishmen could go out in the midday sun because they wore *sola topis*.

Another thing we bought at Tandon's was raincoats. Those were big items, especially since we outgrew them every year. The raincoats were a necessity because monsoons were heavy and lasted for a couple of months after school started. Technology for rain gear was more primitive than what we have today. Raincoats were made of canvas or rubberized cloth as described in <u>From Here To Eternity</u>. Some raincoats leaked and you got wet from the rain. Then there were others that were very effective against the rain but did not allow any air exchange. In the warm monsoon weather you got soaked from your own sweat.

The Tandon's shop, typical for the time and place, was small and narrow. Clean white sheets were in the front part. The owners sat on the floor leaning on pillows. The customers sat on small chairs in the veranda. The store went back quite a distance. There were shelves along the walls and there were servants sitting in the second story of the store where most of the goods were kept. There was an opening in the ceiling. When the brothers shouted the orders up to the servants, the item magically dropped from the "sky."

That kind of shop contained a large amount of merchandise in a small space. The key to its success, of course, was the ability of the owners/salesman to keep track of their inventory. They knew what they had in the store and presumably knew when to re-order. Before computers and globalization these men knew their business and their inventory perfectly. These types of shops still exist. I saw them in Yusuf Sarai near the Institute in the sixties and seventies, and again on my trips since I settled in the U.S. There seem to be fewer and fewer of these shops in the cities, but they do exist in the small towns. The big malls make it difficult for such shops to exist. Chain stores with their huge numbers of choices, brands, and varieties do not allow the old fashioned type of shopkeeping. In those days, we, who were well to do, only had a pair of tennis shoes, one pair of sandals and one pair of closed shoes.

I still enjoy shopping in the older stores. The connection with the shopkeeper is so much warmer than dealing with a smart, well-dressed impersonal salesperson in the malls. Aminabad, Chowk, Daligunj etc. were the old markets of Lucknow. Except for the Tandon's in Aminabad, I don't remember going to any of them as a child or even as an adult. It was during my "discovery of India" in the eighties and nineties that I visited these older markets. I am no sociologist but I can see the bond that these places create. For years I wondered why people continued to live in such places even when they had money and education. Now I can see, or at least understand, the draw of the familiar. I do think about, and hope (fantasize) about a really effective birth control program that would leave intact but much less crowded the Chowks of Lucknow, Budhana gates of Meerut, and Chandini Chowks of Delhi.

I have another vivid memory of Aminabad. It must have been in the mid forties when Dada Sanwal was city Magistrate. There was an exhibition and sale in the park in the middle of Aminabad. A major fire had destroyed most of the stalls. The fire apparently started when someone was cooking right in the middle of those shops, which were made of wood and full of clothes and other flammable goods. Dada for some reason took me along when he went to check on the situation. I remember the charred stores and their merchandise. I also remember a shopkeeper who lost *lacs* worth of shoes. (A *lac* is 100,000 rupees. Our house was bought for 35,000 rupees) We talked to the fire fighters who described how they were focusing on the gate because, they felt, if that caught fire and fell towards the main shops the disaster would have been compounded. The shopkeepers wanted them to focus on their own shops. In 1987, I went to Aminabad again with Dada, this time accompanied by my ex-wife Joanie. It was quite an experience to see this place of which I had only vague memories. She too was fascinated by it. The crowding, however, was overwhelming.

Like the Tandon store in Aminabad, another unforgettable stop was at the Indo-Burmah petrol pump. Papa had a long relationship with the gentleman who owned and operated it. The current term "petrol or gas station" would not be appropriate or accurate. Just outside the posh Hazratgunj shopping area, in one of the back streets, was a single petrol pump. It had two jars made of glass, each one gallon in size. When Papa told the owner how many gallons of petrol he wanted and gave the needed coupons (petrol was rationed for many years when I was growing up), he would move a handle back and forth to fill one of the bulbs. He then let the petrol flow into the tank and started pumping the handle to fill the other bulb. He went on alternately filling each bulb until we got all the petrol we needed. The pump was in the corner and right behind it was the office, a small room with a desk where the owner sat. It was personal, he knew us, talked to us a little and we were on our way.

I forgot to mention one other old market experience - the wholesale fruit and vegetable market. A few times I went to this Mundi near Kaiserbagh where fruit and vegetables were brought in from the surrounding villages and sold wholesale. I also remember large handcarts full of vegetables being rushed to the market early in the morning, with five or six people pushing the cart, laughing and seemingly enjoying themselves. Anyway, at the market we checked out the mangoes, and bought a large amount - probably for a party. The mangoes were served with ice cream. They were cooled by putting them in a basket and lowering them into the well. The well was chilly and allowed us to cool the mangoes without the use of a refrigerator.

The city was small and quiet. There were large areas with no construction or buildings. This allowed some sounds to be heard at great distances. The zoo was probably 2-3 miles from our house, but the sounds of the animals came through to

Nandinee, our home. We could hear the lions and monkeys. One particular monkey was loud. We all called him "hukkoo" from the sound he made. Hukkoo was quite a draw when we went to the zoo. He could be provoked into shouting hukkoo, hukko if someone made that sound around his cage.

The zoo was spacious, there was no through traffic, and it was a great place for picnics. In those days, there was no entrance fee, yet only the well to do went there. Whatever the psychological or social dynamic, it was quiet and uncrowded because the unwritten rules made it a place for us and our type. In a recent article in the *New Yorker* (June 27, 2011, p. 43) a similar phenomenon was reported by Alice Walton at her Crystal Bridges Museum in Arkansas. When she started bringing in school children to visit, "They say, 'We didn't know we could go to a museum,' 'We thought that was for rich people,' 'We didn't know they would let us in.'" By the sixties and seventies "our" zoo was discovered by people who were not rich; it became crowded with buildings, museums, shops and lots of people. The barriers were broken and the effect of the increased population became quite clear- as it is in the whole city (and the country). There is more crowding but less sanitation - even in the affluent parts of the city. Hazratgunj, the elite shopping area, has more shops, more cars, and more traffic in general. This is inevitable with more people, a larger middle class, and changing attitudes.

For me, also, many of the landmark stores are gone. The Universal Book Depot closed because of litigation within the family. Mayfair, the last movie theater that showed Hollywood films, could not find the clientele. The nicer restaurants closed and the rich started using the restaurants in the new five star hotels. There were some changes that had to happen, but for the nostalgia-prone person much has been lost. It is different and it is not what I remember.

***

Chapter Ten
Sociology and Religion

As we were growing up, the world around us was full of contrasts, contradictions and for me, after all these years, a feeling that it did not happen, or perhaps could not happen. And I know there were inconsistencies in that world that would be hard for many others to believe. George Orwell once wrote that he was born in the "lower-upper-middle class, not grand by any means, better off and better educated than tradesmen, to be sure, but without the social cachet of people who might mix with ease in high metropolitan society." We were in that class too.

The contrasts were visible in our day-to-day lives at home, in the neighborhood, around the city, and in the villages that we went to occasionally. We lived well with a house, garden, electricity, flush toilets and running water. We had a dining room, pantry and all that goes with it. In addition, each person had his own bedroom.

Our servants, some of whom had several children, had much less. I know about the living conditions of those who lived in our servant's quarters; they each had one room with a verandah and a small yard. That is what they got regardless of the size of their family. They had no electricity, and for toilets they used fields near the house. There was one tap for all the servants; it was in a shed open on all sides. As life is relative, it should be noted that many people and the servants of many of our friends had even worse living conditions. I know nothing of the living conditions of the help who lived on their own. They were the ones who came to do specific tasks like scrubbing the pots and pans, cleaning the bathrooms, and sweeping the outside of the house.

We got a good education. The servant's children, like a majority of the poor Indians, got little education. Thinking back I am not sure if they had any. As far as I knew Papa did not support their education or encourage them to send the kids to school. He did support and help one student through his medical school. He was the son of Papa's laboratory assistant and a very hard working and dedicated man. In the current generation, Neetu and Meera have made it a part of their mission to provide some education to their young servants or their servants' children.

The walled compound we lived in was kept very clean. The house, the garden, the driveway, and the courtyard in the back were all swept at least daily - leaves, scraps and dust cleaned out meticulously. There was a wall separating the servants' area from ours. Behind the wall it was not so clean. There were sheep tied to a tree, there was a compost pit, and overall it was quite dirty. Just outside the wall too there was a lot of trash on the road - street cleaning was not a part of the municipality's priorities. Just about a hundred yards from our gate was a major intersection that was the hub of the neighborhood. There was a barber shop, "panwalis" shop, a small provision shop and the halwai's shop. Next to the pan shop was the garbage dump. There was a trashcan about 3 feet high and 2 feet in diameter. Needless to say, a lot of trash was dumped <u>around</u> the trashcan. Dogs were scavenging there regularly and small kids defecated around it. In the smaller streets around the neighborhood there was a lot of trash, which was removed irregularly at best.

Some of my teachers lived in the area and I had the opportunity of visiting their homes because their children were friends. One of the more talented teachers who was close to us lived in two small rooms with his wife and three sons. It was cramped but not dirty. Two teachers lived in bungalows similar to ours.

The contrasts however were there in so many other places; the conditions of the Police Lines are another example. There were hundreds of police recruits that lived there in the barracks. They had limited facilities, especially the toilets. There were maybe a dozen latrines for all those men. They were the "dry types" that were cleaned in the evening, with the waste dumped into big containers attached to a cart pulled by buffalos. It was stinky and must have been awful to use and awful to haul away. But think about the billion plus Indians of whom probably ten per cent have flush toilets. How can they keep clean and feel clean! Even with flush toilets there is the issue of water supply and keeping the toilets going. As an aside, when Indians meet in the U.S. they seem to be able to find a connection. Someone they know seems to know the person they have met. Everyone wondered how this can happen in a country with a billion people. Well, the answer came when it was realized that it was not that all Indians knew each other, but all Indians who had indoor plumbing knew each other!

Working conditions offered many contrasts. There was a lot of work done by manual labor. These people worked hard for long hours on a limited diet. Of course it's true that a large amount of work is still done by manual labor. Anyway I saw a lot of heavy work being done by men. In our house the gardeners worked from morning to evening with a short break. Once a week, the garden was watered. Two men came with two bullocks and drew water from the well all day. This was probably normal - it happened and was done everywhere.

There were two instances of extreme labor that still haunt me. Both involved boatmen and I saw them both when we were on a picnic. In those days, the rivers flowed more freely than they do today. There were fewer dams and silting was not a major problem. The rivers were used to transport a lot of heavy goods. What I saw were large barges being moved upstream, one time by a man who had a long punting pole. He put the pole into the river bottom and then "walked" the boat. He stood at the front end of the boat facing backwards with the pole dug into the river bottom. As he "walked" towards the back of the boat he pushed the boat with his feet. When he reached the back of the boat, the barge had moved one boat length. He took the pole out and went back to the front of the boat and started all over.

The other time a lone man had a rope tied to the barge and he harnessed himself to the rope and pulled the boat along. Recently, I saw a painting by a nineteenth century Russian painter which showed almost the identical scene of emaciated men pulling a barge. I guess it was not that unusual a phenomenon.

Volga Boatmen. They reminded me of the two men I saw who were both pushing or pulling their boats. single handedly.

I have described the comfortable life we lived and some of the lives of the less affluent under the heading of "Nandinee," the house we lived in for 20 years.

Western influence on our family was quite strong. Papa grew up in the small town of Meerut, which had limited western influence even into the 1970s. Now, several members of my mother's family are working and studying in the U.S. and excelling in their fields. They have helped to provide more western influence on the family in Meerut and other parts of India.

As a child, after moving to Lucknow, I was exposed to a lot of western influence through Papa's career. He had had English professors when he was in medical college, had spent two years at London's postgraduate Medical School, and then worked in Lucknow Medical College under and with several English professors. Of course the British were running the country, and an important way of doing well in one's career was to impress them with a lifestyle similar to theirs. Many educated, professional, and well to do Indians adopted the western style. The nature, degree, and depth of this adaptation had different forms, and the combination of the Indian and western styles, values, and manifestations makes for a good study if analyzed from a distance. How distant I can be is not for me to determine. I will try to describe what I saw and remember in my family and around me and throw in my opinion about those. The judgments I make are influenced by changing attitudes and changing times. Papa (and we) lived in two worlds - the Indian and the British - the traditional and the modern.

Papa always dressed properly. He wore suits in winter and even in summer unless it was really hot. He used good tailors and in later years some of his suits were stitched in London. He wore garters to keep his silk socks up and also had garters for his shirts sleeves to keep them inside his coat. He had a pile of clean, washed and ironed hankies on his chest of drawers and took a new one everyday. For tennis, he wore clean starched white pants and white shirts. The tennis shoes were cleaned and painted white after each evening of play. He had a big collection of shoes (I would estimate they occupied 8-10 feet of wall space). The ones that were striking were the butler shoes; these were brown in the heel area and on the toe. However, they had white in a complex pattern between the heel and the toe. They must have been the style for a while. I even wore the hand me downs a few times. Papa also had a dinner jacket and patent leather shoes for Rotary Club meetings.

Soon after independence we were having a conversation about ties. Papa, who had numerous neckties, was lamenting that soon his ties would go out of favor. I asked if the congress government would ban them. He said, "No, it will be by convention." Well that did not happen - more and more successful Indians continue to wear ties and western style clothing.

At home and in the evenings he wore Kurta pajamas - Lucknow *chikan*, (finely embroidered fine muslin) of course. On some occasions I remember him wearing *Sherwani* and *Churidars* (formal Indian clothes). We too had proper clothes for school, for games, and for boy scouts. We had our blazers and ties and shiny "Naughty Boy" shoes. We were judgmental, especially Santosh, my classmate, who was very self-conscious about style. He criticized boys who wore un-ironed shorts or badly tailored clothes. Indian style was only acceptable if it was of good quality like silk or chikan. Of Papa's colleagues, Dr. Bhatia had very well tailored clothes, while Dr. Yajnik, a simple but brilliant man, wore shabby clothes often with buttons missing.

Our teachers in school were poorly paid. They tried to maintain a style but often ended up with tight fitting, not very clean clothes. They could probably afford one good piece in many years and had to make do with what they had. Some wore *Sherwanis* for formal occasions, others wore western clothes, but often these were shabby and poorly made.

The western/British influence went well beyond clothes. The social scene was still quite important and influential. The Oudh Gymkhana Club was a part of our social scene. It was the club for the non-military society of Lucknow - the place for Lucknow's elite. It offered the usual facilities for cards, bar, billiards. Papa was mainly involved with the tennis. In his forties and early fifties, he played tennis regularly. As I said, he played in proper white pants during the warmer months, but during the winters they wore flannel pants, which had light yellow/off white color. They wore blazers after the game. Shorts were only worn by the more aggressive younger players. During the monsoon season, there was no tennis because the lawns were too wet. Those were the days before nylon strings. All racquets were strung with catgut. During the rainy season, the catgut changed its tension and there was a risk of bending the frame. Every year in July Papa would take a blade and cut the strings. They were restrung in September. It seemed to me to be a wasteful thing to do. Papa looked down on the bridge and billiards part of the club's activities. We did enjoy the kebabs that Papa brought home from time to time. Yes, the kebabs and *Rumali rotis* (very thin breads, a specialty of Lucknow, named for the quality of a fine handkerchief) from the club used to be a great treat for us all.

Talking of kebabs reminds me of the different kinds of meat eaters in our community. There were strict vegetarians, who ate nothing related to meat or even things like eggs. There were some who even considered onions and garlic to be taboo. The less strict ones would take the gravy from meat or even eat *keema* (minced meat). There were some who would eat kebabs but not pieces of meat. We did eat meat, but only regular meat dishes and not kidney or liver. We even were hesitant to eat the marrow from the bone until we followed the example of our friends, the R.S. Lal family. Many of the Lucknow specialties like *pasanda, Kakori kebabs,* and *sheermal* were not served at our house.

Another food related interaction is important to bring up at this time. Papa and Amma both grew up in Meerut in vegetarian families. All of the family in their generation remained vegetarian. Papa started eating meat at some point in his life. I do not know when exactly, but certainly after he returned from England he was a meat eater. We children started eating meat at a very early age, but Amma remained a vegetarian. Some time after her death, this topic came up and he said to us with no apology or sense of irony that when he first brought a meat dish from outside to the table, she threw up, but then "she got used to it." The dominance of the head of the family was obviously not to be questioned.

Food at home also had a western influence. We ate dinners of soup, cutlets and desserts about once a week. It did depend on the type of cook we had. Some cooks or bearers (*baira*) could cook both western and English food; others cooked only Indian food. When we went out to eat it was almost always for western style food - usually at Mayfair restaurant (later Kwality). I remember going to a Chinese restaurant close to Mayfair. It was a long and narrow place. I have no recollection of the food. I was probably 8-10 but recall Papa telling us how in the Chinese restaurants in London, the waitresses had to run around so much that they used to get all sweaty. (It is just intriguing to me what trivia I remember and why.)

We ate the western food in the proper style with knives and forks, I was closely supervised by all the members of the family – a "privilege" of being the youngest. Papa even ate his *rotis* (Indian flat bread) with a knife and fork. We ate peas without turning the fork over. Our social circle included some westerners and westernized, more or less, Indians. Sir George Thomas, a retired judge, and his family interacted with us fairly regularly partly because their daughter, Dr. Mary Thomas, was a gynecologist at the Medical College. One memorable event was the visit of Professor E. J. King, Papa's mentor at the Post Graduate Medical School.

Many other English and American visitors came to the house while they were visiting the Medical College. Yet we ate Indian food with our hands. Papa, despite his Westernization, was also a patriot. During one of his trips, he was in a dining car on a train. He was sitting next to a snobbish American. The American asked Papa what he thought of American food. Papa, probably to annoy the man, said, "It's OK." The man was appalled. Then, to further shock him, Papa described Indian food and said that we ate our food with our hands. The man said, "Don't your hands get dirty?" Nonchalantly, Papa said, "Sure, but we have taps and we can wash our hands."

The daily use of English, the collection of books almost exclusively in English in our library, and the insistence on the proper use of words, grammar, and phrases marked our family as westernized. When Meera was in school in Benaras, one of her classmates asked her if she dreamed in English. I do not know the answer to that. We were asked to be careful about the use of "I shall" versus "I will" or "May I" versus "Can I". We were informed that the correct way to address a woman was through her husband's name. Thus, my cousin Vimla was not Mrs. Vimla Mohan, but Mrs. Ramesh Mohan, the wife of Mr. Ramesh Mohan. Her whole identity was through her husband.

We, of course, had Hindi in school, and I read some Hindi books. Most of our reading, however, was in English. Hindi teachers in school received less respect than the English teachers. The revolutionary writer, Yashpal, wrote in Hindi and we had his books. I don't know if Papa read them. Later a Dr. Surender wrote some books on medicine in Hindi, which were given to Papa to review; they were in our library. Again, I don't know if Papa read them. Around age 12-13 I read the Forsythe Saga and a few other classics. I was encouraged to read the standard English works but never even asked to develop fluency in Hindi.

Our being comfortable with English made us feel confident in many of our day to day interactions, and gave us an extra advantage due to the importance of English in those days. The advantage continued after independence and, as far as I can judge, remains today. In fact, with the globalization of the nineties onward, the disproportionate advantage of those who speak good English has increased.

During this pre-teen period when I was being encouraged to improve my English skills, Mohini Bhabhi told me to pick one word from the dictionary every day. She said to make a point of using that word at any opportunity I could find. The word would then become a part of my vocabulary. I never did that! I was too lazy! However, there was no suggestion to improve my Hindi.

The emphasis on English was no accident; it had been a part of a systematic effort by the British. In the 1830s, Thomas Babington Macaulay, the Governor-General of India, wrote a memo stating:

It is impossible for us, with our limited means, to attempt to educate the body of our people. We must at present do our best to form a class who may be interpreters between us and the millions whom we govern; a class of persons, Indian in blood and colour, but English in taste, in opinions, in morals, and in intellect.

By the 1850s, there was an independent class of Anglophile Indians who dominated Indian society. Their power persisted through the next hundred years of British rule in India - and it still persists.

In the 1940's, our advantage often expressed itself as a sense of superiority over those who were not comfortable in the day-to-day use of English or the western style.

We made fun of those outside our circle who were not as conversant with western culture. We did not tease them, but noted their lack of sophistication or awareness of "important" things. There was a man in Ram Bhyya's circle who asked, "Where's Shanks?" We found that funny and considered this man to be uninformed. In those days not too many people had flush toilets. The most common, maybe the only, flush toilets were made by Shanks, and the word "Shanks" was written prominently in the toilet bowl. This man was probably trying to show off that he knew what Shanks was and it backfired.

We were also told to use phrases like "May I wash my hands?" rather than to ask for the toilet or the bathroom. We thought poorly of those who were more direct. We definitely criticized those who spoke English incorrectly - be it friends, colleagues, teachers, or acquaintances. I remember one man in particular in Simla in 1946. He said, "You was winning." To us it indicated that he did not belong in our circle. Another friend pointed out that the man was trying, and that just a few months earlier one could not even get a sense of what that man meant to say. That changed our attitude somewhat.

The way we looked at people who did not know English was different from the way we felt superior to those who knew English but were not good at it. It was acceptable for the less fortunate not to speak English. But for the educated professional not knowing proper English was a bad thing. The word sophisticated had an interesting connotation for us. On the one hand, we wanted people to be polite, observe proper manners, and speak proper English. On the other hand, we regarded sophistication to be a problem if it reflected 'airs' or suggested lack of understanding of other people's needs or feelings. I remember Usha di saying about somebody, "She is so nice and unsophisticated." I am not sure exactly what that meant. I do not remember who she was talking about but there was something odd about her telling us about her.

Our mixed reactions to sophistication and westernization were shown in Raniket in 1950 where we went on our first summer vacation in many years. We stayed in a guest house called Essex House, a set of small cottages close to the Ranikhet Club. The place was run by an English woman named Mrs. Ferguson. We were served western food every evening - proper three course meals, served by bearers in uniform. We dressed for dinner, not in dinner jackets, but in clean shirts, shorts, and coats. We learned about a number of English foods.

Mrs. Ferguson had broken her foot. One day we children were standing around and the landlady came by. We were a bit awkward in her presence. Neetu broke the ice and asked, "How is your foot Mrs. Ferguson?" She gave some answer and we had a brief conversation. After she left, we told Neetu how smart he was and how brilliantly he had carried out a polite conversation.

Mrs. Ferguson was not considered to be well educated; Mohini Bhabhi pointed out that the only adjective she (Mrs. Ferguson) used was "nice." Not good enough for our family that had many members with Master's Degrees in English.

Other events illustrate our mixed westernization. Also staying at the Essex House was another Lucknow family, the Sahnis. He was the head of the Geological Survey of India and was using Ranikhet as a base for his survey of the region. Mrs. Sahni was a strong woman and a prominent person in Lucknow society. They had two daughters, seventeen and fifteen, and a son several years younger. Both daughters were brilliant, talented and striking. We became friends and did a lot of things together: went on picnics, ate meals together, spent evenings at the club playing tennis, table tennis, badminton and occasional billiards. We went on walks around the town and generally had a good time.

Once during an evening walk, we went past the Army Officer's Mess. A general was visiting Ranikhet and there was a dance at the Mess. As we passed by, the band started playing the Blue Danube. It was such a thrill. We had heard the Blue Danube on our 78 R.P.M. records played on His Master's Voice Gramophone, but never live. We were at the bottom of the hill from the Officers Mess but could hear the music clearly. We just sat down on a parapet and savored it for as long as they played. Western music was very much in our blood.

The club also had a party in honor of the General. It was quite a gala and we got to go. The General had been married recently to a young and glamorous wife. Her name was Pearl, and she was obviously the center of attention - and criticism. The event was a formal ball in the English style, and we were on our best behavior. Everyone there was "westernized." Since the ball was held just three years after independence, many of the officers had been trained by the British and were, as they say, more British than the British. We were duly impressed and thrilled with the evening.

We were in Ranikhet because my cousin Usha di was posted there with her husband - a civil engineer in the early stages of his career. A prominent U.P. politician and minister was visiting Ranikhet while we were there. Papa, who knew the minister, arranged for Mr. C.B. Gupta to have breakfast at Usha di's house. The purpose, I guess, was to enhance my cousin and her husband's prestige in the community. Taking advantage of connections is something we were not averse to.

The Ranikhet trip was a happy one. I played on regular tennis courts for the first time. Before that, I had been playing against the wall in our house in Lucknow. I had a decent idea of the game but was not very good. I did fairly well on the courts. Most importantly, I enjoyed it a lot.

We returned to Lucknow at the end of the month and got back to our routine. But meeting the Sahnis brought about a lot of changes in our lives. We developed a new social circle. Theirs was a family more westernized than ours. They were all avid readers and involved in the arts. They painted, sang, participated in plays and debates. And in contrast to our family, they were into the arts. We were a family into science and medicine.

The Sahni girls studied philosophy, English, psychology, and the like. They were outgoing and friendly. Mohini was about a year older than I and I developed a big crush on her. I was in 10th class after the vacation -a big year with a state level examination that was supposed to impact one's career. I was expected to focus and concentrate on my studies. Well, I was distracted by Mohini and had some problems with focus. One time I went to their home in the afternoon. I walked about two miles to be there and then told Mohini that this was an "off the record" visit. She was not to tell Papa because I was supposed to be studying. Well, their household was very open and everyone told everyone everything. Mrs. Sahni was very upset. She thought that Papa disapproved of us visiting the Sahnis. Nothing came of this misunderstanding, but it showed the difference between the two families. Whether it was illustrative of openness versus secretiveness, or a matter of partial westernization where for us socializing with girls was OK only to a point, I am not sure. We remained friends and we continued to socialize but with restrictions and limits.

One time we were looking at each other's family pictures. They showed us a picture of Dr. and Mrs. Sahni when the two had just met but nothing was "official." Papa asked Mrs. Sahni in an incredulous tone, "You allowed a picture to be taken with him at that time?" The Sahnis were open. Mrs. Sahni had an admirer who visited them on a regular basis. He spent a lot of evenings with her. He was a prominent professor at Lucknow University, one of the pioneers in sociology. There seemed to be no tension there, though the children made fun of "Duppoo" the nickname for Professor D. P. Mukherjee.

Through the Sahnis we got into a music club that gathered at different homes to listen to western classical music. The music group was an expression of our elitism and westernization. Professor Mukherjee was a part of the group. One time, we were listening to Beethoven's third symphony. I was the technical expert and started the record before the group was fully ready. When Duppoo realized we were listening to

Beethoven's third symphony he said, "But I never heard the knocks," referring to the beginning of the piece. So I had to start the record over again. Gradually, the families drifted apart. I have seen Mohini only a few times since.

Our attitudes towards our religion also illustrate the times and our bicultural life and upbringing. We were a Hindu family brought up by parents who were from traditional Hindu families. My grandparents were followers of the traditions, values, and beliefs of what is called "Hinduism." Yet there were many aspects of our lives that were not quite traditional. There certainly was no prejudice against Muslims. There were, in the previous generations, family members who had good friends who were Muslim and came to visit them on a regular basis. Interestingly, however, I was told that they were served tea in cups that were kept separate from the rest of the dishes in the house. This behavior was done openly and the Muslim friends apparently accepted it without rancor as the norm.

At the railway stations one could buy food and water. At the big stations there were two separate water carts, one for Hindus and one for Muslims. The Hindu cart was clearly marked *Hindu Pani* (Hindu water). It was probably acceptable for a Hindu to go to the Muslim stand, but Muslims were not allowed to get water from the Hindu one. One wonders if the *Hindu Pani* was available to lower caste and untouchable Hindus. My guess is not. In my school also we had a Hindu mess and a Muslim mess.

In 1921, there were Hindu-Muslim riots in Agra. Chachee, my aunt, was a young housewife. A Muslim came to her house injured and bloodied by a Hindu mob. Chachi took him in, helped him clean up, dressed his wounds, gave him a glass of hot milk, and allowed him to leave when the situation had cooled down.

Yet we did have our prejudices that showed up even in my generation in the sixties. We looked down on many Christians because they had converted from low caste Hindu families and were therefore "inferior." One cousin even said we had to clean the chairs in the living room because a "low caste Christian" had sat in them. It is difficult to say if this was a joke or an indication of deep-seated prejudice.

We in our family did not visit temples except as tourists. One occasion was in Fyzabad, the alleged birthplace of the god-king, Ram. I remember a pilgrim taking a liquid offering from the priest, drinking part of it, and pouring the rest on his shaved head.

We did celebrate many of the traditional festivities and rituals. We lit the house with *Diyas* - traditional earthenware oil lamps - to commemorate the return of Ram after his exile, or, as some said, the triumph of good over evil. (We accepted both.)

We as kids worked hard to prepare the lamps, set them along the walls and parapets and lit them as dusk came on. But we did not have an altar or *pooja* for the occasion, as many friends and family members did. We certainly played with zest with colored water on *Holi*. We enjoyed the special foods and sweets that went with those occasions; those foods were only prepared during that celebration. Now those special foods are available all year around.

The special day for brothers and sisters - to reaffirm the support and love among them - was a big occasion. The sister demonstrated her love by tying a hand made string bracelet around the brother's wrist and feeding him a sweet. The brother gave her some money as a token and promise of helping her in time of need. We were five sisters and three brothers (counting cousins), and this was a major time for a family get- together.

Another time of gathering was *Karua-Chaut*, an occasion when married women fasted for the long life and health of their husbands. To us, as kids, it was again a chance to enjoy the special foods that went with that holiday. Other religious celebrations and rituals were very visible around us; nearby temples and small shrines attracted many devotees. We saw them and accepted them, but never participated in those activities. That was something "they" did; we were not a part of it.

A commemoration of *Hanuman,* the monkey god, took place at a temple not far from us. The pilgrims - all adult males - came from their hometowns and villages. They wore just a red loincloth and a garland. They measured the whole route with their bodies. They held a small stone in their hand, stood-up, joined their hands in respect to the god and prostrated themselves on the road. They placed the stone where their hand reached, stood up and repeated the ritual from where the stone was. They repeated this again and again all the way to the temple. This was in the month of June with temperatures in the range of 105 degrees Fahrenheit (40 degrees Celsius). Sometimes they had a mother or wife with them who fanned them and gave them water and encouragement. I saw one of our servants performing this ritual with his mother by his side. Why this ritual? When did it start? I do not know.

The temple was about half a mile beyond the main road in our area - the University Road. It was a major thoroughfare and in the days before the central celebration, the main road, not just the pedestrian paths, was full of the pilgrims, causing traffic problems and danger to all. We never went to the temple during the celebration where thousands collected. I did go there later and saw the temple from outside and a place where a shopkeeper made puffed rice and roasted *chana* (a legume) in hot sand. It was fascinating to watch how he put the raw grain into hot sand for a minute and then pulled it out with a sieve to let the sand escape - a hot, healthy snack. Many years later, in the late '80's, I visited that place with Joanie. It looked just like it had when I lived in Lucknow thirty years earlier. But the city had grown much beyond that area with a lot of new housing and shopping centers, even modern shopping malls. I doubt if that place still exists!

Probably the biggest public religious event is that of the *Ramlila*, a yearly reenactment of the story of Ram. Events are held in many communities, with a major one at one of the city's big parks. The ceremonies last for ten days, culminating on the last day with a big battle and the burning of an effigy of the evil king. I remember watching one time as a small child, before Amma died. We were watching from the roof of some family friends' house. An ember from the burning effigy floated towards us and set fire to Amma's *dhoti*; luckily, it was put out easily without damage.

Other interesting people that I was able to see on my trip to Lucknow in 2007 were the *Kanwarias*. These were people who collected the water from the Ganges and carried it in earthen pots back to their villages. The stipulation was that they were not allowed to place the pots on the ground. So they carry beautifully decorated tripods that allow them to rest without putting the pots on the ground. They still follow that tradition and I saw a few dozen of them carrying the pots. Many such little traditions continue in India. What it says and means to the culture is hard to say. But it continues in an age when computer classes are held in the small alleys of big and small cities, cars are causing traffic jams, and there are bars and disco joints in the cities.

All these religious events occurred around us, but we were observers not participants. We were secular and a-religious, but nominally and culturally Hindu.

Despite the western influence in our lives, we did not go to any churches either. If Papa's English professors or friends went to their churches, we never went with them. One exception was when we went to a Christmas party at the house of a Christian friend of Papa's. They had a Father Christmas and carol singing and also a group that sang Christian songs in Hindi. They were animated and the music was accompanied with a variety of Indian instruments.

I vividly remember a *Muharrum* (Muslim) procession. There were scores of young men carrying knives and hooks which they used for self-flagellation, even to the point of bleeding from their chest and back.

The treatment of men and women, boys and girls has undergone many changes, as has the degree of interaction permitted between them. These were and are differences between cultures and families. Among the poorer Muslims, women regularly wore a "Burqa" which covered them from head to toe, with only a mesh-like opening for the eyes. None of our friends' sisters or mothers wore a burqa. On the other hand, the upper class, rich women stayed in the Zenana, the female wing of the house. When they went out, the car or the tonga was curtained. I am not sure what they did when they were walking.

Many Hindu women also covered their faces. Most of the women in my mother and aunt's generation had their head covered all the time. In the presence of certain people (I am not sure of the rules) they pulled down the head covering to also cover their face. In our family, my generation did not follow this rule, but many others did.

Social interaction between boys and girls was limited, especially during teenage years. Family friends, of course, were different. With sisters of friends, one could have some interaction, but there were still many restrictions. In any case, most of my friends did not have sisters. The few who did, (like my best friend Salman) had rules that allowed no interaction. Even in educated liberal families, there was a double standard.

Our family was liberal; boys and girls had equal degrees of education and many pursued careers. But the girls had more restrictions. They were not allowed to go out on their own; they had to be escorted by one of the boys or a trusted servant.

Public displays of affection were not acceptable. Once, when Ramesh Bhyya returned from a year in England, Vimla di, his wife, was with us at the railway station. He stepped out of the train and greeted everyone. He said hello to his wife awkwardly, but there was no touching or hugging.

Today some members of our generation maintain these traditions. Some follow the rituals, others believe in the power of Hindu gods, and even interpret the Hindu myths literally. Some may have suspicion about Muslims, but overt prejudice is not a part of our family's thinking.

Despite my close friendship with Salman, my understanding of Muslim culture and its problems after independence and partition was skimpy at best. When Salman just disappeared one day, I did not really understand why the family had left. But I recently, in February 2011, had the opportunity to talk to Aftab, Salman's brother. He too had written a description of his family and ancestors. I had read it and that helped to provide a framework and background to my pleasant, informative and lengthy conversation with him.

I went over to his house. He is widowed and spends a lot of time at his daughter's place about an hour away by the Metro. He does maintain a house in NOIDA close to many of his childhood friends. We had a delicious lunch and then started talking about the old days, and also about his family, his parents, and the older generation. We talked a lot about Islam in general. Aftab, in recent years, has studied Islamic literature and history. Some say he has become more observant in recent years, and that he has had some conflict with a childhood friend who is a Muslim. Either way, it was very helpful to me to learn and clarify many aspects of Islam and my interaction with Salman and his family.

He described the Muslim culture of North Central India in the late 19th and early 20th century, and the growth of the Muslim League through India's Independence and the formation of Pakistan in 1947. After the fall of the Great Mughals in the early 18th century, smaller Muslim kings and landowners, often called Nawabs, dominated North India. Lucknow was one of the larger kingdoms, and culturally the most advanced. Aftab's family, from both his mother and father's side were upper class from towns within 50 miles of Lucknow. In a simplified way, he said there were two broad groups amongst them. Some concentrated on the lands. They collected taxes from the peasants, oversaw the land, worked to keep their property rights. The laws of inheritance were somewhat complicated, but the eldest son got the bulk of the property in a system called primogeniture. Customary law, however, was for all sons to receive a reasonable inheritance. Girls also inherited property and were given a dowry. Property disputes, however, were common. Salman used to tell me that many of his relatives had legal disputes going on for years; in the meantime, the families continued their normal interaction. Aftab confirmed this.

On his mother's side, two generations earlier, there was more emphasis on education. Her parents and grandparents had been civil servants, judges and surgeons. On his father's side, there was more emphasis on land ownership and less on education. Aftab's father was the third son and expected lesser inheritance, so he got a degree from Lucknow University in Arabic, Persian and History. He followed this with a law degree, also from Lucknow University. As best as I can reconstruct, Aftab's father spent most of his time in the villages where he owned land that he managed. In the early fifties, when we were all mid to late teenagers, their family lost a lot of their property in a major land reform. I do recall they (Aftab, Salman etc.) had a period of adjustment.

Going back to some historical background. In 1858, after the British defeated the most powerful and rich Nawab of Lucknow and the king in Delhi, the British were vindictive towards the landed Muslims and many lost their land, property and in some cases, their lives.

Rosie Llewellen-Jones in <u>The Great Uprising of India 1857-58</u> describes in some detail the looting and repression of the Indians during and after the uprising. One passage is worth quoting:

> *Search parties sent out on treasure-seeking expeditions were bound to cause alarm and dismay among the civilian population. The Prize Agents were not simply taking discarded arms and ammunition from captured forts, as part of the spoils of war, but searching house after house, street by street, in some of the richest and most sophisticated cities of northern India. The rewards were immense, but so were the opportunities for corruption, self-enrichment at the Company's expense, intimidation of householders and general ill-will towards the government that allowed plundering to go for weeks until there was nothing left to take. 'The Atrocities committed by the Government native Troops [the mutinous sepoys] serve, no doubt, as severe punishment, but no one ever thought that the capture of Delhie by Englishmen would be attended with more cruelty to the general population, than that by a Nadir'. wrote Sannat Nana from Mhow in November 1857. He referred to the last sack of Delhi by the Persian ruler Nadir Shah in 1737, when the fountains in the main street, Chandni Chawk, ran red with the blood of its slaughtered inhabitants, and the troops were hardly able to carry their loot, including the Peacock Throne, home with them. By the middle of the nineteenth century the inhabitants of Delhi might have hoped for fairer treatment than their predecessors had received 120 years earlier. After all, British politicians and missionaries were frequently emphasising the benefits of 'Christian civilisations over heathen cruelty and purposes', but when it came down to it, it didn't seem to make much difference whether the looters were Christian, Muslim or Hindu.*

As time went by, the system of land ownership reverted to the old feudal system. Land was owned by a few - Hindus and Muslims. The peasants in most cases tilled the land and paid taxes to the land owners. The landowners had great power over the peasants. Extra-judicial control was maintained with the help of goons and bribes to the government officials who were supposed to track the production of the crops and collection of taxes. It was this system that was reformed in the early 1950s when Aftab's family lost significant amounts of land and income.

The Muslim population of the area had a heterogeneity to it. Aftab described them as less educated, caste ridden, and focused on religion - often put under the umbrella term "traditional." But there was an educated group amongst them, and amongst the leaders of the freedom movement were many Muslims of repute and importance, mostly from the same North Central part of India. Sir Syyad Ahmad Khan is the most prominent amongst them.

The reasons for India's partition, the Hindu-Muslim divide, and formation of Pakistan is still being analyzed by those who were there and by historians. One of the points that Aftab made during our conversation was that Nehru, and particularly

Gandhi, paid more attention to the Muslim religious leaders because of a misreading of their power and influence over the Muslim populace. Aftab pointed out that in Islam there is only one God. Mohammad was a man (a prophet but not god), unlike Jesus who is considered a god by Christians. The Mullahs and other religious leaders do not have any superiority over the average Muslim - at least in theory. Secular Muslim leaders like Jinnah would have worked towards an India with Muslims and Hindus sharing their life and country. It was the religious leaders who created the atmosphere of suspicion that lead to the partition of India.

In terms of Hindu-Muslim and men-women interactions, Aftab had some interesting observations. He said Purdah was common amongst Muslim families (as amongst Hindus). However, in his family, it was not that strict. For example, their family lawyer was a Hindu, but he was a family friend and Purdah was not observed with him. In general, his mother did not observe strict Purdah and his sisters never observed Purdah. However, mixing of boys and girls was limited. Their family in the village had Hindu friends - similar to my family who had Muslim friends in Meerut at the turn of the 19th century. And in a similar way, when they came to visit, separate dishes were used. Aftab's family even had a Hindu cook. The lifestyle and customs that Aftab describes explains why we did not interact with his mother or sisters, though they were all well educated.

***

Chapter Eleven
The Neighborhood

It is just another road in Lucknow. I guess it was built in the twenties when the New Hyderabad area opened up. It started at University Road, skirted the property of my school, and branched into a number of roads going towards and away from the Gomti River. Its southern branches joined the road along the Gomti. That road was unnamed for a long time, but later was named in honor of Dr. Birbal Sahni who was probably the most famous scientist associated with Lucknow University. The branches to the north, away from the Gomti, ended in a number of smaller streets that went through bazaars and lower income neighborhoods. They ended at the bustling *Nishat Gunj*, the papermill road, and the Fyzabad Road.

We lived on Rai Behari Lal Road. The house address was No. 1. Later we named the house "Nandinee." It was number 1 because for a long time it was the first house when you went from University Road towards New Hyderabad. A lot of my life was centered around RBL Road. It was my way to and from school, Gunj, and places beyond. Many of my friends lived on RBL Road and its branches.

At the corner of University Road and RBL Road were some of the houses for the teachers at Colvin and a bicycle shop run by a man with vitiligo. It was our belief that vitiligo or leukoderma was a form of leprosy, and we were very careful not to touch him. However, we used to watch him, fascinated by his skills. We depended on him to fix punctures, repair chains, fix pedals, align wheels, pump air and whatever.

Behind the bicycle shop was a large property that later was a motor workshop run by Papa's friend's son. When the workshop was opened Papa's Ford was the first car to be serviced; it was garlanded and had teeka applied to it. I don't think the shop did too well and disappeared fairly quickly.

Just beyond these shops was Colvin on the right and the Police Lines on the left. That part of the Colvin property was mostly unused; it had some empty horse stables, a deep pit which had been used for horse training in the old days, some servants' quarters, and, from time to time, a garden for corn and wheat. There was a gate to the property that was open only sporadically. If it was open, we used it as a short cut. When we rode our cycles through it, it was quite an adventure. Seeing the back of the hostels and the abandoned buildings was a thrill for us because we were generally regimented and followed strict rules. Sometimes the dirt wall broke down and we would climb through the low areas as a short cut when we were on foot. That was an even bigger thrill and we only did it if we had company. One time there was a partial break in the wall. It was flanked with cactus and other thorny bushes. We needed a running start to get over it. Shankh went first and made it through. I went after him but my hand was caught on something sharp. I got a gash at the base of my right middle finger. It was deep enough that some of the fascia came out. It so happened that a short time before that Papa had brought a rabbit brain for Meera to take to her Biology class. The brain, to me, was a white glob that came from the body. So when I saw the white stuff coming out of my hand I immediately shouted: "Oh my god, my brain has come out." I still have the scar. I wonder if I got sympathy or a scolding when Papa saw the cut!

Opposite this gate were the latrines for the Police Lines. These were tin sheds with a pan at the bottom. All through the day there was a stink coming from them. In the late evening, however, they used to be cleaned. Three or four black carts designed like a drum with wheels would collect the waste; it was manually put into these carts and hauled away in buffalo drawn carts with a man sitting on the carts. The poor guys had a thick wrapping of cloth over their faces to protect then from the stink and splatter. At that time the stink was awful and spread all over the area; one had to rush by or stay back to avoid the awful stench. That was, and probably is, the way of the world without flush toilets.

The rest of the Colvin property on the right was uninteresting. Nothing happened on it. On the left, Police Lines were active. There were lots of police trainees. There was no boundary wall and for a long time not even a wire fence. The police trainees were all over. The band people practiced in that area. The bagpipes, which I never liked, played all day. The drummers used to sit or stand over any kind of ledge they could find. They went on with their sticks on bricks for hours practicing their marches.

Opposite our house were some houses for the junior officers of the police, the *subedars* and *jamadars* (sergeants etc.). They were important people as far as the regular policemen were concerned. They controlled the police and enforced the rules laid out by the senior officers. The *subedars* were probably from the ranks - rugged, village folks who rose to their positions of authority because of their toughness and smarts, not necessarily by their education. One time two boys from this group got into a fight and beat each other up. The father was quite casual about the whole thing. He just said, "Go inside and put some iodine on the wound." No sympathy, no regrets, just a matter of fact action. I was reminded of that event when I read <u>Temur Lane</u> by Justin Marozzi (p 203).Temur Lane's son, the heir, died in battle. On his death Temur was said to have shown no emotion.

We did a lot of things in the Police Lines. The grounds were available to us to play hockey. We played with some of the children of the policemen. We used a ball that was used for horse polo, which was apparently made of the root of bamboo. Even though these boys were tough, I do not remember any fights. One time there was a fire in one of the houses on the Police Lines; it was put out by the people before the fire engine arrived. Good thing, because when the fire engine did arrive there was no water to feed the hose.

We saw demonstrations of riding skills, parades, and crowd control. At that time I had no idea of what those skills were all about. One was called "peg sticking." The horsemen rode at speed and picked up pegs stuck in the ground. Later I realized this sport was based on the skill of removing pegs of tents in order to trap the enemy when the tent collapsed. The riders were skilled and rarely missed; they made it look easy. Sometimes during the practice sessions we got whiffs of tear gas, depending on the wind on the police grounds.

The police dug tube wells. I was fascinated by the process, which was mechanized to some degree. They raised some heavy metal tools with pulleys and let them drop to make a hole. The dirt was removed by hand. Later, as the metal tube was sunk in deeper and deeper, they used buckets that went into the tube. We watched this every day to and from school, and, lo and behold, soon they were pumping water with electric pumps.

There was a *subedar* who used to come to the house regularly. He was a dignified looking man with a large, well trimmed beard. He used to lead some of the parades. He let me sit on his horse a few times. There was also a friend of Papa's who was from the Indian Police Service. Anand uncle was a young Indian in this service - which in those days was mostly British. He rose to a senior rank. Last time I met him was in Sikkim, in 1969, when we was the head of the police there.

A memorable event was when we saw a dozen or so horses that had been shot in the head and were being carried on handcarts — blood dripping form their mouth. As Neetu explained to me, (he was the source of a lot of my information), they were shot when they became old. They could have been sold for the horse drawn tongas that were very common in Lucknow. However, the police felt that they would not be as well taken care of by the tonga wallas. It was more humane to shoot them. The shootings were performed by the policeman who had ridden and cared for the horses. The carcasses were then taken to the Lucknow Zoo to feed the lions and tigers.

Over the years, as the police lines grew, a fence and a wall were erected around them. The area was not accessible to us. But by then I was older and not involved in things at the police lines.

For years there was no other house opposite the police lines; the first one built there was the Daryabad House, owned by another landlord/Raja/*taluqedar* from U.P. The son was in my class. I think the only name we had for him was "Daryabad". The house was fairly large and at the center of the front façade there was a large semi-circular hole. We called it a clock tower. We learned later that they had planned to put an idol of some god or goddess there, but that never happened. We once went to their house for some kind of traditional dance drama - *Ras Leela*. Daryabad, the boy, was musically trained. During our laboratory experiments in our physics class we did experiments with tuning forks and strings to put them in the same pitch. All the boys did this using small "rider" which amplified the vibration of the string; that was our end point. Daryabad was the only boy who put the tuning fork to his ear and plucked the string to match the pitch. Frankly, I had no idea what or how he did that. Now I have some idea of what he was doing.

After crossing the open sewer, which we called the *Nallah,* one came to an empty triangular plot, which was used by the poor people in the neighborhood, including our servants, for their toilet.

After the *Nallah*, came a cluster of four bungalows that were built in the early thirties. The first of these was Nandinee. We lived in it for a few years before Papa bought it from a General Habibullah. As I remember, he paid Rs. 30,000/- for it in the early forties. The four houses together went for 100,000. Nandinee was my home for twenty years - all through school and medical college. More about Nandinee later. I am guessing that Nazli, our friend and the wife of one of my classmates, is the grand-daughter of general Habibullah.

One interesting anecdote about the road itself: Hem jiji married Dada while he was city magistrate. It so happened that RBL Road was being repaired soon after they were married. Rumors started going around that Dada was favoring his in-laws. Apparently he stopped the repair work to prove to people that that was not the case.

Another time on the side of the road they had upturned drums of coal tar (asphalt) which oozed out slowly during the winter months and were to be used for retarring the road. I saw these drums with a 2-3 foot flat layer of coal tar on the ground. I tested one spot - it felt firm - and walked across this black goo. The next step was disaster. My foot and *chappal* sank in and, as you can imagine, I got into trouble.

We played a lot at the next door neighbor's house. The Roy-Chowdhry's were eccentric, not very visible, and had a good-sized yard, which was unkempt. They had a few trees including a cotton tree, which shed a lot every year. Since the yard was unkempt, it was all right for us to play in it without risking any damage. I don't think I ever saw the father, a well-known sculptor who had been commissioned by the British to make sculptures for King George and Queen Victoria. The elder son was also a sculptor and a recluse, but I did see him on and off. The next brother was Deb Brat Roy-Chowdhry - Kaju - who was in Neetu's class and was a quiet fellow. There was another son, Jhontu. One time I saw him buying fish from the vendor who went house to house. One of the fish had a big, oval, white structure inside it; Jhontu wanted the vendor to burst it.

We played cricket and *Gilli Danda* (which could be called the simple Indian version of cricket) at their house. During one of the cricket games, a splinter came off the bat. FDR had recently died, so one of the boys (Pradip Banerjee or Ratin Sen) said, "We could have used this to splint Roosevelt's brain." Another time after playing *Galli Danda*, I was returning home, dusty and grungy. Papa saw me and I got quite a scolding about my appearance.

Kaju was our age and participated in some activities with us. He was a tall, lanky fellow and was wicket keeper for one of our local cricket teams. As I started to write about Kaju, a very minor but vivid memory popped up. This kind of trigger for small events is quite interesting: once I start thinking about someone, vivid visual memories come up. In this case, I remember a time when Kaju was wicket keeper and a ball hit the tip of his gloves, bounced up, and was caught by one of the slips. A very minor incident just popped up. Kaju had a collection of some kind of reeds with a tight top - something I had not seen before, but it too has stuck in my memory. One time at *Holi*, which was a group activity, Kaju and I were the only ones left in the neighborhood. So we devised a game in which we pretended one of us was a passer by and the other one attacked him with a load of paint.

Near the main *chauraha* (crossing) was a small room in which a man known only as master ji lived. I have no other information on him. He made bows and arrows and Neetu said he once saw master ji shoot an arrow all the way through a door. I did go to his house once, and was struck by his rather dirty pillow, which was quite flat but went all the way across the bed.

We all played with bows and arrows. We used old LAC (a kind of resin) bangles and made arrowheads with them. Babu James, our bearer, told us stories of *Bhils* (a tribe) who used bows that were as big as an adult. They were so powerful they had to be pulled using the whole body while lying down. The feet were placed in the middle of the bow, the arrow between the feet. The string was pulled with both hands and the arrow went for miles. We, of course, were thrilled and impressed with the implausible story.

There was another older gentleman who was called "coach." He coached our cricket practice and matches. However, he had no control over us. If a ball bounced and was caught, we said "How's that?" and he would say, "OK, bat in hand," and compromise. Coach was just there. I remember him mostly in a field at the other end of the RBL road, near Anadi and Tappan's house, close to Babujee's Normal school.

One of the prominent people who lived in the neighborhood, not exactly RBL road, was Professor Birbal Sahni. His road, along the Gomti, had no name in those days. Later it was named *Birbal Sahni Marg* (at the same time the Birbal Sahmi Institute of Paleobotany was established). Professor Sahni was a Fellow of Royal Society. At that time, C.V. Raman and he were the only FRSs from India. He was an unassuming man who wore *khaddar churidars* and *achkan* except when he went to Europe or America; then he wore khadi suits. Papa thought he looked much more dignified in Indian clothes. I remember that even Nehru wore suits when he traveled outside India, at least in the earlier years.

We went to Professor Sahni's house a few times. They had no children and the house was immaculate. I remember being asked to be extra careful about our behavior there. He gave us paperweights made of fossilized corals - which broke and were lost. Mrs. Sahni used to come to the house for some shots that Papa gave. In those days, ampoules had to be cut using a file. Dr. Sahni was concerned about powdered glass going into the syringe, and inspected the ampule with a pocket magnifying glass - the mark of a geologist.

One time a nephew of theirs was visiting and we went to play with him. He flew kites and had a match with some local boys. There was some kind of argument about the rules of the match, and the nephew was critical of those boys. He also washed his hands by closing the outlet of the sink and filling it with water. This was appalling to us because we washed our hands in running water.

Unfortunately, the multiple floods in the sixties destroyed their road and their house.

Later in life we became friends with the family of Dr. M.R. Sahni, younger brother of Birbal Sahni. Uncle Sahni was also a geologist and retired as Director General of the Geological Survey of India.

Just beyond our house was the first crossroad on RBL Road. It was the "downtown" of the neighborhood, and was where the *paan* shop and the garbage dump were located. In the corner was Gajraj Hair Saloon where we went to have our hair cut. Gajraj came to the house to cut Papa's hair. The barber shop was the hub of a lot of activity. I was too young to understand what was going on, but looking back I think there was a lot of political activity. Those were the days of the freedom movement,

World War II, and the Indian National Army. The Hindi papers were available there and read out aloud to those who could not read. I remember stories of Subhash Bose and his links to Germany and Japan.

Next to Gajraj was Mahesh Halwai's shop. We were not allowed to eat there because of the flies and filth. Once in a while we got *jalebi* (like a funnel cake). It was done in a special manner. One of us went with a plate. The plate was weighed then the hot *jalebis* were put into our plate without touching any of the containers in the Halwai's shop. I used to watch with awe the whole ritual of mixing the dough, the cleaning of the previous days pans by putting them on the fire and removing the scum, and the skill with which the liquidy batter was squeezed out of the old cloth to make the squiggly and delicious *jalebis*.

There were a few other shops in this SE corner, all of only one room, selling all kinds of things, usually with family living right there. At *Holi* this was the place where the bonfire was lit. It was the main crossing in the area. A green plant was set up in the center of the intersection a few weeks before *Holi*. Big logs were piled up. The night before *Holi* the fire was lit. Crowds watched. It was still hot the next day when we played *Holi*. The singing groups started from there and went around to different houses. They did come to our house – I am not sure how welcome they were but they did come. We played *Holi* all over the neighborhood. Papa participated with a little bit of *gulal* (dry colors).

There was cruelty in the social structure. There was a young boy, maybe 10 or 12, who had been working at the Halwai shop. One time some people from his village came to Lucknow. As they were leaving, he requested that he be allowed to go home with them. The powers that be would not allow him to go. He was pleading and crying. To add to the cruelty, after his village people were gone all the adults started to shout at him to go. The poor boy lost on both accounts. I seem to recall seeing him later doing his chores - sad as can be.

At the Northeast corner of the intersection was Unity Lodge. It was a large compound, containing a very large house and the large Misra family. The patriarch was Bade Chacha, a bachelor, a prominent member of the police. He was in the Criminal Investigation Department. He had captured a notorius *Dakoit* by dressing up as a *Sadhu* (a wandering holy man.) However, I think the CID in those days was mainly involved in keeping tabs on the freedom fighters and other anti-British activities. The other members of the Misra family included the senior widow "Bhabi" and her five children. Pravash was with Neetu and Pushpa was my contemporary and one year junior to me in Medical College. There were other uncles, cousins, nieces and nephews. It was a major joint family similar to the joint family of my Mama in Meerut. We spent a lot of time there - hanging out, playing badminton, hide and seek, board games, etc. We were all afraid of Bade Chacha. He was, like Papa, strict and aloof, but he was out of town often so we could play at Unity Lodge more than at Nandinee.

Going somewhat geographically the house after Unity Lodge was where the Nigams lived. Suresh was in our class. I knew him a bit but the only memorable thing was that one of the parents had a bad temper.

Opposite the Nigam's was an empty plot, and next to that was Mr. B.C. Pal. He was an engineer and his house was built while we were kids. We watched with interest the construction of the house. It was very modern with a curved verandah, which was quite a unique thing. In those days cement was a new material, and the cement companies put out glossy magazines with pictures of fancy houses made with cement. Our house was made with a mortar that was limestone based, and the stucco was also limestone. The stucco houses had to be painted every year with a lime based emulsion that was washed away by one good rain. The cement houses never needed repainting. Later, when there was remodeling at Nandinee, we had cement on the interior that was painted with "distemper" which lasted much longer. Most older houses had a blue interior color which came from copper sulphate - *Tootia* as it was called. The workmen who applied the stucco were generally simple village folk, while the distemper was applied by more sophisticated painters. The stucco was a suspension and had very different characteristics.

Anyway, I remember the workmen putting rocks into the foundation of Mr. Pal's house, and then pounding them in layer by layer for each wall. They used a large bell shaped iron tool with a flat bottom attached to a pole. They worked barefoot, lifting and dropping this piece again and again on the rocks to pound them in. I wonder how often the poor chaps landed the heavy iron weight on their feet. Then there were the old men and women using a hammer and bare hands to break the stones into 1-2 inch rocks for that foundation. We used to go to Mr. Pal's and he came over to talk to Papa regularly. I have a vague recollection of some scandal but that is too vague to make any sense of. Maybe Meera or Neetu will know something.

Opposite to the Pal's was a duplex with a Bengali family in one of them. There were 2 boys slightly older than me, maybe Neetu and Meera's age. They were active in the R.S.S., a right wing Hindu group. I recall them in khaki shorts and white shirts with a Gandhi cap. I think they went to Jublee College. After Gandhi ji's assassination they were arrested. What happened later I do not know.

The next few houses also had Bengalis. There was Mesho Masai (uncle) and his wife. They had no children but they welcomed the children of the neighborhood. We played *Kabbadi* in their lawn. One time Tuku was on the team opposite mine. There was a disputed critical point and we argued about it for a while and finally I said, "They are weaklings, let them have the point." This infuriated Tuku who started beating me up for insulting him. The fight went on to the street and I was chased to our house. I guess it resolved and I remember no long term animosity.

Another time Neetu got angry at me and hit me a few times. Mesho Masai and Mashima rescued me. I had swelling on my back. When I took off my shirt they were shocked. I remember them saying *"Bhison Gumbah"* (what a large swelling). I don't think that was reported to Papa.

Next to them was Shankh Banerjee's house. I have written about Shankh in my stories of Colvin. The corner house next was Dr. J.G. Mukherjee's, who was Papa's mentor. He was called *Dak Saheb*, which just meant respected doctor. After he retired he devoted himself to gardening, and was Papa's inspiration and guide in that too. Many mornings he came to the house, had a cup of tea, and went around the garden with Papa and Makki Mali. I was not too interested in the gardening but sure was struck by his personality and his charisma. He had a big cactus garden and so did we, but his garden had a lot of exotic plants and was impressive. We went there a few times. He had an electric pump for watering the garden; we had bullocks come once a week to draw water from the well. One time his motor stopped working and his garden suffered terribly because it took a while to fix the problem. We had no problems because the bullocks kept working.

Dr. Mukherjee was a man who must have been great. I knew him only as a child so I cannot judge. He was in the pathology department and had acted as chief when the British Sahebs weren't available to head the department. The Sahebs apparently came to these positions based on their seniority in the Indian Medical Service, not based on their qualifications as pathologists. It is reminiscent of the Indian Administrative Service officers who take over projects without qualification in the relevant field. He certainly was a well-respected man. He never practiced medicine after retirement, but was a mentor and guide to many doctors and neighbors. I don't think he ever went into medical college politics.

One time, some relatives of his organized a performance of music and plays at his house. It was held in the front verandah with the audience in the portico. The things one remembers! I remember a tableau by kids, which took a long time to arrange. When the curtain opened there were children depicting the descent of Sita into the lap of her mother - mother earth. The scene was repeated for effect. What I remember most is that even the repeat scene took a long time to arrange.

The other performance I recall was a *Tabla Tarang*. My memory of it fits well with my musical ability or lack thereof. To me it was a man surrounded by a semicircle of *tablas*, which he played in some odd sequence. It was only in the last few years that I realized that he was playing a *raag* on the *tabla*. At least now I understand what was going on. This performance was in the general time frame when I tried to play music by turning the volume control of the radio!

Dak Saheb died when I was quite young. Papa came home very upset that Dr. Mukherjee had had a stroke. He told Neetu and me that he wanted to see us. We went there and waited in the driveway. We were informed he had gone into a coma and we never saw him.

Dr. Mukherjee had two daughters Aruna and Usha. Usha-di had one son, Tuku, who was Neetu's age. I have a very clear memory of Tuku being given a sword as a present by Papa. He was wearing it as he left our house by the side verandah under the bougainvillea. We were not given too many things and definitely not swords or guns. I'm sure I was jealous.

I met up with Tuku when I was in Medical College. Shashi Mathur started to introduce me to …Ganguli, who had come to Lucknow University to do his M.Sc. in botany. Anyway, he walked up to me and said, "I'm Tuku." I knew who he was. We met regularly while he was in Lucknow, but never became friends.

In the sixties, when I was on the faculty of the All India Institute of Medical Sciences, I was introduced to Usha di, Tuku's mother. I had an interest in bird watching and she was a prominent bird watcher in Delhi. She wrote a book on the birds of Delhi and introduced me to some well-known bird watchers.

Usha-di got ovarian cancer and I helped with her treatment. More importantly, I helped her fulfill one of her life's desires. My childhood friend Sudha and her husband Krishin were posted in Sikkim. We visited them and took Usha-di with us, giving her a chance to see Sikkim and the birds. She was continuing her chemotherapy so I gave her her treatments there. She was such a great lady, and everyone in Sudha's household loved her.

One the way to Sikkim we stopped in Calcutta and stayed with Tuku's in-laws. In Calcutta, we talked about our plans for hiking in Sikkim. Tuku's father-in-law said when he went hiking they used to rub their socks with Sunlight soap - the real stuff, not the new detergent which had just been introduced in India. My own technique was to wear a thin sock with a woolen sock over it. Maybe I will write about the Sikkim trip sometime - I do have some notes.

After Dr. Mukherjee's death, his relatives lived in the house and focused on keeping up the garden. Both daughters were married to successful men, Aruna-di to a pathologist in Saharanpur and Usha-di to an economist. Usha-di's husband was vice-chancellor of Delhi University in the 60s.

On the other side of the street lived Mahender Shah and some cousins. They were older. I think they were a rich industrial family, not much into studies. I had little to do with them. Next to them lived Dr. M.L. Bhatia who was in the University, possibly in botany. He was friends with Papa. The children were older and I had little to do with them. It was at the Bhatia's daughter's wedding that the gifts were displayed, and was one of my early experiences about the negative aspects of gift giving.

RBL road had a lot of cross roads, many without names. We did not go on many of these - they were out of our area. The end of the straight part had an interesting configuration. One side went straight towards the Gomti and the other side made a wide "U" also ending at the river. The two houses at this crossing had a number of tenants stay there. Our friends the Mathurs stayed there for a while when they had a very small car with a sunroof. When Mr. and Mrs. Mathur and the two boys got in, Ravi, the elder one had to stand up and put his head out of the car. One of Meera's classmates also lived there for a while.

The next house had a politician who lived there for a while. When that house was empty it was the perfect place to play hide and seek or cops and robbers. We made it quite an elaborate game. The objective was for the cops to catch all the robbers. So as each robber was caught he used to call out in code as to where the cops were headed so we could delay being caught. We took this very seriously!

The next house was that of Dr. B.B. Bhatia. He was a close friend of Papa and his two younger sons were classmates and friends of Neetu and me. One of them, Ravi, is Neetu's brother-in-law. Theirs was a big house with a large compound. The front lawn was a large rectangle with a "U" shaped driveway and a gate at each end. In the early years, the driveway was made of soft rocks, later it was cemented. One day Raji, the youngest, held onto his father's car's rear bumper with the idea of running with the car until he could not keep up. He apparently had done this before without Dr. Bhatia knowing about it. I was watching while Raji's fingers got caught in some projection in the bumper and he was dragged on the rocks for a while. Luckily, the gardener saw this and was able to get Dr. Bhatia to stop. Raji had a lot of bleeding and required dressings. Dr. Mathur used to do the dressings; I remember Raji shouting a lot during the procedure.

The Bhatia house had an unusual plan. The whole house was in a single row. Starting from the left was the kitchen with a small courtyard and covered path to the large dining room and its pantry. The drawing room was partially combined with the dining room creating a sort of "L" shaped room that was really large. Each room then led into the next through a door, but all the rooms were in a row. All the bathrooms were at the extreme right hand side. I learned in 2006 that this was designed by a well known American architect named Griffen. Some Australian Architecture School students came to look at this house, about which they had read. Luckily, they went to Ram Advani Booksellers, one of our relatives, and got the correct directions and information. They had a meeting with Bhushan, Dr. Bhatia's eldest son.

There were two back verandahs with a small lawn between them. One was enclosed and had a table tennis table. We played table tennis, had long political discussions, and even tried our hand at boxing. We used socks filled with more socks to make gloves. We were not good and not cut out for boxing.

The back lawn was our major gathering place. It was huge and a good six feet lower than the level of the house, providing a large surface for tennis wall practice, and also a back for cricket practice so we did not have to chase the ball. The lawn was not maintained as a lawn so it was all right for us to play there. During one of our cricket games, the shot hit a watering can that was called a *hazara*. There was a famous cricketer in those days named Hazare. We thought we were very clever when we made the link. The lawn was big enough for a tennis court. We played quite often, but had to prepare the field with a spray of water. We did this with what was called a "stirrup pump" - a mechanical device which had a handle that had to be pumped to get the water out. The pump was immersed in a *hazara* and one person pumped away and the other sprayed the ground.

Ravi had an air gun (BB gun). We shot at targets, trees, and occasionally at birds and squirrels. One time Ravi aimed at a solitary bird that was pretty high in the tree and, surprisingly, hit it right through the neck; it fell straight down. We felt really sorry and gave it a decent burial. The Bhatias had lots of board games and gramophone records. One of our favorites was "*Door hato ae dunia walon*" which they transmitted to us by phone.

Opposite the Bhatias was another Chatterjee family. They had one son, about our age. Biru was different. He came to our birthday parties but always hid his face in his hands and did not talk. Even at his own birthday, he just covered his face. I don't know what happened to him.

Going back on the other limb of the "U" was the house of Dr. Sehgal. He looked older than the other fathers. Maybe he was, or it was the beard; I don't know. He was head of the Hygiene department, what would now be called Community and Preventive Medicine. He smoked a *hukkah* sitting in a reclining chair. He had a horse and buggy. One time the reins were not properly secured and the horse ran off with the buggy and caused quite a stir.

Mrs. Sehgal was a petite woman. When her youngest son was born, for some reason, we visited her. I was informed that she was having abdominal pain. My response was that when Kunti gave birth to Karna she must have had a lot of pain in her ear. I did know my Indian mythology!

Our beat was confined to the main stretch of Rai Behari Lal Road. We had some friends who lived further back on the narrower, dirtier parts of the area. My memories of our friends and neighbors as I remember them have generated a lot of interest in my family. As a result of their jogging my memory, I added a few anecdotes. I had fun writing this, and hope you have enjoyed it too.

On my later visits to the neighborhood, I saw a very different picture. Most of the family homes, including ours, had been demolished and replaced by multi-story complexes. The Bhatia house was just about the only single level house left in the area.

***

Chapter Twelve
Nandinee

Nandinee was number one Rai Behari Lal Road. The road was our way to get to school, to friends' houses, to *Hazratgunj*, to visit relatives, and to travel via the Charbagh Railway Station. Nandinee is the first house I remember living in. Papa bought it for the sum, huge for the time, of Rs.30,000. It was a struggle for him to come up with the money. He used to have cash, which he kept in the house, to be given as payment in installments over a period of time.

When one of the servants stole cash from the chest of drawers, obviously there was consternation. The man was caught, put in jail, and the money recovered. The justice system's arbitrariness was shown by how the case ended. The *kotwal* or *daroga* told Papa that the man had already been punished (beaten) and had spent time in jail. Did he really want to pursue the case, especially since the money had been recovered? Papa agreed not to pursue the matter.

There was another servant theft issue, although perhaps it may have been the same one. I am not sure. What I remember is there was a servant who said he had diarrhea and he kept running to the servants' quarters. The next day he disappeared and was found to have stolen stuff from the house.

Another theft was by the fancy, accomplished, Babu James, our bearer. He did not steal in a big way, but pilfered small items. I remember a pair of scissors disappeared for a while. One day I noticed the impression of the scissors on a cushion from one of the garden chairs which we often took out to play with. Sure enough, the scissors were on the chair. This was probably the only scissors in the house, and therefore sorely missed and needed. Anyway, the scissors disappeared again till one day I saw Babu's daughter Miriam using them at her house. There was no confrontation that I can recall and they kept the scissors.

Papa sometimes used to ask me how many bananas I ate on a given day. I thought it was because too many bananas were bad for you. Later I realized that it was because he was concerned that Babu was stealing bananas. Obviously bananas were too expensive for the servants in those days. Continuing with Babu, briefly: he came to us after the British left and brought with him a lot of style and food from the Sahebs. We ate a lot of Western food while he was with us. More about him later.

There was another case that illustrated the honesty amongst the servants. Kul Bahadur was a Nepali servant who was loved by everyone. After WW II started, Kul Bahadur disappeared without a word. When his room was checked his personal stuff was gone but the bicycle that had been given to him to use, was sitting there - something he could have taken. Kul Bahadur came to visit a few years later; he was in the army and very happy.

When I started talking about Nandinee, I said it was No.1 Rai Behari Lal Road. The letters were addressed that way and it gave me a feeling of superiority. Later, after papa bought the house there were ideas exchanged about the name. One of the suggestions was "Mangalik Villa." We made fun of the relative, Chote Babujee, I presume, who suggested that name. It is the name of Indra's garden. A lot of kids asked why a name. In some ways it was a come down from No.1.

Where do I begin talking about Nandinee? I keep saying "talking" and I think it is the right word. I am narrating in a fairly free flowing fashion, so I will stick to "talking". Since I started with some of the servants, let me go on with that theme.

Over the twenty years that we lived in Nandinee, there were many servants – long term, short term, cooks, bearers, gardeners, laboratory assistants - and the turnover was frequent. Some of the servants were major players in our life; others did not work out so well. By far the most prominent was Makka Mali. He came with the house and died with the house. His wife, Malan, died when Amma died, and he died soon after papa died. Makka was papa's confidant and the man who implemented the plans for the garden that Dr. J.G. Mukherjee - Dak Saheb -and Papa came up with. He did not just follow orders but gave his own informed input, which was usually heeded. He had his own way of pronouncing the names of the plants and shrubs but he knew what he was talking about. He knew the colours, the growing conditions, and the aesthetics. Mali lived alone, worked hard all day, and remained a part of the family. He lived in the servants' quarters, a single room with a small verandah, which was also the kitchen.

There were six servants' quarters, all pretty much the same, with a small courtyard for each. They had one common tap, which was their only source of water. They bathed under the tap and drew water from it for all their needs. The tap was at a lower level than the rest of the taps in the house. Since the water pressure in the taps in Lucknow was generally low (till Dada Sanwal fixed the problem), when the servants turned on their tap, the taps in the house ran dry. Often, while we were bathing we had to shout from our bathroom *"Are' Bamba Band Karo"* (O' turn off the tap). The servants' tap was covered with a tin shed. The floor was made of a soft brick and over the years a depression had been created under the tap. They had to empty out the dirty water with their feet. The water from the tap drained into a bed, which had banana trees and further down was a compost pit kept wet by the surplus water. The water from the tap where the pots and pans were scrubbed with ash also drained into the bananas and the compost pit. Makka Mali took care of the whole garden and was the overseer of the other servants. However, I wonder how he and Babu James (a bossy man who worked for us for a few years) interacted.

I will switch to the physical description of Nandinee. It was a generous and comfortable place. The house had a complete boundary wall and was a *bigha* in size - about half an acre. There was an iron gate that was painted blue-green. The driveway curved right beyond the gate, went along the front of the house and curved again to go into the garage. A wide paved path along the side of the house was used for turning the car and also for a weekly washing of the car.

We had a few servants who could work on the car. The garage was designed with a service pit. It was a thrill to go under the car and see it from the pit. Thick wood planks covered the pit, but from time to time, despite the planks, one of the wheels of the car went into the pit.

To the left, as one entered the gate, was a cactus garden and the well behind it. Along the wall was the sloping ramp that the bullocks used when hauling water from the well. Between the ramp and the driveway was the canna bed. There were two large palm-like trees near the front entrance of the house. These plants grew new shoots from the center and the old ones on the outside slowly died out. Each year the main stem grew as the old leaves fell out. These Cycus trees had been present in the days of the dinosaurs! The leaves were at ground level to begin with. Year after year as the old leaves were cleared the plant grew. By the time I left Nandinee it was about 3-4 feet in height. In December 2012, I was in Buenos Aires, Argentina, and saw Cycus plants there.

Front view of Nandinee taken from the main gate.in 1986 just before the house was demolished to build multi-story flats.

There was a front lawn with flowerbeds around it. The lawn was bordered with bricks. The dahlias grew along the boundary wall, and sweet peas and other plants along the curving driveway.

The east lawn was protected by a hedge of chandani (a sweet smelling plant whose blossoms opened only in the evening) and was the private part of the house. We entered it by walking under a bougainvillea arch. The side verandah and the east lawn was the major family area. Except during the monsoon and the height of winter, we spent a lot of time there. Morning tea, afternoon tea, and even dinner were on the lawn; many parties were held there. We even slept there during the hot weather. The lawn was green and thick and the pride of Mali and Papa.

Papa had a fungus infection in his feet. Every few days he sat on the lawn and scraped the dead skin from his feet and clipped his nails. He also shaved sitting on the lawn. Often he entertained visitors while carrying out these activities.

In the back part of the lawn was the pond in which I nearly drowned, and in which the grandson of one of the tenants later did drown. The pond had lotus blooms and frogs. There was another lawn on the west side with a rockery along the wall and under the *gular* (fig) tree. Behind the courtyard, in the very back, was the vegetable garden, the guava tree, and along the back wall a whole row of lime trees. We were surrounded by a lot of green and a lot of color. Neetu's house in NOIDA also has a long row of lime trees.

The house had a simple but practical design. Four large rooms formed the core of the house with a passage that we called a gallery separating the front two rooms. To each large room a smaller room was attached. The living room (drawing room) to the left of the gallery opened into Papa's office. Papa's room to the right opened into the guest room. The back room to the right was Amma's room and later Neetu's and my room; a dressing room and bathroom were connected to that. The dining room was at the end of the gallery to the left with the pantry next to it. The pantry led through a covered path to the kitchen and the storerooms. There were verandahs on the front, back and the east side. The *angan* (courtyard) was behind the back verandah surrounded by more storerooms and enclosed with a wall. In the far corner was the shed for cleaning the pots and pans. The servants' quarters were further back behind the shed and the storerooms.

Let me go back to the servants. There were some that were with us for a short time, others were there for longer periods and had a greater impact on our lives.

Apart from Makka we had another junior Mali named Dwarka. He did the heavier work under Makka Mali's supervision in later years. He was nowhere near as smart as Makka Mali. He had a son who had his neck turned to one side and Mohini always got a good laugh from that. Of course she had a good laugh from anything!

Ganga Ram was the *ooper-ka-naukar* (he did the house cleaning and serving of meals) when I was very small. He took me to school on the bicycle and was with us on the Mukteswar trip. There was cook, who could catch dozens of flies with his hands at one time and then throw them down into a bowl of water. He used the kitchen bowl and I am surprised it was not considered unclean. A fly going into any food, after all, was considered dirty.

Thinking of the kitchen, we had all the cooking done with *Patthar Ka Koila* (hard coke). The large chunks were broken up and stored in a special *kothri* (store room). The fire was started with wood chips and the coals were put into the *chulha* (hearth); it took a while to catch fire and produced lots of smoke. For some reason only a small amount went up the chimney and the whole kitchen used to be full of smoke for a long time. The kitchen walls turned dark brown and there was a lot of deposit on the doors and windows. An expert once came to study the problem and suggested that the window behind the fire should be kept closed in order to get more smoke up the chimney. I don't know if that helped. There were two *chulhas* on the platform with an air vent. The vent was useful for drying our socks and also for baking potatoes in the hot ashes. To the right was a platform for making the dough and the *chapattis*. Along the right wall was a shallow trough where we washed vegetables; the water drained directly outside into the vegetable garden. The mint was planted there and it flourished. Along the back wall was a thick slab on which the cooking utensils were kept.

One of our bearers (baira is how we pronounced it) was an older man. What I remember of him was his pride and joy - his bicycle. He spent a lot of time cleaning and shining it up. He used to go up and down the space behind the pantry with a cloth on the rim to keep it polished. When it rained he kept wiping it again and again.

The *dhobie* (washer man) brought the washed clothes once a week and took the dirty clothes back at that time; he was illiterate and had a rudimentary sense of numbers. The washed clothes were counted and checked in the *dhobie* book. When he counted the clothes he could not simply count 1-2-3-4. He had to go 1,1,1 - 2,2,2 - 3..... because he needed to keep repeating the number until it went from shirt pile to the general pile. Further, he washed clothes for many homes and had to have a system to keep them separate. Since he could not read, he kept a system of dots, dashes, and crosses to keep the ownership of the clothes straight. The system worked; he hardly ever lost our clothes or mixed them up. Another interesting point, as I said earlier, was that in Medical College, Papa had two pairs of pants. When I was in Medical College, I had fourteen - enough for two weeks. Every week the *dhobie* brought seven clean ones and took away the seven I had used. I wore a clean starched pair of pants every day. This first generation *dhobie* worked for us for many years and started a family tradition. The later generation still work for the family. One time one of the kids disappeared. The mother came to the house crying. She had heard that kids were being kidnapped and served in restaurants. She had graphic descriptions of someone finding a little finger in the food. The boy was found a few days later!

Babu James was a major player in our household who introduced a lot of new things to us; he was efficient and knowledgeable, but also combative and difficult. He had worked with the sahibs so he could cook a variety of dishes, which were new to us and that we enjoyed. He introduced baked goods - cakes and pies - to the house, delicacies that only came from Benbows before that. He made little Christmas trees and talked a lot about the sahibs. He had six children. The oldest were boys Neetu and my age. We played together a lot. Many years later, in December 1966, Asha and I had gone to Bombay to pick up our car. We were having dinner at Kwality. Munno was working there (his name was Samuel) and recognized me. We talked for a while. Only thing I remember is that the eldest brother was sick with tuberculosis. I did not ask about going to see him. I don't think I was ready; in fact I am not ready even now to go into the slums and see their condition. Just driving around NOIDA I am uncomfortable with the filth and poverty. I don't think I could be like Suketu Mehta and learn first hand about the conditions of the urban poor.

Another younger son of Babu was about 4-6 years younger than I and very afraid of our sheep, which used to be tied up right in front of the servant quarters. Once after *holi* when I had changed into clean clothes I went to the servants' quarters, as I often did. The poor little boy threw a glass of colored water on me. I was mad and I picked him up and took him close to the sheep. It was a bullying, power play, but I was afraid I would be scolded for dirtying my clothes. Babu talked to me and said I was wrong; the poor boy just wanted to play *holi* with me. He was right.

Despite his efficiency Babu was a problem and finally was made to quit at short notice. Apparently there was something that Papa gave to another servant and Babu came to Papa and said, "That was my right; you cannot give it to anyone without my permission." That went over the edge and he was fired. He also beat his wife and children.

Another big part of the household was Majeed - Abdul Majeed Khan Aghouri. He was a very capable laboratory technician who worked in the pathology department. He came to the house and worked in Papa's laboratory at home. He ran the laboratory all by himself, making culture plates by boiling the agar, drawing blood from and injecting the sheep, rabbits and guinea pigs. He operated on the rabbits for the pregnancy tests, did the serological tests, stained the slides and whatever else was needed. In 1952, when Papa became dean, he quit his practice and Majeed's visits became social rather than work related. He worked very hard at the department, at our laboratory and at Dr. S.P. Gupta's laboratory. He had one ambition - to make his son Musheed a doctor.

Musheed studied with me in preparation for the pre-medical test. He did get into Agra Medical College. He became a pathologist and joined Lucknow Medical College. He was on the faculty of pathology while his father was still a laboratory technician at the same place.

Some time later Majeed told me how Papa handled the situation of a father who worked hard for the success of his son, and the responsibility and expectations of both father and son. He told Majeed that whatever he did for his son was great, but Majeed should not expect the son necessarily to be grateful. The son should have his life; he, the father, should not expect anything in return. He told the son that the father had devoted his whole life to his son's education and that he must support the father in his old age! This was a masterpiece of managing human relations.

Majeed brought us meat and *sevain* (noodle pudding) for *Eid*, which we enjoyed. On Muslim festival days he wore a fez. We referred to the two *Eids* by the food served. Majeed was Papa's confidante. Once Papa was having his haircut in his bathroom. Majeed came with the news that a servant had contracted syphilis. The decision was made and implemented that the servant had to go. After I moved to Delhi Majeed always came to see me when I returned to Lucknow. He looked older and weaker each time, but he continued to visit into the 1970's when he died.

We had another laboratory assistant who helped Majeed. He used to work every evening except on Saturday evenings when he used to play in a band. He played the bass, which I think they called JAZ. I was quite confused between the instrument and Jazz, the style of music. I think his name was Ishwari. Once he came to the house before his performance all dressed up in a black suit and black bow tie. We did not see bow ties too often. Papa, on occasion, did go to Rotary dinners dressed in a bow tie.

Talking about the laboratory help, let me describe the laboratory itself. The laboratory was an enclosed part of the front verandah. There was a small door into the verandah for the patients who waited there. The laboratory had a table along the outside glazed glass window. Papa had his microscope there and a small sink to stain the slides. He did the blood smear examinations and the differential counts. Before the availability of mechanical counters he drew a grid of 10 by 10 squares and wrote down P-P-L-P-L as he did the counts. Sometimes he had us fill the grids while he read out P-P-L. Whether this was to help him or to get us involved in his work I am not sure; nevertheless it was a thrill. The grids were made on used paper and the slides also were wrapped in used paper. Papa used to talk about Dr. Jal Patel, a well known (society) pathologist in Bombay. Dr. Patel used fresh, new paper to wrap the slides, and had some device to remove the cover from the microscope.

As a side story, it was said that in 1946-47 when negotiations were under way about the partitioning of India, Jinnah (the main Muslim leader) was sick. Dr. Patel was the pathologist and made a diagnosis of tuberculosis. The book <u>Freedom at Midnight</u> states that the diagnosis was kept secret. It was speculated that if it was known that Jinnah was dying of tuberculosis, history might have been different.

The back wall, the one that was the wall of the drawing room, had a table and shelves where the scale and chemicals were kept. The surgery on the rabbits for pregnancy tests was also done there. A cigarette tin was partly filled with cotton and ether was poured into it. The rabbit's face was put into it to anesthetize her. The surgery was performed on the table. The level of anesthesia was adjusted by moving the tin closer or further from the rabbit's nose. In most other places the rabbits were killed after examining the ovaries for follicles, but Papa re-stitched the rabbits and used them again and again.

The laboratory was quite active in the mornings and evenings. Blood, urine, and stool samples were collected, processed and tested. One of the tests was the fractional test meal. The patients had a tube put into the stomach through the mouth and they gagged a lot as it went in. We got to watch. Subsequently they sat in the armchair in Papa's office spitting out their saliva. They had the stomach contents sucked out at periodic intervals. Later the samples were analyzed for their acidity. That was the fun part. A drop of Phenolphthalein was put in with a biuret. The liquid turned colour but it changed back as the beaker was stirred. Finally the end point was reached when the red color stayed. This was all charted on a graph to see the amount of acid in the stomach.

We had *chowkidars* (night watchmen) who were supposed to be up all night with a lantern and a stick. They used to beat their stick on the ground and make noise to make their presence known, but they sometimes went off to sleep at night. Papa would catch them sleeping, hide their stick and give them a scolding in the morning. There was never a robbery in our house, or any amongst our neighbours that I can remember. But the threat must have been real. One *chowkidar* sticks in my memory because he did not bathe or wash his shirt. I had to hold my breath every time I came near him or even rode my bike by him. For some reason I gave him a pair of socks, which I realized later were socks I needed for myself. So I exchanged another pair with him. Knowing his state of hygiene, I took the socks from him, poured alcohol on them, then washed them several times before I could wear them.

When Papa became the Principal and dean, he got a *chaprasi* assigned to work at the house. Brinda came as a raw, frightened young man. Very quickly he became the main *Ooperwalla nauker*. He cleaned the house and supervised and served the meals. He used to peek from behind the pantry curtain watching for our needs - Meera found this habit annoying. Because he was good, he was responsible for the special jobs. When we got stainless steel *thalis* and *katoris* (tableware) it was Brinda's job to wash and clean them with Vim - as opposed to *rakh* (ash), which was used to clean the other metal dishes. Brinda stayed with us for many years. He was still there when I came back from Delhi during the holidays and - to everyone's consternation - pulled out my packet of Panama cigarettes from my pocket. He was a Medical College employee and went back to the office when Papa retired.

We had brought a young boy with us after our trip to Mukteshwar. He did odd jobs around the house. He had a brown cap like a Gandhi Topi. We used to tease him by putting his cap on the grass when Mali was mowing the lawn. There was plenty of time for Mali to stop and it caused no direct harm. One time I got over aggressive and threw the cap close to where the front of the mower was. Mali could not stop in time and the poor chap's cap got torn. He was sad and I did feel stupid and sorry. I don't know if he got another cap.

For a long time we had an old *jamadar* (he cleaned the toilets). He had a big bushy beard and was a dignified character. Later on we had his children work for us. We also had a *jamadarni* who was completely bent over. Her back was parallel to the ground and she walked with a shuffle.

The front entrance to the house was through the gallery. It was not used too often; family and friends came through the side entrance under the bougainvillea archway. The gallery had a hat stand which pretty much sat there with a few walking sticks and an occasional raincoat. It was a standard British style piece. It was the passageway through which I remember Amma being carried on a stretcher after her stay in the hospital.

Papa's room to the right was formal and properly done up. There was a large chest of drawers (that Neetu has now) where he kept his shirts and other laundered items. On top on the left there was a stack of clean, ironed handkerchiefs. The small drawers had cufflinks and things like that. A comb and a brush were also kept there neatly arranged. To the left of that was a door that was kept shut and behind which he had his ties hanging from an expanded metal spring. On the opposite wall was the wardrobe for hanging suits and his many sweaters. A large shoe rack was kept near the door leading to his bathroom. His cabin trunk from his ocean trip to England was on the floor on the side of the door leading to a guest room. There was another door connecting his room to Amma's room. Sometime later a Godrej steel *almirah* (armoire) was added to the furniture. This had a safe and a secret compartment.

The guest room came off at an angle from the far side of Papa's room. We did have some guests, mainly external examiners, who came for short visits. I also recall Professor and Mrs. S.P. Sharma, friends from Agra, stayed there for a while. Chote Babujee stayed with us for a somewhat extended period one time and we got to see his morning rituals of shaving, *amla murraba* (preserves) and the overall slow process of his getting ready in the morning.

Hem ji ji and Dada spent their wedding night there. In the morning Usha di made Dada's tea with salt - a common trick. Dada was aware of it and just tasted it and gave it to Hem ji ji who took a gulp and immediately spat it out. It was the talk of the house for a while. Mungo bhaiya also lived there for a while. The guest room had its own outer entrance so he could have his own hours. These were the days he had a motorcycle. I cannot put it in any context of time.

The other bedroom was Amma's but I have no recollection of it except that it was where she was when she was sick. I presume that Papa and Amma slept in their own rooms. When Neetu and I shared the room we had our beds against the wall with the door that opened into the *kothri* (store room) where quilts and other woolens were kept. It was a small, unventilated room with a large wooden box and shelves. I am told that one day when I had a tantrum I hid in that *kothri* under some quilts and was found all sweaty but calmed down.

Neetu and I had desks on the other side of the room. We used to do our homework every evening. We also had tutors who used to help us. On January 30, 1948, Papa came back from his tennis quite agitated - Gandhiji had been shot. We turned on the radio and the news was confirmed. Our tutor was there and he kept on repeating, "He died very bad." His poor English struck me, and that expression has stuck in my mind.

The next day there were funeral processions in all cities across the country to coincide with the funeral in Delhi. It was a massive affair. We were all in *Hazratgunj* and then went to the grounds near Monkey Bridge. There were orations by, amongst others, Acharya Narendra Dev. The lines I remember are "... *woh Gandhi hai*" (that is the Gandhi) which he repeated with different preambles. On the grounds were some of our teachers who were emotional and crying loudly. Papa was a non-believer, but on that day even he fasted. We also heard Nehru's radio address -"... and a light has gone out." Later on we discussed whether there would be an autopsy. It was felt that, despite Gandhiji's religiosity, there would have to be one to determine the path of the bullets. The funeral was on radio with Melvile de Mello as the English commentator. I remember the talk about sandalwood for the pyre, which appalled me. The immersion of the ashes in Allahabad thirteen days later was also on the radio. What I remember is that nine *maunds* (400 kg) of milk were poured into the river with the ashes and that bothered me. Also the Hindi narrator, who was not close to the immersion site, went on talking about irrelevancies when the actual immersion was being done. Melvile de Mello was at the actual site and he was quite irritated when he got the mike. He had to describe the immersion in the past tense because the Hindi commentator did not give him the mike at the right moment.

Another tutor who had taught us Hindi was quite an interesting man in that he challenged us. He brought up the discussion of "the pen is mightier than the sword." He shot down our arguments from either side and made us think. He also brought up the issue of the exile of Sita and again made us look at the arguments from both sides.

While at our desks we did our homework, but Neetu sometimes read his comic books and had a clever way of hiding them under his books when Papa came to our room. Neetu asked me to help him memorize his civics and other lessons. "...Hence Mr. E.M. White of America describes civics as..." After Neetu left for the Academy, I had my desk alone.

An unrelated event may be appropriate to describe now just because it happened in that room. We had some distant relatives, whose son, Guppoo, came to stay with us for his Pre-Medical test. Guppoo tried two or three times but did not get in. He was an odd fellow, awkward more than anything else. Once there was some conversation and laughter going on in the dining room. Guppoo went from our room to the dining room and wanted to know what was going on. What I remember clearly is Neetu berating Guppoo for being nosy, and Guppoo saying repeatedly that he was just asking by the way - and Neetu did not accept that.

Guppoo's brother also stayed with us for his PMT, and got in without difficulty. He came to the house regularly and when he was doing his house job in ophthalmology, did my eye examination. And one time he helped me back home because the dilated pupils blinded me. Billoo, I understand, was interested in marrying Meera. He died of hepatitis around 1950, just a few months before I got hepatitis. There was lots of concern because of that.

Thinking about Guppoo's failure in the PMT exams brings to mind our expectations. Thousands took the examination every year and only a hundred or so got in. No one from our family failed; we just seemed to take it for granted that every one succeeded. We just saw no other side of it. Years later in Albuquerque, Abbas said about his children, "An A-minus is not acceptable." Examination grades and success in a career was and is very important in the culture of our family circle.

The dining room was an active place. We had all our meals sitting down, properly served and in proper stages, if not courses. The idea of *aam-roti* (mango burrito) as per Khazanchand, a friend of Papa's who had an informal style, would not have gone over well. For years we had a cement-topped (mosaic) dining table. In the early fifties, when we were old enough to behave properly, it was replaced with a shiny plywood veneer tabletop and chairs inspired by the gates of the Stupa at Sanchi. Neetu still has them more than sixty years later; they look good.

Depending on Papa's mood there was conversation at the table or not. Sometimes the meals were a torture because of the tension. The meals were complete with *roti-chawal-dal-sabzi* (bread, rice, lentils, vegetables) or soup, main course, and dessert or fruit depending on whether it was Indian day or English day. There we had small get-togethers with family who could easily fit around the table. Bigger groups had stand-up meals. Some important people including Drs. Khanolkar, Wintrobe, and Blumgart were entertained there. Wintrobe's visit helped me get a fellowship and enhanced my career. We have pictures of the Wintrobes and the Ira Pandey (Pant) family in the dining room.

Dr. Maxwell Wintrobe (third from right, with glasses) and his wife (on his right) at our home in 1956. Wintrobe was a pioneer in the field of clinical hematology. I trained with him ten years later.

The dining room had a mantle piece with a picture above it (Hope or Picasso's *Guitar Player*) and three pieces of china. I understand that the bigger centerpiece was an antique while the other two were more recent. One day the string holding the picture broke and shattered the antique piece. The string had been eaten away by the rusted nail.

The fridge was near the door to the gallery. We had the same one for a long time. It was one of the few fridges even amongst our friends. The Bhatias were the only others I can recall who had a fridge. Ours was a D.C. model, because ours was one of the few houses with direct current. Back then the fridge had to be serviced regularly, and defrosted frequently in the rainy season. We had rules about not keeping the door open for too long because of the humidity, and also not to open and close too often because the door, being mechanical, was liable to break - which it did. At one time we even had a lock on the door. The servicing was fun because I got to see the back of the working parts; the motor was opened, the armature sanded and the carbon brushes checked. We changed to A.C. in the fifties when we did extensive repairs and an electric overhaul.

Talking of electricity, there was time when our electricity bill was too high. The electrician came and hooked up some device to the mains and cranked a handle on his meter and burst out laughing. He explained that the reading should be zero and was registering infinity. As a result, we had to change the entire wiring and all the electrical appliances that had motors.

We kept water in bottles that did not have caps, and were kept standing by the side of the freezer compartment. Some people complained that the water had a "mediciny" smell. I think this was in their imagination. Yes, some samples and reagents were kept in the fridge but they were all sealed.

I remember one traumatic event related to the fridge. It was on the first day of my high school examination. I was under tension. I wanted to feel special and be pampered. I reached for a water bottle and pulled on it. A milk bottle, which was short, was in front of it and fell to the floor and shattered. I got a scolding and that hurt. A short digression here. We were getting our milk from Kailash's Dairy. This Kailash was an educated man doing something that was not done by that class. He had a farm and he sold milk. We visited the farm, and we got lessons in agriculture. Walking around the farm he said the amount of manure they are putting out is not high enough in nutrition. (I do remember some strange things). To explain the milk bottle: Kailash also had a milk bar with ice cream, milk shakes etc. The place looked clean but had the smell of stale milk.

Back to the layout of the house. The wall between our room and the dining room had a sideboard purchased from some British officer who was returning to England. The walls also had built in cabinets for the formal crockery. The dining room opened into the back verandah where we had the hand-washing sink. When we put in a neon light in the dining room, that was considered quite revolutionary and controversial. From the dining room Papa enjoyed a view of the garden, especially at teatime. Later, during refurbishing, curtains were added to the doors and he was sad that he could not see the flowers.

When we had parties - and we usually had one big one every summer - they were held outdoors. The whole east lawn used to be full of people. These parties were events in the medical college. As head of the department, and later as dean, Papa invited a large number of doctors, their families, and probably other important people. Dr. C.S. Chaterjee of Radiology also had similar parties. What I remember of the Chaterjees' party was that Dr. C. went around to the kitchen telling everyone to hurry up and serve the food (*Sheeghir karo, Sheeghir karo*). The pattern of all the parties was similar. Everyone came in, talked for a bit, food was served and then everyone left. In those days alcohol was not served in good homes. The pattern remains the same except that now alcohol is served on a regular basis.

At our parties the preparations were extensive. The whole family was mobilized: Meera, her friends, our cousins, our servants, and even servants of friends. In addition there were special cooks. There was a man who specialized in kebabs. He prepared the kebab meat by using a knife to cut it into very fine mince without use of the mortar and pestle that the other cooks – *khansamas* – used. (This was before there were food blenders.) Another man specialized in western food. He made mayonnaise from scratch using salad oil and water and two forks to fluff it up. I guess we served exotic foods; I know we served the best. At one level I accepted all this as the norm and enjoyed it. At another level I had a problem with it, had my little protests, and did not partake of some of those foods. I still have that kind of conflicted reaction and action.

We did have some small elegant dinners when American or British scientists were visiting. The best crockery was used and elegant foods prepared. There was a careful balancing of Indian and Western foods to give the guests a taste of our culture but still allow them to be comfortable. A lot of planning went into these refinements; they were part of the image and style that contributed to Papa and K.G. Medical College being regarded as top rate.

Sometimes at the smaller parties or if there were last minute guests some of the food ran low. Meera invented a code. If a family member asked for a dish that was running low, she would say F.G.S. This stood for Family Go Slow and we all understood that we should skip the dish or take only a small amount.

Other minor incidents stick in the memory. Dr. Indu Mohan Gupta, a demonstrator, was visiting Papa and sat for tea. The poor guy was nervous and shaking his torso and head a lot. We made fun of him after he left. The Mithal family came from time to time. When Annu and Neelu were small they were at the dining room table and put salt in the *dahi* (yoghurt.) They put in too much salt and decided that the only way to eat the *dahi* was to use the small spoon from the salt dispenser. We were never allowed to do things like that, and I was afraid that all of us would get a scolding. We had a brass stand with three cups and a small spoon for salt, pepper and I don't know what. During the rainy season the salt became gooey and reacted with the brass to form a greenish mess.

Another time bade mama ji, mami ji (my mother's eldest brother and his wife) and a few of the clan came for a visit. Mama ji was in the verandah and Papa was talking to his wife about his obesity. His diet was analyzed and discussed and papa was explaining the risks of obesity. " Toast, even with a small amount of butter, is okay for breakfast." Mami ji said, " *Sun lain ge*" (speak softly, he will hear you)." Papa said, " That is good; he needs to." Of course mama ji never went on a diet, and died a few years later of a heart attack and pulmonary embolus. Obesity was a major problem on that side of the family.

I have a lot of memories of the drawing room. It was a standard room for years, with two small windows facing the side lawn, and blue walls colored with copper sulphate emulsion. The sofas were along the walls and there was a brass topped table in the middle. There was also a table that revolved with the radio on it, and a standard lamp. There were bookshelves with, amongst others, my favorite encyclopedia, "Pictorial Knowledge." The bookshelves were tan colored with sliding glass doors.

In the early fifties, major changes were made. I do not recall if this was one job or several jobs over a few years. The big change was the creation of large French windows. The color of the walls was changed from the copper sulphate emulsion on plaster to light distemper on cement. The wiring was put into the wall, giving clean lines instead of the thick wooden strips we had before. The arrangement of the curtains was changed. Instead of having the curtains hang from the doorframe, pelmets were added so that the curtains were flush with the open doors - and thus visible whether the door was open or closed. The curtains themselves were of a new silk flowery material.

Then came the furniture rearrangement - a big step. The sofas had always been along the wall, like those seen in the news when Asian leaders (near or far East) entertain visiting heads of state. Kishin came up with the idea of putting the sofas close together around the fireplace and coffee table. Everyone was skeptical about it. But we did try it out, and amazingly we all approved. The room remained like that for the rest of Papa's stay in Nandinee. With the new furniture arrangement, the fireplace became meaningful and was used fairly often. A pretty fireplace screen was designed by Mr. Khastgir from the Art School. The fireplace screen is with me in Albuquerque now. Also a portable grill was made for the fire.

At another time an aquarium was set up. This led to designing of a place to display it. I did this. It was a great design if I may say so myself. It was L- shaped and it created another cozy space complementing the new furniture arrangements. During the remodeling, I had objections, at least in my mind, about the changes. I guess I am not too fond of change.

The events I remember in the drawing room include the chance to talk to Dr. Khanolkar when I had just started my medical studies. He was well known and talking to a famous pathologist was an honor. While sitting there he pointed to his bald head, took out a cap from his pocket and said, "It gets cold." Another time a big shot from Rockefeller came for tea. Every one had his best foot forward. Everyone was given a starched tea napkin. I was appalled to see that the visitor put his food on the napkin.

Late in Papa's career when he was working with the Rockefeller Foundation, two professors from Harvard Medical School were invited to Lucknow Medical College to help set up new programs. One of them was Dr. Herman Blumgart. His wife was very interested in music and wanted to learn about Indian music. Papa arranged for our family friend, Shanti Hiranand, to act as teacher. Shanti was quite well known as a musician by then (she became famous later). Unlike most Indian musicians of that time, Shanti was educated and spoke fluent English. She probably understood Western music too. Shanti came with an assistant who was a *tabla* player. The two demonstrated and performed and Mrs. Blumgart asked a lot of questions. In the end, she had a smile and she said, "Now I know why I don't understand Indian music."

Amongst the changes in the drawing room was the acquisition of a radiogram. We used to have musical evenings for the adults; they became the starting point of a music club where we met at different houses to listen to western classical music. During the day the drawing room was where some of my school friends gathered. At that time we played popular western music. In the earlier years I spent time in the drawing room listening to the radio. I seriously thought that I was creating music by turning the volume control up and down! Such was my musical knowledge! I did one time hear a singer repeat the notes that the orchestra had played and I was able to understand that.

I also spent a lot of time with the multivolume "Pictorial Knowledge." I read and reread the Greek myths, read about animals and the marvels of science. During the day I also did some experiments. I knew they were dangerous so I did them when I was alone and hid the evidence before Papa came home. I used a small wooden board and attached one electric wire to a cigarette tin and the other to a screwdriver. I created sparks, first dry then with water in the tin. I went on to add salt to the water to test the effect on conductivity. I was working with naked 220 volts of power. Not smart!

The room next to the drawing room was Papa's office; it had a large desk with a big glass on top. Under the glass were some sayings and photographs. Over that was a blotting paper pad on which Papa would blot the ink from his writing. He also had a rolling blotting pad with a small handle. We used to try to read the mirror image writing on the blotting surfaces. These were the days of dip pens and fountain pens so ink had to be blotted or one had a mess. There was a scale, made of brass and kept shiny, to weigh letters. It had a flat top and a curving, graduated scale. There was a flat ruler and a round black rod that was also used as to make lines. There was a wooden letter sorter with slots for stationery and mail. There was a letter opener. The drawers had all kinds of interesting things. There were two office chairs and a reclining chair. There were a lot of books.

There was a rack for rubber stamps (one said "paid") for crossing cheques etc., and of course the ink pad. The wall was blue with an inch wide white stripe all around the room. One day I imprinted "paid" on the white stripe behind the door leading to the drawing room. Papa saw this when he was with someone else and I said, "Well, Papa has paid for this wall hasn't he?"

Papa spent the morning in his office, preparing lectures, working on laboratory issues, and also doing some of his reading. He also met with the cook and the bearer in the evening to do the household accounts. Next to the office was the laboratory, which I described before. The third door of the office opened on to the east verandah, which was the place where a lot of family activity took place. We were in and out of it all the time. The side facing the lawn was divided into three sections, one of which had an aquarium that did not work too well. In the middle were the stairs leading to the path. The third was over a flowerbed.

The east verandah had doors leading to the dining room, drawing room, and Papa's office. It was the equivalent of the American home's den and a nice place for meeting family and friends. It was also where we slept during the rainy season and had afternoon tea. It overlooked the private lawn with its tube roses and rose bushes. During a rainstorm hundreds of earthworms climbed out of the beds and climbed up the three steps to seek shelter from drowning. They had to be swept out sometimes 2-3 times in day. Boys will be boys, and we put salt on them and watched them shrivel. It was just a great space - probably the most comfortable, physically and psychologically. If there was tension in the house we all retreated to our own spaces - office or desk. Being in the verandah meant every thing was fine. Makka Mali often did his flower arrangements sitting there. One year DDT was sprayed in the verandah and flies would sit on the furniture or floor and after a few minutes just keel over. The floor turned black from dead flies.

Every year we had a major event in the garden. At a time when the grass seemed to be at the peak of greenness and lushness, it used to be scraped up. It was supposed to make it healthy and get rid of some weeds. A team came to do the job. It was an interesting deal. I thought that they were doing us a service and they would be paid. As it turned out this was the height of summer and grass for horses was not easily available. Thus they were paying us to buy the grass from us. The price depended on the early rains and green grass availability in the countryside. Once the price was negotiated, they removed the grass and bundled it off. Makka Mali waited for them to leave, then got to work on the lawn for its next phase. The loose dirt was gathered up and hauled away to sit in the area of the vegetable garden. The roots sprouted and the grass was revived once more. The ritual went on. A few weeks later the loose dirt that had been piled up was brought back and spread over the lawn. The rationale was that the weeds were mostly in the surface layers and were removed with the scrapings. Leaving them sitting in a heap was thought to destroy the seeds.

The pantry was off the dining room, and had a door leading to the covered walkway to the kitchen. It had a lot of shelves for everyday crockery and serving dishes. The most interesting item was the wire mesh cupboard. It was a small thing that sat with its four legs resting in bowls of water. It was the place to keep items that attracted ants and flies.

The back verandah was enclosed in wire mesh with a door opening into the *Aangan* (courtyard). There was a large sink in the corner near the pantry. This was used for washing hands before and after meals, and also for washing crockery. The teakettle and toaster also went there. The most common use in the early years was as a space for the tailor - there seems to have been one there all the time. One tailor stands out in my memory from when I was around ten. He used to tell me how the earth would come to an end and the sky would turn to steel. He could not believe that humans evolved from monkeys. He said, "If that is so, how come no monkey changes to human now?" Things have not changed much. Many educated people in the U.S. do not believe in evolution either.

The *aangan* was quite large. It was on the south side of the house behind the *jali wala* (back) verandah. The kitchen and the kothris (store room) were all on the far end separating it from the vegetable garden and the servants' area. To the west was a wall for additional privacy. Near our bathroom was a *Haar Shringaar* tree that produced lots of small flowers with pink stems and white petals and a sweet smell. Sometimes those flowers would be placed on the mantle piece in the drawing room where they looked pretty for a few days. I had not seen *Haar Shringaar* flowers in a long time. In 2006 I was in Delhi in October and saw two trees in bloom; it was really nice.

The *aangan* was surrounded by the *kothris* and in one corner was the shed where the pots and pans were scrubbed. The *Bartan Manjne Wali* used to come and scrub the pots and pans using the ash from the kitchen. Next to that was a room whose original purpose I am not sure about. For many years it was used to keep the guinea pigs that were used in Papa's laboratory for their blood, which I realized later was the source of "complement" for serological tests. The blood was drawn from their heart.

The guinea pigs were held by two people holding onto the legs and arms, a needle was put into the upper abdomen and blood was obtained by puncturing the heart. They squealed and struggled but seemed no worse for the trauma. They jumped right up and went scampering. The floor of the room was covered with freshly mown grass clippings which were removed every few days. The used grass was then put into the compost pit. Every thing was used to the maximum - a habit that I have maintained. The grass used to turn yellow and had a strong odor that I thought was caused by the urine and feces from the guinea pigs. However, when I started composting grass clippings in Albuquerque, I realized the grass clippings themselves produced the same odor- and made me quite nostalgic.

The guinea pigs were fed *channa* (garbanzos) soaked in water. We were all fascinated by the guinea pig babies who were born with a full fur coat, and were running around soon after they were born. We used to take the guinea pigs and play with them on the lawn. We also had rabbits, which were kept in a separate shed with a dirt floor near the vegetable garden. The rabbits bred freely and produced small helpless, pink babies that slowly grew to be cute. The rabbits dug deep burrows going down for many feet and showing up when the ground collapsed.

Next to the guinea pigs was a small low roofed shed, the *koile-ki-kothri*, with a small door. Here the big lumps of coal were kept. Every day the cook would break the lumps into smaller pieces that could be used for cooking. There was always coal powder on the floor of the *aangan*. We played tennis against one of these walls.

Next was the wall of the *kothri* where the cots were stored. We used the cots during the summer and monsoons to sleep outdoors or in the east verandah - and that itself was quite an operation. Every evening the cots were taken out and placed in a row on the lawn. The bedding and mosquito nets were put on each bed. At each corner of the mosquito net a bamboo pole was tied. The nets were kept in place by crossing the bamboos and hooking them to the bed posts. In the morning these devices were removed, the nets wrapped around the bamboos and stored for the day. The procedure was best done by two people working together and wrapping the net from each side. There were ways of doing it single-handed, but it was more awkward. During the early monsoon and occasionally during summer, rain or dust storms made us move into the verandah. Again quite an operation. The nets had to be taken down, each bed lifted by two people and rushed into the verandah. The servants were usually called in from the servants' quarters, the *chowkidar* pitched in, and we all did the job together.

During those summer days the contrast between the lawn and house was great. The house felt like a furnace. Even though the houses were designed for the hot weather - they had lots of doors and windows and sky lights with strings to open and close them - the rooms were hot in the summer; the contrast was most striking because the lawn was cool. One of the debates amongst the family was the relative difficulty of the hot dry season and the humid but relatively cooler monsoons. Since we had the *khas tatti* which provided a simple method of cooling in the dry weather, and because I sweat a lot, I preferred the dry season. Others said the fans gave a cooler breeze once the monsoons came on.

We had *nawar* beds made of canvas-like strips. The servants had beds strung with *baan* (coarse hemp). *Nawar* was made of tightly woven thick cotton strips like a bandage. The bed was woven with a neat cross weave. The *nawar* stretched and from time to time had to be tightened row by row starting from the head end, usually with one servant on either side of the bed. Because the position of the weave moved, the dirtier exposed parts of the *nawar* contrasted with the cleaner covered parts. I found that quite interesting.

The *palang wali kothri* (shed for beds) also was the storage place for our bikes. Neetu and I had bikes as our transport throughout our stay in Lucknow. School, movies, sports, visiting friends etc. were all reached on bikes. We got new bikes as we got bigger - all of them basic and utilitarian. All our friends had bikes. The repairman was on our way to school and we used him as needed. We did not know how to repair our own bikes.

During the war, with the petrol rationing, more people tried bicycling. Papa bought a Raleigh; it was green, with the chain and the entire driving mechanism enclosed in a cover. It had three speed gearing. In those days, the gearing mechanism was inside the hub of the rear wheel. I never understood how it worked. I don't think Papa used it too often. Babujee did use his bicycle a lot. In Lucknow, after retirement, he did not have a car and used his bike through the whole neighborhood. When he was in his late sixties, he had a dizzy spell and fell off his bike. There was no significant injury, but his doctors did not allow him to ride his bike after that.

Next was the kitchen complex. It has its own verandah and the passageway connecting it to the pantry. The verandah was where the *masalas* (spices) and chutneys were pounded and mixed. One time Mrs. Asthana helped us by boiling and filtering *ghee* that must have come in bulk. There was a small *kothri* (shed) in which wood chips and crushed coal were stored for easy access from the kitchen. Next was a large store room in which *atta, dal, ghee, chana* etc. were stored. It was also used as a sitting room for Amma's guests. I do not recall any context or details, but I remember Bari Maami sitting there. One of my younger cousins, possibly Nippu, was playing around with us. He ran to mami ji and she started breast feeding him. I remember how that was criticized. I am assuming that this was when Amma was alive and that is why mami ji was in the kitchen area.

On the outside of the kitchen verandah, towards the family lawn, was the aviary where we had parakeets and *munias* (finches.) It was a room constructed by building a wire mesh enclosing a corner space. It had a rod bent as an "L" that acted as a perch and there were small *handias* (earthen pots) with side openings for nests. One of the Makka Mali's duties was to clean the birdcage. He used to climb in carefully, not allowing the birds to escape, and then sweep the floor. Apart from the bird droppings, there were skins from the *daana* (bird feed) that the birds were fed. The skins were mixed with some intact seeds so Mali used to collect them in his palm and blow on them to get the skins out and reuse the intact *daana*. The birds were with us for most of our stay in Nandinee.

We had another bird perch for pigeons in the family lawn tucked away beyond the tank. This was a cement pole with four compartments on top, each with sliding doors with a small wire mesh window. Many of the pigeons were eaten by some cat or cat like creature, and were abandoned soon after.

The family lawn and its surroundings were quite elaborate and were used a lot. The lawn was shielded from the public eye by a thick, neatly trimmed hedge. The beds in front of it had crotons and many-hots and jerberas. The walking area for the bulls ended in the corner towards the Roy-Chowdhry's house. In that small space, there were cacti and a century plant, which only bloomed once every few years but the blossom was striking. It had a long straight trunk coming out of the top of the plant with white flowers which lasted for a week or so. There was also a pine tree growing in that corner. Quite a rarity in Lucknow. It survived through the hot Lucknow summers. There were lantana bushes along the wall trained like creepers. There was a *nali* (gutter) built into the wall to take water to the family lawn, the tank, and the vegetable garden. In the back part of the lawn was the pond with lotus and frogs. It was also the reservoir for watering the potted plants during the week between the visit of the bulls.

We had a variety of vendors who came around. Some sold wares, some offered services, and some were specially asked to come to the house while others just went around the neighborhood looking for business. We, of course, were interested in the ones that offered food. There was the Bengali *mithai wala* (sweet seller) who walked around with a tiffin carrier in one hand and a basket in the other. The tiffin carrier had layers of *rasgulla, pantua, sandesh, cham-cham,* and *malai chop* - delectables that I can still see in his trays. They were variations on a theme of very sweet milk based sweets. I don't see these variations of *cham-cham / malai chop* anymore, but I have to acknowledge that I don't spend too much time in sweet shops or Bengali sweet shops. The basket had *samosas* and *suhals*. We were expected to choose just one or two items, and that was a hard decision to make. The way the Bengali sweet man called out his wares still rings in my ears. He said something like "*garmik-samose-mitai, Bengali mithai.*" In winter we had the *moongphali walla* (peanut seller) going around with large sacks of peanuts, and a *handia* (clay pot) with burning coals to keep the top layer warm. He had an oil lamp, which looked like a cigarette tin with a spout, and it had a thick wick. He called out "*do dubble pawwa*" and "*moongphali badaam wali.*"

We also had a variety of vendors who were totally out of bounds because of unhygienic conditions. Top of the list was ice cream and *kulfi*; we did want them but they were absolutely banned. One time Mungo Bhyya got *kulfi* from somewhere. After dinner he asked the servant to serve the *kulfi*. Papa was there and he said, "*what kulfi-kulfi kya?*" Mungo did not realize it was a banned item and thought Papa had not heard him. So he says,"*Arre kulfi.*" Then of course all hell broke loose.

Lyya Ram Dane Ki, Budhia-ke-Bal, Neembu pani, Golgappe, Dahi, pink and yellow coloured balls of some kind were all going around – those were so far out of line that we did not even think of them. *Chana jor garam*, we did get to eat once in a while from narrow conical paper containers folded on top and bottom. I am not counting the *sabziwala* (vegetable seller) and *machchi wala* (fish seller), who were a different category.

The services provided were interesting. The *dhunia* (cotton processor) came before the winter. He would set up his workshop in an empty servants' quarter. He hung his "*Shiv Dhanush*" (big bow) from a hook in the ceiling, put a cloth over his mouth and nose and got to work on the old compacted cotton and went "*Dhun – Dhun*" with his thick stick with dumbbells. The vibrating of the bow string fluffed up the cotton. There were cotton flakes all over but the cotton was nice and fluffy. It was then filled into the *razais* and *gaddas* (quilts) carefully and thick stitches were put in to keep the cotton from bundling up.

The knives and scissors were sharpened on wheels with sparks flying. Periodically a man came to work on the *sil – batta* (grinding stone). Chutney and *masalas* (spices) were ground on the *sil – batta* and the stones gradually became smooth. The man would use a hammer and chisel to make a small depression to increase the efficiency of the grinding. He made some designs on the *sil* and plain lines on the *batta*. I guess we ate some of the stone as it gradually ground down slowly into the *masala*. I wonder if modern researchers would classify that as a health hazard in this day and age!

The one I watched with the greatest fascination was the *kalai wala* (tin plater). He came only once in a while and it was an event in the kitchen. All the cooking *bartans* (utensils) were collected in one place for him to work on. He dug a pit to put the coals in then made a channel into which he put a tube, which was fixed to the ground by patting wet mud around it. This was attached to bellows. The bellows were shaped something like a samosa with a slit on one side. The slit had loops for the thumb and fingers. After the fire got going he worked the bellows. In one smooth movement he would open the slit, inflate the bellows and close the slit and bring the bellows down to pump air into the fire to make it glow red-hot. Then he started the job. Each *bartan* would be put into the fire and heated uniformly. A small bead of *ranga* (tin) was put on one spot and spread around the whole pot using a cloth pad with a small cotton pad on it. The whole pot became silvery bright as the *ranga* spread a thin layer on the surfaces which came in contact with food. Once completed the pot was immersed in a bucket of water. I was allowed to try my hand at the bellows once in a while. Recently, when my friend Ellen was visiting Delhi, we went to Chandni Chowk area. There we saw a man doing the *kalai* just as I remember it back in Lucknow sixty odd years earlier. I am sorry I did not look closely to see if he had the same kind of bellows.

There was a man who came to print *saree* borders. He spread the plain cloth on the floor and prepared his paint. He mixed the thick gooey paint using two sticks and put it into a metal mold with patterns on one side and an open end with space for a plunger. He placed the box on the border and pressed the paint with the plunger to make the pattern on the *saree*. Once done, he sprinkled some silvery powder on it. And you had a pretty *dhoti* with a border.

There were Chinamen who brought clothes for sale in big bundles loaded on bicycles. They came in twos. The bundles were neatly and tightly packed and put on the carriers on the back of the bike. The bundle was higher than the head of the salesman. They came to a home, showed their wares, did or did not make a sale, repacked, and were on their way.

I have mentioned before that Makka Mali was a servant, but he was really quite a presence and part of our lives. I do not remember any time he was not with us. Makka Mali was the gardener and guardian of Nandinee. The most striking memory of him is of the morning rounds he made with Papa and Dr. J.G. Mukherjee (Daksaheb to everyone). They went around the garden checking on what was doing well, what needed more care or what needed to be changed. They spoke a common language of flowers and beauty and the technical aspects of gardening. They were an unusual trio: the retired, truly retired, Professor of pathology who was in his quiet way the father figure of the Mohalla; the new aspiring pathologist on the faculty of the Medical College who was owner of a new house in the New Hyderabad Colony of Lucknow; and this young Mali, fresh from the village, illiterate, but competent and enthusiastic. These three went around the garden. I saw them make their rounds with a bond based on their love for flowers. Although Mali did not know the names of the plants, he knew what they were and had his own names for them, which were his versions of the English names that Papa and Daksaheb used. I don't think the limited English in anyway interfered with their communication, which of course was in Hindi. Makka Mali did not make much money. The flowers and plants cost more than what he made. What did he think of that! Makka Mali did not just take orders; he was an active participant in the planning or the changes made. He was an equal partner in this area. The actual doing was his thing. The mutual respect and understanding of the roles each person had was striking. I saw them, overheard some of the conversation, but was more interested in seeing what was being done.

Makka was quiet, hard working, kept to himself but knew what was going on. I watched with fascination the things he did. The big weekly job was watering the garden from the well. The bulls came in the morning with a man. Mali took charge. The bulls were harnessed, the rope measured and the job began. He did all the parts of the job. When he drove the bulls he made them walk fast and had a short turn around time. He cursed and beat the bulls. His language at that time was very different from his usual demeanor. He did, however, increase the output of water from the well. When he pulled the bucket to empty it he did it with finesse. When he actually did the watering in the garden he moved quickly to add lengths of the pipes, add angled segments and generally spread the water around. He worked with swiftness and efficiency. Compared to his helpers he just had an air of confidence and worked as if he knew what he was doing.

He also did delicate jobs around the garden. He treated the seedlings and flowers with kindness. The seeds were planted in small trays and once they sprouted he moved them very gently one at a time into another tray with the delicate touch of a craftsman. The watering of the new seedlings was also a careful job. He filled his palm with water and dripped small amounts onto each seedling, tray-by-tray, rack-by-rack. As the seedlings matured they were again moved to the beds, in neat rows with due consideration for their size. He did the transplant, and he knew what each plant needed in space, water, and soil. He had skills that came from an intelligent understanding of the plants.

How old was Mali? To the five, ten, fifteen year old he was old. Later his years did start showing. I assumed for a long time, for no reason, that he was as old as Papa. Now I feel he was younger, maybe in his twenties when he joined us.

He was more than the gardener. He was the Mali of the house. We had a turn-over of cooks, bearers, *chowkidars* and other servants. Makka Mali was there all the way through. He had seniority, he had respect and charisma. I was too young, too removed or too busy to have intimate knowledge of the workings of the servants' quarters to comment on the specifics, but I can make some generalizations. Makka was a quiet wise man. He observed and learnt. He showed emotion but in a controlled manner. He did not shout and he kept his assistants in control by example rather than by coercion. As with the bulls for watering the well, if other people did not do the work right, he would show them how to do it. Because of his seniority he was the man who kept the other servants in check. Papa often went to him if there were problems with other servants. A word from him was able to keep discipline in the ranks. He was not a spy but he kept his pulse on the servants and kept Papa informed. At one time we had a bearer who came from the old British household. He was quite a domineering man and because he was familiar with the ways of the English he considered himself superior. I can only speculate that there was some tension in their interaction.

Mali was married and had a daughter. His wife died quite early, close to the time Amma died. Malin used to weave baskets with designs very similar to Navajo designs. So he was left with a small girl to take care of. Gurdevi was just a year or two younger than I. To make things worse, the poor girl's foot was crushed under a cart during a fair. Crushed feet are hard enough to fix even these days; in those days there was nothing. She had a deformed foot and walked with a limp. She was married off early - I guess around age ten. She did come back from time to time; I don't think she had any children. The way our lives were structured I never knew what kind of life she had. Reading about abuse of young brides these days one can't help thinking how this young girl fared. She had no mother, a deformed foot and no child. These questions and more come up now. I don't even know what kind of family and village ties Mali had. Did he take time off to go home to see brothers, sisters or parents? What kind of life did he have? He worked from morning to evening except for a break for lunch. I recall him talking to and meeting with a few men who may have been from his kinship. It did not seem to be a common occurrence. He worked hard by himself; only much later did he have an assistant.

Makka developed a strong bond with our last dog. He had shown no interest in our previous dogs. Ernie however, became his companion and friend. Ernie and Makka were stranded on the roof of Nandinee when the flood of 1960 hit. They were rescued together and Ernie died soon after Makka did.

I remember his lunch break because I used to go to his room in the servants' quarters. He had one room with a verandah and a courtyard. The verandah was partially walled off to make the kitchen. The kitchen was a single *chulha* (hearth) and a few pots and pans. He mixed what seemed to be a huge amount of *atta* (dough) and made 2-3 half-inch thick *rotis*. He put them on the *tawa* (griddle) till they were firm enough to stand close to wood fire. He cooked slowly and then ate his meal slowly with some *chutney* (mint sauce.) He drank water after he finished his meals. I remember his lunch ritual vividly. I suppose I watched it on an ongoing basis. I don't recall talking to him during his meals. I would not be surprised if he did not talk during his meals and just suffered me as an observer to be tolerated.

He was skilled and efficient with the small number of garden tools he had. One was a *Khurpee*, a metal device with a long stem, a wooden handle at one end and the stem flattened at the other to make the blade at right angles to the stem. The blade was strong, sharp enough to dig through moderately hard soil and wide enough to turn the soil. Mali used it to dig up plants, make holes in the ground and to remove weeds. The skill was the key, the tool was simple. Makka worked and walked without shoes. The skin of his sole was very thick. From time to time he got thorns stuck into his sole. If the tip broke off inside the skin, he developed calluses around them. He used the *Khurpee's* edge to carve out the callus; it seemed to me the gouges were a quarter inch deep.

Thinking back on the servants' quarters and their amenities it is somewhat surprising that an enlightened person like Papa did not provide electricity or toilets for the servants. It was not the norm in those days, but still I wonder.

Makka asserted himself when it was appropriate. Papa generally focused on flowers, shrubs and exotic plants in the garden. Even though the vegetable garden was not given too much importance Makka, on his own, kept it up. One year corn (*maize-makka*) was planted. When the crop was ready we had an influx of a large number of monkeys - more than were usually around. They devoured the crop. We were very young and cruel, as children can be. We went around teasing poor Gurdevi, Mali's young daughter, with a taunt: "*Makka ko Bandar kha gai*," the monkeys have eaten Makka. We drove the poor girl to tears. Makka Mali told us in no uncertain terms that we were wrong to tease her, and we did stop. He was composed but firm; that is the way I remember him.

Talking about monkeys, Mali had a sling that he used to drive monkeys far away from the house. The field near the house had a lot of monkeys. When he drove them away from the house they would go to this field and come right back. He devised this sling with which he could throw big clods of dirt or stones great distances to drive them far away from his garden. He used the sling with great effect.

Even though Papa's focus was the flower garden Mali took pride in the vegetables. We enjoyed the products that he brought us - the vegetable garden was his. He was also, however, a master at arranging flowers. His arrangements had a casual elegance, a blend of colors and types of flowers. The artist and the sophisticates in the family admired his flower arrangements.

Makka Mali was a simple, straightforward man, but by no means uninformed or stupid. He did not know how to use the phone but with help was able to take the few calls he got. I cannot remember or figure out who would call him. I do remember him holding the phone awkwardly when he first used it. When we were gone he did not answer the phone. He was good with his hands, could fix broken fences and garden tools. The lawn mower was his tool and he could dismantle it, remove defective parts, fix them or take them for repairs. He regularly lubricated the gears and adjusted the tension of the cutting blades. He had a small number of implements and he used them with skill.

More importantly, despite his simplicity he had a profound understanding of the world. He was aware of the world, asked questions about the war and medical issues. He showed his understanding of the realities of society at the time of Independence. My brother, who was fourteen, asked him what he thought of the coming Indian rule with the departure of the British. His response was a reflection of the life he had seen. I wonder if he had faced oppression when he lived in the village. He simply said what difference would it make to a poor man like him. Congress or the British, he felt, would not change his life. My brother who was idealistic and believed that freedom would change our life got upset. He criticized Mali for thinking negatively and said that it was people like him who were keeping India down. I don't think Mali said anything. Well, he was with us for another fifteen years and I don't think his life changed in any meaningful way. And in the years since he died the lot of the poor is as it was then. There is some change, there is some progress, but there remain large numbers of poor living by manual labor and living on just enough calories to survive.

Mali was also the moralist and chaperone. When I was engaged I sometimes came to the house with my fiancée when there was no one else at home. Mali was watchful and somehow managed to come into the house to make sure we were behaving. Did he have a sex life? Did he have a life outside Nandinee? I doubt it very much.

I am writing about Makka Mali nearly fifty years after his death, and seventy odd years after he came to Nandinee. It would be more accurate to call these impressions rather than memories. Yet, I remember some events clearly, some images are there clear as can be and some statements seem vivid. Regardless, he was a strong man and genuinely a part of Nandinee and our lives. The last time I saw him was when we went to Lucknow after Papa's death. He was admitted to ward IV in the Medical College for a lung infection. We talked about Papa's death and he said, "Malan (his wife) died when bahuji (my mother) died and I will die now, now that sahib had died."

I never saw him again.

I have written down some descriptions, and recalled events and people as they happened or as I think they happened. It was interesting to put these thoughts together and was a great way for the family to connect during my extended stay in India in 2006-2007. It is a collection of information that probably means nothing to most people, but there it is. The last time I saw Nandinee was when it was ready for demolition. It was Joanie's first trip to Lucknow and I was able to go down memory lane with her. Now there are highrise apartments.

***

PART FOUR
THE SCHOOL AND EDUCATION

Chapter Thirteen
Colvin Taluquedar's College

I was lucky and privileged to have a good education. Colvin Talequedar's College was founded in 1899 and was named after the Lt. Governor of Northwest Province (Agra) before the formation of the united provinces of Agra and Oudh. The foundation stone stated that the school was founded especially for the education of the sons of the *Taluquedars* of *Oudh*. (The spelling later changed to Avadh to reflect the Urdu pronunciation of the region in central Uttar Pradesh.) The inspiration for the school came from Captain Nelson Davies, the jailor for Bahadur Shah Zafar, the last Mughal. Davies said, "First and most essential requisite is to give the lads breathing room and separate them from the baneful atmosphere of bigotry, superstitious ignorance ….etc." (from William Dalrymple The Last Mughal).

23rd November 1908, (Colvin Taluqdars' College) Elephant drill for the Viceroy's procession

A procession of elephants at Colvin College, 1908, during a visit of the Viceroy of India

***

Colvin had become a prestigious private school by the time I was enrolled. I spent 12 years there - from first class to intermediate. I finished the 12th class and passed the UP Board Exams to enter Lucknow Medical College. To paraphrase Charles Dickens, it was quite a time. A lot happened to me and a lot happened in the world in those 12 years. There were good things and bad things. World War II ended as I finished 5th class. India became independent when I started 8th class. Amma died when I was in 2nd class. I wrote an essay on Independence Day in those turbulent times. I adapted to the changes at home and continued my studies and life with classmates, family, neighbors, teachers and family friends.

A lot of memories of that period have kept coming back to me. V.S. Naipul once said he could not write a novel set in India because he does not understand it well enough. I cannot write a novel set in Lucknow, Colvin, or New Hyderabad because…. that is the way I am. My memories may mean nothing to others but I have not read anything describing that life so I am indulging myself and recording them. They say old age leads to loss of recent memory and enhances the remote events. Having reached 70, that thought does occur to me. However, I still have a good recent memory and a good comprehension of current events, so I will not worry.

I spent a short time in the English Medium School, St. Agnes Convent, run by the nuns, and transferred to Colvin when the petrol rationing prohibited the convent from running its bus. Colvin was next door to our house, so I could go there on foot or bicycle. My early memories of Colvin are patchy. I remember being held back in second class and I was happy that I would have a new set of classmates. Sushama di reminded me of this and teased me about it later.

I took part in the school's annual celebration of the birth of Krishna. I memorized and was to recite *"Manus hoon to'….."* in praise of the time of Krishna when the world was perfect. I got on stage alone and could not remember my lines. Mr. Bharadwaj had to prompt me line by line. It passed and I remained close to Mr. Bharadwaj and met him again about 10 years ago. He was still active and productive. In his eighties he was writing and producing a play. He remained a part of my life all through the 12 years at Colvin and beyond.

The school grounds were extensive. In the early days the rich kids were treated like the royalty they were. *Taluquedars* were landlords with immense wealth and, more importantly, with despotic power over their tenants, who were almost like their subjects. The grounds in the old days had stables, servants' quarters, a field where crops were grown and, of course, space for football, cricket, hockey, and track. We never had a shortage of space for our games and sports. We also had a covered swimming pool.

The front of the main building of Colvin

The principal lived on the premises in a good-sized house; the other teachers were on their own. Mr. Davidson, an Englishman, was principal when I started. Later a retired inspector of schools, Mr. Kichlew, became principal. Mrs. Davidson was like a "mama" for the younger kids. Once while playing and running around the fields I fell and cut my eyebrow. For decades that scar was my distinguishing mark on passports and other identity documents. When I fell, I was taken to the principal's house, and Mrs. Davidson herself cleaned and dressed the wound. She told me not to let anyone open the bandage. That evening Papa asked his friend, surgeon Mathur, to check the wound. To me, Mrs. Davidson's instructions were most important and it took a lot of persuasion from Dr. Mathur and Papa before I allowed them to remove the bandage!

The personal touch and bond with the teachers was strong. Outside the classroom we had a lot of interaction with teachers who offered advice on issues, games, and scouting. Mr. Misra and Mr. Bharadwaj even visited us at home. Amma died soon after I started at Colvin and we received a lot of support from Mr. Bharadwaj, Mr. Misra, and Mr. Chaube who took us under their wing.

Neetu was three years senior to me, very much present until I was in 8th class, but I have very few memories of him in school. We never seemed to interact in school! I remember our doing our homework sitting side by side at our desks, and reading comics under the schoolbooks. He took my help when he needed to memorize something. "Hence Mr. E.M. White of America defines civics as…" He corrected my writing and spelling, and taught me such things as the difference between principle and principal. Neetu also told me how ether was manufactured by pulling it from the atmosphere, resulting in confusion for me between ether, the chemical, and the one physicists talked about as a hypothetical medium for transmission of waves.

We day scholars seldom went to visit the hostels. But I did see them and went to the mess a few times. The junior and senior hostels were each built as a quadrangle. The junior hostel also housed the library that also served as the auditorium for plays (where I forgot my lines) and occasional lectures. Each student's room had a bedroom-study, and in the back a dressing room and bathroom. Behind that the outer rim had the kitchen and servants' quarters. Many, maybe most, of the hostelers had their own servants.

Apart from the library, the common room, and tennis, visits to the hostels were limited. One evening I remember being there for "*Sandhya*" (evening recitation of *bhajans*). How and why I was there I do not understand; I was supposed to be doing homework and studying every evening. In the back of the west hall Sharma ji was leading the singing. One of the boys came late, apologized and immediately joined in the singing with his hands clasped in front of his waist. I did not know any of the songs, but I stood there listening. I had very few opportunities to hear or sing *bhajans*. This chance only came after I moved to Albuquerque in my fifties. There I went to the Guptas' *puja* a few times.

I did use the library regularly. I don't think I read too many of the English or European children's books. The book I remember best is "*Bal Bhagwat*" - children's religious stories from a variety of sources. I checked it out many times and read it again and again. I think it was my version of fairy tales. Reading the *Bal Bhagwat* certainly did not make me a devout Hindu.

The junior hostel had houses for the English teacher, and the warden, Mr. Sharma. The English teacher was, for most of my years at Colvin, an English lady. One was Miss Lawson, who left (or was asked to leave) after she got married. I do not remember her in the classroom, but as the only English person (apart from Mr. Davidson) in the school, I do remember her. Mr. Sharma was a prominent member of the staff. He taught Hindi, English, and math in the junior classes. His sons studied at Colvin also.

The teachers' children can be stereotyped to some extent. Because Colvin was a private school, most of us came from affluent families. The teachers' salaries were low. The teachers' children got a break in tuition fees, and many of these boys had cheaper clothes than most of us. The boys were as much a part of the school as others; there was no prejudice or favoritism. Of the professors' children, the Sharmas, the Bhardwajs and Mr. Misra's son were brilliant and went on to do good things in life. Some others were not so smart.

As I said before, the junior hostel had the library that also doubled as the auditorium. The big event every year was the school play in August for *Janma Ashtami* (to celebrate the birth of Krishna.) Apart from my disaster with recitation, I did one more play in my final year at Colvin. I wanted to be college prefect and even hoped to be college captain. In order to show my multi-talented self, I needed to be in a play. As it turned out, I got the role of Krishna, who of course was the center of all the *Janma Ashtami* plays. I have no idea how I was as the hero, but I did become a college prefect. I did not make college captain because I was a day-scholar. Papa did not want me to live in the hostel. I was terribly disappointed, but so it was. Rajinder Shah became college captain. He was not good at studies, was not athletic, and did not act in a play! However, S.V.M Tripathy and Shankh Banerjee, both top athletes and brilliant students, did not attain that position either. Maybe because they too were day scholars.

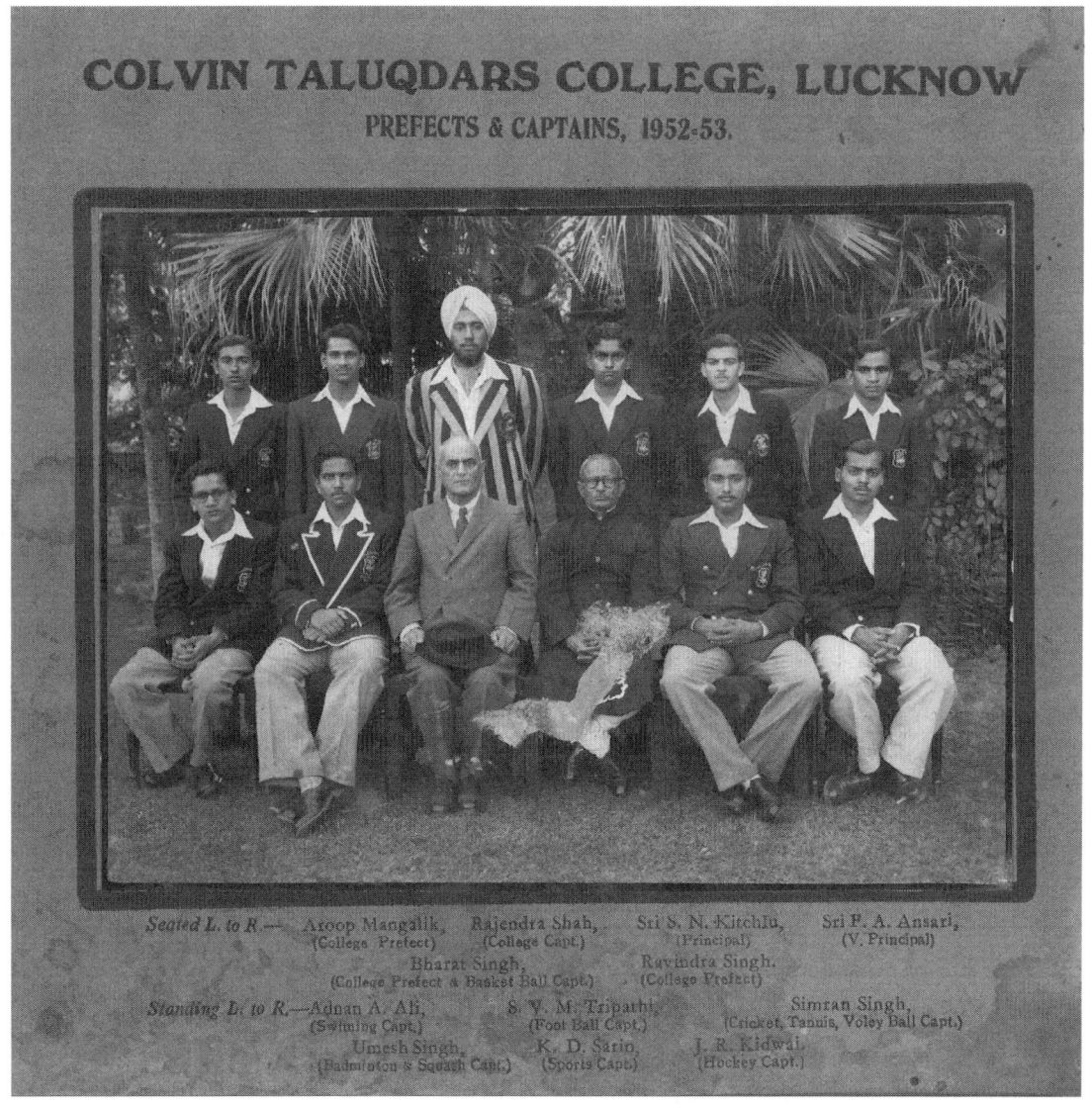

Prefects and Captains, 1952-3. I am on the far left, seated.

The senior hostel had the tennis courts and the common room. I did play tennis and, as in all my athletic endeavors, I was OK but never good. The common room had some simple athletic equipment, and we also had some classes there. Mr. Tiwari was involved for all my years at Colvin. He was the all around coach, athletics, gym, and sports teacher. He also taught the hygiene classes. We had to maintain a daily diary of healthy habits - washing, bowels, truth telling, and the like. In class Mr. Tiwari was strict and sat in his chair with his leg bouncing and tapping with impatience. In the field he taught the whole school, guided us in running, jumps, football, hockey, and swimming. He led the school during annual sports day and the prize distribution ceremony.

The warden for the senior hostel was Mr. Fasih Ahmad Ansari. He was a small but dignified man; he never taught me, but as vice-principal, he was around. His son, Zubair, was my friend and I visited his house. I have a vague recollection of having a glimpse of the *zenana* in, what I assume, was a traditional Muslim home. Zubair was the director of a play we did for our cub scout group. The play was written in Urdu; Zubair dictated my entire part to me so I could write it in Hindi and memorize my lines. I don't remember how the play went, but I remember I needed a lot of help with the Urdu words.

Each hostel had separate Hindu and Muslim kitchens (mess). The Hindu boys thought the Muslim mess was unclean. I do not recall ever eating in a mess, but did go there a few times. I think I was told that they were eating beef.

Another hostel related incident was during the routine air-raid preparations. Even though there were no Japanese around for a thousand miles, we went through these exercises. Somehow I was still at school after school hours and three of the scouts were making a bicycle stretcher. I ended up watching them put the stretcher together: two bicycles in the back and one in the front. The stretcher was suspended with ropes and bamboo poles. I got to ride on the stretcher from the school grounds to University Road. The air raid siren went off and we all hid under the archway at the University Post Office.

Scouting and "cubbing" were a part of my stay at Colvin. I was a cub scout early and became a senior sixer in the fifth or sixth class. We had evening activities that included marching, knot tying, and message delivery. We learned a lot of knots: reef, bowline, clove hitch. Some were easy, some were hard, but we did spend a lot of time practicing them. The bowline was difficult for me then and remained a problem (surmountable) when I tried rock climbing. Our skills at knot tying were tested with a relay race in which we had to tie a designated knot behind our backs as we ran from one end of the hockey field to the other. Pass the message was a test of memory. Each team had to pass on a given message through four stages to the next person, testing the fidelity of the process of oral transmission.

As a senior sixer I was expected to participate in all activities with the group. Once there was an outing to the Botanical Gardens in Sikandra Bagh. I was informed of it in advance, but was scared to ask Papa, so when the day came I was not in my uniform, did not have my equipment, and had no food to take with me. I think it was Mr. B.N. Singh and Mr. Sharma, the teachers in charge, who insisted that as a senior sixer I must go on the trip - and I did. I had a coat over my regular clothing. When we stopped for lunch, I took off my coat and left it there. After I realized this, I said, *"Arrey Master Saheb, mera kot!."* (Oh, teacher, my coat!) I went back and picked it up - no big deal. However Mr. Singh later made fun of me— *arrey mera kot*. I do not remember any repercussions from my going on a trip without Papa's permission. Maybe the teachers talked to him. It is interesting that we had to ask permission for everything, even school related activities. I also think this happened after I was scolded for going to see Miss Chandy after school without asking.

As I am writing this in long hand and talking about Mr. B.N. Singh, I am reminded of my English writing class. Mr. Singh worked hard on my handwriting. He was especially distressed about my r. Here is the r he wanted me to write: ↱ And here is the r I wrote and continue to write: ⱴ Well, I never got the point. My r remains my r - despite the fact that we used four line notebooks for English with strict rules about how each letter was written. I also had a lot of pressure from Papa to improve my handwriting.

As boy scouts we did similar things as the cubs, but also went on camping trips. The first one was to Talkatora, just a few miles outside Lucknow, and we marched there in formation. The camping grounds were on land owned by the Talwars, factory owners who had three sons at Colvin at different times. At that time only the youngest, Yogi, was in school. We had tents set up for us during our stay of a few days. The Talwars were rich and reckless, with studies a low priority in their life. One of the older boys, Sunny, had been in a motorcycle accident. It was hardly an accident, since he was riding the motorcycle lying down and steering it with his feet. At least that was the story I heard. Thinking about it now, it makes no sense because you can't keep the throttle on with your feet! Anyway, Sunny did come to visit us, and I remember listening to him talking to Mr. Pandey, our scoutmaster. He was bandaged up and had to go through some major maneuvers to scratch his nose. Geeta from the Talwar family married our nephew Arvind.

Plastic cups had been introduced around that time. Our set at home was a hit and a novelty. I took one of those cups on the scouting trip. Trying to be macho, I hooked it onto my belt. In the process I dropped it a few times. Ultimately the "unbreakable" cup broke, so I was left with no cup for the rest of the trip. Someone took pity on me and did loan me one.

There were two other camping trips, but neither involved staying in tents. The trip to Nainital was mainly for our cricket game with Sherwood, when Tariq Saeed Jafrey was the hero. We stayed in some kind of a guest house, and I don't recall any scouting activities. But I do remember I had a political discussion with Nair who was anticommunist, and I was defending Mao and General Chu-teh.

The third trip was to the Jhansi area. Again we were guests of an old boy, a former student. The Kunwar Saheb of Orcha, the heir to this state, was our host. The Kunwar Saheb of Orcha owned a Jaguar, which made quite a hit with the students. We stayed at a guesthouse near a river with a small dam. We had a lot of open country in which we explored, hiked, did scout things, and had campfires. We bathed in a tank by the side of the dam with fresh flowing water. In those days I did not wear glasses and did not know much about them. Salman gave me his glasses for safekeeping when he went swimming. I don't know what I was thinking or what I was reacting to, but I got very upset at one of the boys who sprayed me with water and got the glasses wet. At one level I was concerned that by getting the glasses wet I was betraying Salman's trust. I had an idea that getting them wet would take out the "electricity" from the glasses and render them useless. It is interesting now, nearly sixty years later, to think of what made me so upset and if there was something else going on. What was the true nature of my relationship with Salman? We remained best friends all the way through my medical school and his BSc and BA. He switched to BA because he did not do too well with math. But he was my advisor through my "puppy love" days of Mohini, the trials with Nila and Shubhada, and so on. Even on to the days when I got interested in Asha, he was an advisor. I did not realize then that he had an even more Victorian attitude than I did.

But, getting back to the glasses, Salman had very poor eyesight all along. For a period of time he was hooked up with a quack who claimed he could fix his eyes so he would not need glasses. Apart from exercises, one of the requirements was that he wear his glasses as little as possible. So when we went *Gunjing* (Saturday evenings when we walked up and down the pavement of the fashionable *Hazratgunj* trying to spot girls), he would not wear his glasses until I spotted someone. He would then put on his glasses and get his eyeful. I told Salman about the intricacies of anatomy, physiology and pharmacology, and he would explain to me his new knowledge of catenaries and dynamics. He also described to me his observations of the girls' hostel that his room overlooked.

Although Salman was my best friend and shared lots of adventures with me, I was shocked when one day Salman disappeared; he immigrated to Pakistan. (Only his brother, Aftab, who became a senior officer in the Indian Police Service, remained.) In the years of our close relationship I regularly went to his house, but I never talked to or even met his parents. I saw his younger sisters a few times, but never talked to them. I went to pick him up regularly to go on our outings to *Hazratgunj,* but always waited outside. On the other hand, Salman and many boys came to our house regularly. Salman and I were together through the turbulent period of Independence and Hindu - Muslim riots. It is important to remember that at the time of partition Lucknow was quiet and Salman and I spent every evening together. Salman died in 2005 at age 71, about the time I started writing about my memories of Lucknow and Colvin. After Salman was gone, I had wanted to talk to Aftab about his memories of partition. In 2011, on a trip to India, I had that opportunity. His recollections are included here in Part C, Sociology and Religion.

The trip to Orcha was the most outdoors type trip I had had until then. We went on a full day hike along bullock cart tracks, sometimes flooded with ankle deep water. There was talk of panthers in the area and also *dacoits*, so we had night duty in two-hour shifts to protect the camp. One night our campfire went on longer than scheduled and my duty was cancelled. However, Nilamber, who was on before me did not know of this and woke me up very early in the morning saying it was my shift. Half asleep and sure that I was not on duty, I thought he was asking for my *jooti* (shoes), so started looking for them around my bed. I guess we resolved the issue somehow.

We went to Jhansi by train, in a reserved "inter" compartment that was the full length of the *bogie* (coach). It had three rows of benches, and we spread out our boxes and bedding in a way that we had a long continuous bed. Nilamber said he was going to try an experiment and sleep standing. I told him that was not possible because I 'knew' the muscles relax when you sleep and he would fall before he could go to sleep. He did not like being contradicted by a youngster. A few years earlier Nilamber was learning to ride his bicycle and did not know how to get on it. He was at our house and asked Meera to help him. Somehow in the process he fell and fractured his arm. Meera felt guilty about this.

The campfire at Orcha gave me a glimpse of other sides of life: singing; silly comic shows; spontaneous creation of lyrics to make fun of friends and classmates. Khalid Sultan gave a puppet show. He had two sister dolls, Gulabo and Sitabo. He carried out dialogues between them that ended in the two having a fight. Khalid was not a friend in those days. I knew him as one of the boys who was not good at studies, therefore not my type. He was also older. Twenty years later, I was at a wedding chitchatting under a big tent. From somewhere in the tent I heard a laugh and knew it was Khalid. I found him, and we have remained good friends since. He became a professional in the field of entertainment as well as a television producer and actor.

This might be a good time to recall some of the other boys I knew in those days. Some were friends with whom I have kept in touch, and others I remember from some events, but have no idea what happened to them. Some I knew well and interacted with a lot, but then nothing.

Amrender Dutt was outgoing and prominent, but not so good a student. He came from a Christian family, and was the leader in sex education for many of us. One time I was invited to his birthday party. As often happened, I had not asked for permission to go. I waited till the evening of the party when Papa came back from work. Then I was allowed to go. A servant took me on a bicycle, and I arrived after the party was mostly over. Amrender took me to meet his mother who was in her dressing room putting on make-up. She said, "Oh, here is the late *Latif*." This phenomenon of my fear of even asking to go to friends' houses or doing other simple things went on for my entire childhood. I remain constrained in this regard even now as a grandfather at the end of my career!

Shankh Banerjee was a classmate, the top student in the class. A typical *Bong*: good in math and hockey. Thankfully in the last two years he went into the math section, allowing me to become the top student in my biology section. Shankh must not have had the personality to make prefect, senior-sixer or troop leader, but he certainly was smart and an athlete. Once I got into medical college we lost touch. Even though he was a neighbor, I got no news of him after I left Colvin. Shankh told us that the existence of soul was proven when a dying man was sealed in a glass case. When the man died there was a crack in the glass proving that his soul escaped at that time.

In early 2012 I connected via email with Shankh. In November her was visiting his daughter in Colorado while I was visiting my son. We met and had a meal in Winter Park. It was great to reconnect after 59 years.

Talking of neighbors and Bengalis, we had a number of Bengalis in the neighborhood. Shankh was the only one in my class from those *Bong* families. One of them was Mr. and Mrs. Mesho Masai, which really mean Mr & Mrs Uncle. That was the only name we knew them by. They were a childless couple. Their house and lawn were a major playground for us. We played *kabbaddi* and cricket on their lawn and they were tolerant of our antics. One of the boys explained that the reason they had no children was that he was too big to get into her!

Going back to the classmate friends at Colvin, I will describe them with no particular plan or sequence and see how it goes. Santosh Tandon was a big part of my life. He was many things I was not. He was very interested in clothes and fashion. He had suits and "combinations" - lots of them. When we went to the movies (our biggest outing/entertainment event) he agonized about what to wear, what made him look compressed or whatever. He would stand in his bedroom with feet apart, swaying from side to side asking for my opinion while giving his critique and wearing what he wanted. Santosh was a casual guy in general - too casual in some ways. But he was very serious about his clothes. Whether it was suits or casuals he was very particular. Interestingly he hung his pants on a hook, which we were not allowed to do - we put them on hangers. Santosh's fussiness about clothes also included criticism - even ridicule - of boys who did not meet his standards. One time one of the *Taluquedar* boys wore a cotton *bundi* under his shirt instead of a sweater or coat and that was upsetting to Santosh. Another time someone wore an unironed shirt and that too was unacceptable; the standard of the school was being lowered by such behavior. He also had a term, *Bhushar,* for the shabby bush-shirts some boys wore.

Talking about clothing at Colvin, we were expected to be proper and neat but did not have a uniform. Only on special days did we wear the blazer. We wore a school tie with it. Annual sports day - Durbar day - we wore a white shirt, college light and dark blue tie, and dark blue blazer with *noblesoblige* on the insignia. I noted on a visit to Colvin in 1981 that even in summer the boys were required to wear a tie. During Mr. Brotherton's short stay as vice-principal and principal I made a fool of myself with a tie episode. I was explaining to some boys the latest styles in wearing a tie. For some reason I was walking backwards. I did not see a bicycle and tripped over it and fell. Brotherton walked by as I fell and had the English equivalent of a hearty laugh - he smiled.

As with clothing, there were expectations of us to succeed and do good things. However, unlike some "public schools" we were not inculcated with a sense of superiority. I think at home too that was the attitude. It has served me well.

I may mention Santosh's family here. His father was a specialist in tuberculosis and referred to as "TB Tandon" to distinguish him from the other Tandons on the faculty. He had a big practice and was seldom home. Ammyee was a gentle soul who fed us well. His sister Usha was very quiet, around but not interactive. She never married - I do not know the rest of the story. Santosh's brother Tej was great at studies, went to Jamalpur, and had a good career in the railways.

We were the rebels in some ways, but not subversive or disruptive. We rolled up our pants like Raj Kapoor, we went to movies occasionally, cutting classes to catch the matinee. We were friends with Zafar Ibrahim who was another boy who was different. We read comic books, and listened to Western music, knew more about Hollywood than Bollywood (it was not called that then), and had stylish clothes - even I did. Santosh told us tales of his conquests with girls and his escapades with his cousins. (In retrospect I think they were made up to impress us.) Zafar and Santosh supplied me with "hot books" and tales of adolescent fantasy.

Santosh and I once had a project of building a go-kart. We worked with scraps of wood and had a hammer and a hacking tool normally used by the cook to split wood to make kindling. We did not get very far. Santosh managed to pass the inter examination and did enter the University. Again, once I got into the medical college my contact with him was minimal, but I did hear stories of him spending the day riding a scooter, spending time in coffee houses. While I was doing my internship I had a member of his family as my patient. At that time I learned that Santosh died in a scooter accident. He was not wearing a helmet, fell off the scooter and hit his head against a wall. He was twenty-three years old.

Santosh wrote an essay about how one should create one's own path. It was in Hindi, and sounded eloquent. The gist was how most people don't know how to do what they want to do. It struck a chord, I felt, like him, that I never followed my dream - I'm not sure if I had a dream. But I must have had some feelings because it did mean something to me and I remember it. Santosh was, I am sure, troubled. He was not a bad person but he did not do the "right thing." He was a "waster" - one of the terms Papa used for people who were not straight and narrow. I was too involved with studies and proving myself through the period that he was missing classes and roaming on a scooter. It would have been nice if I had talked to him then.

Santosh once read me a poem about the making of the Taj Mahal. It was written from the perspective of the poor who suffered because of its construction and high cost. Santosh sympathized with the poor but said, in a derogatory way, that it was written by a communist.

Talking about essays, there were two that I remember writing and I do wish I had saved them. One was at the time of India's independence. Most boys wrote about how after 90 years of struggle for independence (starting from the 1857 Mutiny), India was entering a new era. *"Nabbe sal ke anant sangharsh ke bad."* I decided and argued that it was after one hundred and ninety years of struggle we got independence. (I dated my war of independence to the battle of Plassey in 1757.) Was I being difficult or just looked at history differently? I don't know. I do remember that I argued with the teacher (Mr. Sharma or Mr. B.N. Singh), and he got frustrated and wrote in my notebook, OK 190 or 1190, or 11190. In that essay I did not write about the glorious days ahead, or Nehru and Gandhi, but about a young boy who was suffering on his march from home and sleeping on the roadside and in refugee camps. The teacher accepted that. I am not sure whether he liked it.

Santosh had written that serious piece about how we follow the beaten path and don't know how to follow our desires. Another situation where he was very serious was as a goals keeper in hockey. He took that role very seriously, though he was not interested in sports in general. For me, sports, games, athletics were something you did - not something to excel in, not a big deal, but a part of life. The "big boys" did the serious stuff. After having played for quite a few years and seen many school matches I discovered the score keeper's book. A big sheet of paper with space for batting, bowling, extras, and what not. I remember watching with awe how the score keeper was able to make all the entries one after another, watch the game, and communicate with the umpire.

The other story I wrote was in English class. I don't remember the assignment, but I wrote about "Who Will Bell the Cat?" I came up with a speech delivered by the head mouse at a meeting where a bunch of suggestions were given. The names were derived from the comic books we read. There were a lot of gadgets that were suggested by different mice. They all had hi tech ideas for others to implement but in the end no one wanted to do the actual belling of the cat. In the last scene the old mouse says "Yes, that is the question - who will bell the cat?"

Getting back to the boys in school, Zafar Ibrahim is logically the next one. Zafar, Santosh, and I hung out together a lot. Zafar had had a major motorcycle accident, which damaged his face and scarred his eye socket, but he was otherwise ok. He was some kind of prince, only son of a widow whose husband had been the 'king' of an island in the Indian Ocean; I never got the name straight, possibly Laxadweep or Maldives. He lived in a small flat above a tailor's shop just outside *Hazratgunj*. His sister was married to our dentist; I saw no other family. He was very intelligent, and much more widely read than myself. He seemed to have read Marx and Engles; he talked about the theory of communism - very impressive. He was, as mentioned earlier, the supplier of hot books. I seem to recall he went into the police and was in Bihar, but I have not seen him since our inter-exams in 1953. Zafar impressed me a lot, mainly because he was smart and talked about so many things. Despite that I don't remember too much about him.

Going on randomly to other classmates, I'll bring up Rajju Bhal. Rajju started with Neetu and flunked several times to end up in my 6th or 7th class. He was a nice guy, always helpful, smiling, pleasant, pretty good at sports, and enthusiastic. He obviously did not do well at studies. His father was professor of zoology, a well known figure and researcher and author of the book on the earthworm, Pheratema. It was our textbook for intermediate and, more importantly, for the premedical test because he was the examiner. I presume professor Bhal was disappointed with Rajju's performance in school. I am guessing that he hired Mr. Bharadwaj to reform Rajju. What I do know is that on several occasions Mr. Bharadwaj humiliated and beat Rajju with his hands and with a ruler. I can still see Rajju trembling in fear as the blows came crashing down with the whole class watching.

Rajju was also an expert tree climber. We had a clump of trees in our playground. Most of us climbed partway up some of the trees. Rajju could climb to the top and then circle on the top of the trees and made a full circuit at tree top level.

These were the days when learning disorders were not understood and it was presumed that all Rajju needed was motivation to do well. He went on to become a car mechanic and did fine. Around 2001 I talked to Rajju and he said he was dying of heart problems. He had a niece in Connecticut and I talked to her briefly.

Bharat Bhatkamkar was a prominent boy because his father was a big shot, Senior Member Board of Revenue. Some teacher said the father was next in rank to the governor and Bharat was considered to be a decent boy because he did not have airs. I think that was generally true. He was a good cricket player. We formed the M.C.C. (Musketeers Cricket Club) and played in the park near the Monkey Bridge. It is now a hotel. It was close to Bharat's house. Bharat's family was Maharashtrian, somewhat of an exotic group for Lucknow, and I remember meeting his mother who was dressed in traditional *Marathi* style. His house right on the Gomti was elegant. They had a Pekingese. I remember Bharat complaining that when the dog bit someone's fingers the fellow pulled his hand and damaged the dog's teeth!

Bharat and Dushyant joined the air force. I have kept in touch with Dushyant but Bharat just dropped out. Nobody wants to say what happened to him. Bharat's cricket recalls some old memories. He was a good player. I remember him as a bowler and batsman. He was, however, humbled at least once by Etmad Rasul, one of the least athletic of the boys I know. Etmad was bowling to Bharat, it was a very slow pitch. Bharat in his arrogance and impatience came way forward to punish the ball. He missed and was bowled out for zero. Etmad also teased Bharat about a zit on his nose and had some tale about a *Pakora*. Bharat was the first person I knew who had a fracture in his finger and a plaster cast.

Dushyant was a good friend. We did a lot together. He was in biology and a good student so we did have some things in common. His father was professor of economics at the university and a nationally prominent figure. He was really lenient by our standards. At age 15 Dushyant was allowed to drive. It was a typical 1940's car, a tourer as we called it. It was small by today's standards but we managed to fit quite a few boys in it. He even allowed us to drive it. He described driving "gangster style" when he was late - turning fast to balance on two wheels. I never had that experience.

After our inter-exams Dushyant and I had one day before the rest of the class finished their exams. The mathematics exam was on the last day. So we were going around celebrating the end of our examinations. (Why was Santosh not there!) Anyway, we were driving past the Residency and saw a crowd near the river. Dushyant decided to explore the situation. He came back a few minutes later looking pale and saying he was nauseated. He said the crowd had collected because they had found a body in the river; the face had been eaten by turtles. He remained unwell and it ruined our evening.

Dushyant went on to the Air Force academy and did very well. But for his birthday being a few days early (or late), he would have been chief of the Air Force. Dushyant graduated while I was in Medical College. His family had a party that I very much wanted to attend. Unfortunately, the first heart operation in Lucknow (maybe in India) was scheduled for the same time. Anil, who was in my class and a relative of Dushyant's, also wanted to be at the same events. Well, we ended up rushing from one event to the other and missed out on both!

I didn't see Dushyant for a few years but knew of his whereabouts. He married a woman from our *Mohalla* and was living in Agra in 1966. Before that, he had been in the Congo with the United Nations peacekeeping force. When I returned to Delhi in 1966 after my training in the U.S. I drove from Bombay to Delhi in my American car. Since I knew about Dushyant being in the Air Force Base in Agra (maybe Aftab and Mona knew his whereabouts), we stopped at the base and found him. Actually we found his house and were having tea with Parvez when he came home in his full uniform with cap. Before he took off his cap, he warned me, "Don't be shocked." Well, he had become very bald and we were just 30. He explained that while in the Congo, he sat in the cockpit of the plane in hot, humid weather with helmet on and lost his hair soon after. We had a good time and then proceeded on to Delhi. Since then we have met off and on - more so recently, after his retirement. He lives in NOIDA, (a suburb of Delhi) where several of our old Colvin people live. As an aside, Dushyant's father, Dr. Singh, was my patient while I was in Delhi. He died of cancer. The treatment of his type of cancer was quite limited in those days, and still has a low cure rate.

Dushyant's brother, Hemant, was a non-entity youngster in those days. He went into the railways and is now retired and I see him on most of my trips home. Dushyant's father was an economist and presumably in the mainstream. Papa was a socialist and we were seeped in the accounts of the advances the Soviet Union had made, the socialist ideas of Nehru and the stories of the evils of the big industrialists like Birla. Dushyant and I had many arguments about this. In retrospect, I believe he had not read the books he quoted, and I too was saying what I heard Papa say. Dushyant quoted The God That Failed as a major source.

Since I mentioned NOIDA I can talk about those who live there. There are Shashi and Ravi Mathur, Aftab, Khalid, and Dushyant. Vinod Deva also lived in NOIDA, but died a few years ago.

Ravi and Shashi lived in two different houses in New Hyderabad. Mr. Mathur was in physical education. He was a very pleasant man. Of the fathers of our friends he was the only one who talked to us, told us jokes and did not frighten us. Mrs. Mathur was a great cook. Theirs was a warm house and remained so when Ravi and Madhu took over that household. In later years, I played golf with Mathur Saheb. He was not a great player but was good. He was relaxed, natural and enjoyed the game. He was a natural athlete. I remember him explaining how it was important to do exercises with the correct positions and angles and that physical education was not just playing games.

Shashi was a year ahead of me. He was a big swimmer, the only person I remember from school who boasted about the lengths (laps) he did. Ten, twenty - I don't know how many, but that is what he enjoyed while we just played in the water, splashed water at each other and tried our hand at diving. We used the pool at the school, but we had very little coaching in swimming. There was a steel rope swing along the length of the pool with a pulley and belt; this was used for teaching and to give a few tips here and there. We learned survival swimming - swimming with our head out of water and using our arms and legs to keep afloat. The concept of crawl did not exist. We had simple competitions and water polo matches. One competition was to see who could pick up more plates from the bottom of the pool in one breath. Some boy could go almost the whole length of the pool under water. Yadvendra Singh (our camping host) and Ripu Daman Singh came from Mayo School. They were great swimmers and they showed us for the first time a jackknife dive and some trick dives that we had never seen before.

During May and June when school was closed, Papa rented the pool and we enjoyed it with some other family friends. The pool was filled with well water and it was emptied onto the cricket and hockey field - a simple dual use of the pool. They did not use chlorine, just potassium permanent as disinfectant.

Anyway back to Shashi. He was a good friend, but not being in my class in those years we did only a few things together. I have recollections of him rambling on about some chemistry formula the center of which was CH_2SO_4, and referring to *Gautan Dar* in his class - it was not complementary. Shashi was one of the persons who recognized Rajju Bhal's problems and talents, and helped him to become a mechanic - a job at which he was good. Back then, I have to admit I was embarrassed by a classmate of mine being a mechanic.

Ravi was Neetu's classmate. He was the terror fast bowler in the college and later in the University. I remember his cricket boots with studs all shiny white. Not many people had special boots. We did most of our athletics in the same tennis shoes; they were for running, hockey, football, jumping and, for a few of us, tennis. During the war, the quality was poor and we got holes in them in a few weeks. Also during the war, we were forced to wear brown canvas tennis shoes, something which earlier only servants did. Ravi was the butt of jokes related to a tailless buffalo which roamed around the area. What was that all about?

Ravi and Shashi have remained friends and we have been in touch most of these years. Shashi lived in Delhi very close to the Institute where I was. In '62, when I was a student, he brought his fiancé, Bimla, to meet us. Ravi visited us in Denver. Both taught me about geology and Ravi told great tales of his trips into the interior of the Himalayas when he was director of the geological survey of UP. Every trip back to Delhi we get at least one great meal at their place.

Aftab and Mona also live nearby in NOIDA. Aftab is Salman's brother and Mona's sister Rena is a close friend of Mohini Bhabhis. Aftab went into the police service, spent time in NEFA and Madhya Pradesh. He was in Khargaon in the sixties at the height of the dacoit activity in central India. Man Singh, Phulan Devi and many others were active in the area. On the trip from Bombay to Delhi, as we were entering the area, I remembered that Aftab was posted there. I managed to track him down; it was easy because the superintendent of Police was quite a big shot in rural areas. We drove into the huge compound and after confirming that we were at the right place just barged into the house, much to the consternation of the guards. Aftab on the other hand thought we were some rich seedy *seth* - we were in our American car. In those days cars were uncommon in rural India; a fancy (big) American car was unheard of. Anyway, we had a great time, good meal, and a chance to see a game reserve escorted by Aftab's deputy.

During that visit, Aftab told me how he had been offered 1 *lac* as a bribe just to arrange for a mid-level police officer to be posted to a checkpoint between Maharashtra and Madhya Pradesh through which alcohol was smuggled. This was my first direct exposure to corruption in India. In those days one *lac* bought a nice house in the city.

I visited Aftab and Mona a few years later when he was at the police training academy at Mount Abu. The trip to Mount Abu was interesting. I spent a few days in Ajmer and then took a bus. It was not a comfortable journey. I was not well and Pasha was a restless five year old. Asha was in Denver on sabbatical. Aftab and Mona showed us around the temples, which were gorgeous. We got great food and company. We went to a nearby town where we were told there was a guru giving discourses. The man was dressed in immaculate white robes and spoke in a simple manner. I did not understand what he was talking about but I wanted to stand there and listen. It was two or so hours before he finished. I was mesmerized but understood little of what he said. Thinking back, I can just remember wanting to keep on listening. At least now I do understand why a lot of people listen to such discourses, read books by these sages, and follow them. I understand that these people get something out of it - even though I still don't understand what it is they get out of the experience.

The next day we again went back to another event by Bhagwan Rajnish. This one was another discourse, a shorter one, followed by a demonstration of the power he had over people. He explained to the two or three hundred people sitting on ground in the tennis court that they could now stand up and participate in the dancing. "Move as you want, follow the music which will guide you. The music will build up its tempo and will reach a high point, just do what you feel like doing." The orchestra started a pleasant sound from a mix of western and Indian instruments with a *dholak* setting the tempo. It did build up gradually and the audience moved. They were a mix of people: well dressed and shabby; westerners and Indians; twenties into the sixties. Some Indians appeared to be Westernized, others appeared to be from small towns - "native" as babujee used to call them. The tempo really built up and people were moving fast every which way, their sense of exhaustion was visible and then suddenly the music stopped. Everyone just collapsed to the ground. They lay there panting and exhausted. After a considerable period of time the music started again. A few drum beats, a few notes soft and slow. It was like an awakening - the sixth symphony, the day after the resurrection! The crowd awakened slowly, moved a little, became alive then joyous and after another short sermon dispersed.

It was quite an event. It impressed me because of the power of the man's words, of the music, the movement, the incongruous nature of the mix of people. Above all it was different. I was brought up in a rigid environment and remained conventional. It was not just the rebel in me, but the part of me that had never seen anything so different that was impressed. I had heard of the Chicago demonstrations in 1968, Woodstock, and hippies in general. I had seen the hippies who came through India. Some were patients at the Institute Hospital. However, I defended their lifestyle when my friends criticized or made fun of them. But I guess I was never one of them. I observed but did not participate, and I did not judge.

Yet one year in the late sixties the non-medical staff at the Institute put out a list of titles for the faculty. The over ambitious, the brown nosers, the mean and rude were all identified and given titles. I was called "hippie" by these people, the desk and laboratory workers. It was a compliment of sorts. That I was not of the establishment, that I was not arrogant or aloof. It showed that I was perceived as being out of the ordinary, unusual, like those strange Americans who were coming through Delhi.

Going back randomly to the boys in class. Vibhutosh Singh was one of the boys from the *taluqedars* group. We interacted but did not have much in common. My one recollection of him is from our civics class with Mr. Bharadwaj at the time of the British election after World War II. Mr. Bharadwaj asked who was the new Prime

Minister of England. I was so proud that I knew it was C.R. Atlee, and in my arrogance I was sure no one else knew the answer. Vibhutosh was asked and he said "Mr. Clement…." and that confirmed my thoughts about his ignorance. Except he went on to say " Richard Atlee." He knew the full name while I only knew the initials. Luckily I had not shown my feelings of superiority.

The classroom in which this took place was one we used a lot. It was in the old building in the main row to the left of the portico. The walls had posters and sayings. There were names of famous people and a poster in praise of books. The school building was pretty simple. The old wing was one story, raised up about 6-8 steps above the ground. The teacher's room was in the middle at the top of the stairs from the portico. Classrooms were in one row on both sides of the teacher's room. At the north end (left) there was a crossing with more classrooms. At one end of that wing was the art class and at the other end was the room in which Rajju Bhal got his beating.

One time we were asked to draw a picture depicting "every cloud has a silver lining" in pastel. With my talent as it was, I drew a blob of dark grey clouds and drew a sharp white line around it. Mr. Janki Saran saw the work and said you have to draw clouds that look like light cotton balls. Then, he took my pastel sticks and a small piece of cotton. He gently softened my sharp lines, rubbed here and there and he transformed it into soft clouds. In the November 29, 2010 issue of the New Yorker Magazine there is an article about a 15th century panel that has recently been restored. It says, "…the exquisitely detailed but erratically composed panel, eight feet wide and almost five feet high, displays vestiges of medieval style, as in the clunky clouds which contrast with the meteorologically correct ones on the adjoining panels." It brings out differences between the ordinary and the masters like Jan Van Eyck.

Since I mentioned the art class I will go on to my art teachers and my interactions with them. The first one was Mr. Ishwardas. He was an intense guy. I remember him as someone who would be biting his nails while we finished our assignments. I think he even used the ruler on us a few times. Since I was not very good I stayed under his radar. He went on to be well known and recognized as an artist and painter. Many years later Joanie and I saw his paintings at the Thiruvanthapuran Museum. The Thirvanthapuran museum was an odd place, shabby, with a varied collection. The biggest draw was a clock with moving figures and bells. It was largely a collection of stuff put together by one of the kings of Travencore.

The next teacher was Mr. Jankidas. He was more gentle, probably older. (Maybe he had accepted his situation and was more relaxed about life.) We painted themes under his guidance; one was illustrating a story. I did one with a tiger but I can't remember which story. The tiger and the lamb or the tiger/lion and the mouse; I gave it to Sushma di. She had it for a long time. Neetu was good at art, and of course Sushma di was doing leather work, painting, and soap stone sculpture. We had some aesthetic stuff at home but art was not something I participated in, even though I appreciated it.

Art reminds me of a talk on the meaning and definition of art by Mr. Kitchlew, our first Indian Principal. He asked around the room and most boys gave definitions related to painting. Then as now art, artist and painting was what one thought of when talking of art. Music, architecture and design are considered art only when one thinks about it deliberately. Yogi (Geeta's uncle) gave the definition of art as "the science of painting." Mr. Kitchlew's definition made (and still does) a lot of sense. "Art is the expression of abstract beauty in a concrete form." (Another definition attributed to Zola is "art is nature seen through a temperament.")

Mr. Kitchlew was a Kashmiri and very fair. He had retired from the education service. He worked all his life with the British. Even in summer he wore suits, spoke with a British accent, and had somewhat jerky movements. He pronounced Avadh the British way as "Oudh," it sounded more like oodh. I cannot reconstruct how long he stayed, what influence he had on the school, and how he and the school transitioned after independence.

Since I have digressed to the teachers I will continue on that theme. Some of the teachers were just classroom teachers to me. Others had greater influence because of their personality, their involvement in extracurricular activities or their discussing and making us aware of social and moral issues. Some lived in the neighborhood and came to the house as Papa's friends so we had a different relationship with them.

The science teachers Bhatnager, Dube, and Sheobux Singh were just teachers. Mr. Bhatnagar was humorless and strict and that is all I remember of him. Mr. Dube was more interactive. His class was fun because we had a lot of practical experiments we did ourselves. They were focused on sound, heat, light - basics that have served me well. He demonstrated Boyle's law, the barometer, electrical resistance, precision measuring instruments - things we could see and do. The physics laboratory was large with big tables going all along its length. One time for some reason in the pre-exam period Mr. Dube did not show up so we started singing and making parodies of well known songs.

Mr. Singh in biology was a poor teacher with a strong accent. His most memorable lines were, "This is not a Val but a Val." He could not say 'valve' or 'wall' very clearly. Years later, in 1978, I went to Colvin with Pasha. He was the only teacher still around from my days. His hair was dyed black. Pasha said he looked younger than me.

Mr. B.N. Singh taught civics and writing. He was strict and he punished us with a flick of his finger to our ear lobes. His method of teaching was to write the text on the blackboard and we had to copy it. When he reached the bottom of the board he erased the top and continued his writing. He did not talk much. He also had a problem with my 'r.' He smoked *bidis* which we associated with our servants. I don't know how but I heard him talk to someone about renting a house; he said he could afford Rs. 15 or 16 but not 20. If my memory is accurate, it is a demonstration of the disparity between the teachers and us. We were paying Rs. 20 per month as fees and he could barely afford that much for rent. Colvin was an expensive private school but the teachers were not paid well. I recall Vinai Baxi, who transferred from La Martinairre, boasting about how the teachers there were well dressed.

Mr. L.P. Bharadwaj was a major part of my life. He lived fairly close by. He taught English and other subjects. His sons were in school with us. He was a poet, writer, play director and all around visible person. Mr. Bharadwaj had two or three wives, one of whom committed suicide by drowning herself in the Gomti while the youngest boy was sitting there waiting for her. Narendra and Surendra were both on top in their class. Both went into the Army. Narendra got caught up in some episode about ragging and was asked to leave the academy. He went on to join the Indian Administrative Service and did well. Mr. Bharadwaj remained active in the theater. I met him in the nineties when, well into his eighties, he was involved in directing a play he had written.

Mr. P.N. Chaube was a dapper, serious and proper man. He taught English to the senior classes. He gave us dictations and did not speak out the punctuations; we had to figure them out by the length of the break in his reading. While waiting, his knees used to twitch. He too lived in the neighborhood in a large house in the joint family system. I am not clear who was what, but one of his boys, K.N., went to Colvin. The others went to some other school. He used to dye his hair, wore very proper British style clothes and was very particular about accuracy in the language. He, for example, was particular about "May I" and "Can I". He pointed out that our usual Hindi translation of "May I come in" as *"Kya me aa Sakta hoon"* really meant "Can I." The correct form was *"Kya me ander aa jaoon."* I had a hard time understanding the distinction at that time or even for a few years after. Somehow it stuck in my mind and I got it a few years ago. I can say though that I too am particular about precise language in medicine.

Mr. R.S. Misra was also Papa's friend and came to our house regularly. He was the biology teacher before Sheobux Singh. He had a collection of animals in jars. I remember a king cobra that had been shot by Rudra, one of our seniors. One time a snake was caught in the gutter in front of the bicycle stand; it was properly preserved with its head intact, sides slit and put in formalin. Mr. Misra's voice always seemed to be cracking. He was the scoutmaster and somewhat of a "military" man. He took us to a war exhibition. He was strict and I was scared of him. We met him about 10 years ago and visited him at his son's house at Indian Institute of Technology (IIT). Ashok went on to be Director of the IIT.

Mr. R.S. Sharma was warden of the junior hostel, Hindi teacher and a gentle soul. He had two sons in school who were not so gentle. He used to read the stories from our Hindi text to us. He put in a lot of dramatic flair to his reading. I remember three chapters. One was *"Hans ka neer Khsheer vivek,"* a description of the swans in Mansarovar Lake in Tibet. Maybe that is where my fascination for Mansarovar started. The other story was about a professor and his wife and was a sociological and personal account of husband-wife relationships in middle class India. I would very much like to read that again! The third was a very dramatic description of a sunset about the sickle shaped moon stabbing the sun and causing the blood to spill into the western sky.

Mr. T.P. Roy taught English and Mathematics. Neetu was in his math class and did poorly; his performance influenced his decision to go into the army. In his English class he read the story of Girard, a young man who became a priest. This Mr. Roy read to us with dramatic flair. Mr. Roy lived in the house between Dushyant and Salman in a compound with three houses going backwards (deep) from the main road.

A few years ago watching the U.S. open took me back to my tennis experiences, a lot of them at Colvin. The senior hostel had six tennis courts and well maintained grass, and balls provided by the school. I used to watch the seniors play when I was small and by seventh or eighth grade started playing from time to time. Actually we used to play against the wall in the courtyard at Nandinee. Papa used to help us a bit but I never got any real coaching. We lost the ball regularly, either into the vegetable garden or onto the roof of the kitchen. We had a route we followed to get on the roof - climbing on the *Koila Kothri*, the wall of the *Aangam*, the sloping roof of the *palang kothri* (that was a bit frightening) and then onto the kitchen roof.

Knocking balls against the wall gave us the basic skills. We learned to hit with our whole arm, using our shoulder muscles rather than the wrist that badminton players used. We used to watch tennis at the Oudh Gynkhana Club. Papa played there and we went with him from time to time. We also got to watch the championships. We saw Gauss Mohammad, Sumant Misra, and Dileep Singh. Sumant Misra was from our neighbors the Misra family of Unity Lodge. Dileep Singh had strong muscular legs, which, we were told, came from his football (soccer) playing. There was one player who was supposed to have been great but, we were informed, he got married and had his energy sucked out of him. This came to mind watching Andre Agassi today. He and Stephi Graaf have 2 kids. He is thirty six and certainly has a lot of energy in him. Sumant had a terrific serve and at one time there was some concern that the nets allowed in serves to go through them. At one time, Kaul and Chitamber from Lucknow Medical College were said to be doing well in National Championships.

At Colvin we were encouraged to play tennis. Mr. Chaube pointed out that as we grew older we were more likely to continue to play tennis as opposed to football, hockey or cricket. The tennis was organized by "nets" - 1st, 2nd and 3rd based on ability. The players in the 3rd and 2nd net were allowed to challenge someone from the higher net for placement. I was in the 2nd net, challenged by someone from the 3rd net and was leading 5 to 2. However, he came up and beat me 7 to 5. I remained in the 3rd net after that.

The most striking figures in tennis were Anadi Sehgal and Simran Singh. Simran was an all around natural athlete, hero of the school, but as a student failed several times and went from being 1 year behind me to 3 years behind me. He was rich, tall and got the 'full colours' for athletics. The full colour meant he could wear a blazer which was made of one inch wide stripes of light and dark blue – the school colours. Striped cloth was not available, so he bought light blue and a dark blue cloth, had stripes cut from each, the strips were then sown together to make the full colour blazer. His was the only one I ever saw. The half colour was simpler. It had light blue piping around the collar and sleeves on the dark blue blazer.

Anadi was two years ahead of me and amongst the top students of his class. He was not very athletic and while playing cricket was afraid of the ball and had a hard time catching it. But Anadi was really crazy about tennis and used to practice even during scorching summer months. He went on to win Junior All India Tennis Championship. The contrast between Anadi and Simran was striking. Anadi's father died when we were young and I don't know how they managed. Anyway Anadi wanted to go into the Indian Administrative Service. They required extracurricular activities to qualify. Anadi chose tennis as his entry into the IAS. He practiced for hours on the University's tennis wall. I presume he had some coaching also. Regardless, he developed a very steady, if unglamorous game, and was amongst the college's top players. There was a match between Anadi and Simran Singh. There was quite a crowd. Anadi was the underdog because Simran was the glamorous hero. The differences in style were striking. Anadi was the returning machine. Nothing went past him but he did not have the style and, more importantly, he had no support from the crowd. I don't remember who won but do remember the match. The hero worship for Simran struck me as inappropriate, as it does now with regard to sports stars. Yet that is a phenomenon that is real and prevalent. Anadi did join the IAS. I had a brief correspondence with him in the sixties when he was in Kumaon and I was thinking of a hiking trip. I have not heard of or from him since. I found out that he died while playing tennis.

I continued to play tennis all along - never good but enjoying it. Tennis was a big part of our vacation in Ranikhet when I was fifteen. We played at the club where Mohini Sahini played so it was a big thing. I also remember Kishin came for a short time. He was a cadet or had just become a *Piolet* officer. He seemed to be a good player, but what I remember is he was in uniform and just took off his blue air force shirt and was playing a pretty hard game. I never got any coaching and picked up a lot of bad habits that I have even now. I made sure I got Pasha into a formal coaching situation and he has grown into a good player.

Tennis and sports leads us to the annual days, which were quite grand and fancy affairs. It was also called the Durbar Day - a throwback to the royalty of the early days of the school. Some of the more exciting sports events were held that day. The 100 yards, 220 yards, 440 yards and a few of the relays were held for the entertainment of the invited guests and parents. Another big event was the old boys' race. The biggest attraction was Mr. Hammad, a very obese man, who was given a 50 yard handicap for a hundred yard race which he ran (or rolled) for a few yards with his walking stick. The old boys also included some of the younger ones who were athletes in school and in the university and were very competitive. We of course knew the younger old boys and rooted for our friends.

Students assembled for the prize distribution at the annual sorts day

We students waited under the banyan tree near the principal's house. We were separated by our houses with strict discipline being enforced by the prefects and senior prefects - not an easy task given the ages that we were. Durbar Day was Mr. Tiwari's big day. The event was held in December, just before the Christmas holidays. The school was cleaned, whitewashed and the dust suppressed by water sprayed by the *Bhishti*. The teachers were in suits or *sherwanis* - some not in great shape but that was the state of our teachers who earned modest salaries. Mr. Tiwari started the march past with the police band leading. After the march past we had our sports events. At some time in the past apparently horses were involved in the ceremonies.

The game boys, *jamadaars*, and *chaprasis* were in clean uniforms. The senior boys were in gray trousers and blazers with white shirt and dark blue and light blue school ties. The guests sat in the raised part of the grounds on the north side of the classrooms. The lines for the tracks and the bricks were freshly done in white. The guests and the parents arrived and were seated, but we were not allowed to visit. (Thinking back I don't think Papa ever came to this event or any event in school.) The chief guest was always the Governor who came with the usual pomp, motorcycle escort and big black car. After the Governor was seated, the march past began, One of the people who dressed up during this ceremony was Daftary Saheb, who was the eyes and ears of the Principal. He was a man who was everywhere during the school year. He wore a long coat, the muslin *sherwani* and was in a sense an enforcer. Without saying much he kept the students in check. He was not a teacher, not a clerk, but someone we respected because he was stern and yet helpful. During the annual day he was dapper and had a presence.

The house that won the most points and prizes led the march past. Our house Butler, later Taxila, often led the march past. One of the good things about the system was that, apart from the winners in the competitions, we got points for what was called "standards." This was a way to encourage the average and not so great athletes to participate. Each student who participated got points for reaching a certain goal: three points for 15 seconds, 2 points for 16 seconds and 1 point for 17 seconds for 100 yards. Taxila house got lots of students to participate and got a lot of points.

When the races were over, we assembled for prize distribution. This was the highlight of the evening and we practiced for weeks for it. The boys stood up at our stations under the tree. The college prefect shouted the order like a military sergeant and we ran to take our places. We stood by height order in perfectly straight rows. When I started at Colvin, we had three houses and we formed a box. When the school became bigger and we had four houses we formed an M. It was all rehearsed and we knew which boy was to be on either side of us.

The prize distribution for scholastic and sporting events was next. The way we approached the Governor, the way we saluted and took the prizes was also rehearsed and we followed the drill as prescribed. The Governor gave a short speech and we dispersed for tea, which was a grand affair. One of the hazards we faced during the tea was the eagles. They sometimes swooped down to grab the food from our hands. A number of bearers stood around with long bamboos to try to keep them away.

Mr. Tiwari was our coach and sports master. He taught us the different games and sports, field, track, and swimming. To the boarders, he also taught basketball. He was an athlete. I remember him playing squash with a student and putting all his energies into it. I watched once while he was teaching the fine points of the 100-yard race to some senior students. His main assistant was Suchit, who was there to take care of the grounds too. He kept the swimming pool clean, supervised the weeding of the lawn, and laid out the lines for races. He took care of the pitch and all the equipment: the balls, the cricket matting, the leg guards, the discus, shot put and whatever else.

Recently I have been reading Lucknow: The City of Illusion. This beautiful book has photographs of Lucknow just before and after the mutiny of 1857. One of the points that the pictures and the text shows is the destruction of large parts of Lucknow starting in 1858. It seems one of the areas worst affected was Qaiserbagh. Qaiserbagh brings memories of Etmad Rasool and his family.

Etmad was an interesting character: intelligent, short, awkward and non-athletic. I mentioned him briefly in relation to Bharat and his cricket. I call him intelligent because he did well in his examinations. But also he talked about things we did not understand like Indian and American politics. His mother was in the Constituent Assembly, the body that wrote the Indian Constitution. He used to talk about the politics in Delhi. Although I did not understand and do not remember specifics, it was impressive. He went to Delhi and stayed at the Western Court (where MPs reside) and that was another world. His sisters went to the United States in the late forties and he talked at length about the 1948 U.S Presidential elections. Again, I was quite ignorant of the significance of that. His sisters brought back Hawaiian shirts for Etmad and his brother Imtiaz. The boys wore those to school. What a stir that caused. We all dressed in white, khaki or blue and to have these boys wearing yellow shirts with flowers printed on them was shocking. The boys teased them and even teachers commented on "proper dress" and not imitating foreigners. This was clearly before Americanization of India and Lucknow.

I went to their house in Qaiserbagh a few times and seem to remember meeting his mother, Begum Aizaz Rasool. The house was in a courtyard of the wing of

Qaiserbagh palace that overlooked the road connecting Avadh Gymkhana club to the Qaiserbagh Circle. His house then was to the left. It had large rooms but I do not remember more. I will try to visit on my next trip.

Another interesting student was Prem Kumar (Kuki). He was self declared rich and told us that his father owned many factories. If a button broke on his shirt he would say, "No problem my father owns a button factory." He was the only person who had chewing gum and he used to dole it out to us. He stood with his cache and gave out half a stick to each boy. If we went alone he would ask us to bring a partner.

Midhat Kazim was another boy who stands out. He was aggressive, extroverted and not outstanding in studies. He was a performer, at least in the classroom. He did highly stylized boxing demonstrations with loose wrists and sound effects. He narrated *"Jhansi-ki-Rani"* with sound effects, fencing, and other actions. One time I visited his house. (I am surprised that I did visit the homes of my classmates given the rules I had.) I remember a really dirty, disorganized place. Papers and clothes were strewn all over with thick layers of dust on the papers and books. Why I went there, what we did and where he lived I do not recall.

I remember a boy from Datia state. He wore diamond earrings and had a soft voice. He once described in class a prank he played at the railway station. They put rocks on the track and said the carriage hit it and rolled back. Mr. Sharma gently explained to him how dangerous it was. He used an expression something like yes'm.

Satendrajit Singh and his two brothers were in school with us. They were rich *Taluqedars*, very aggressive and show offs. I had a few run-ins with them. Later in the seventies I re-connected with Satendrajit. He was an active hunter and abusive towards ecological or conservation movements. Needless to say, I did not keep up a relationship.

Isanagar was a strange character. He was the heir to the estate of Isanager. In his family the heir was not given a name until he took over the power. He described how young servant girls were provided to him for sex and all he had to do to prevent pregnancy was to make them sit up.

In terms of what happened to so – and – so, the most bizarre is Arun Bhandari. He came from Bahraich from a family of bureaucrats. He was an okay student and a fairly good friend. I lost touch with him. In the sixties, 12-15 years after leaving Colvin, I heard a story about Arun, which was almost frightening. Another Colvin classmate was in Bombay and traveled a lot. Arun came to his office once and offered to pay the premium for flight insurance if Arun was named the beneficiary. I wonder if he would have blown up the plane if the fellow had agreed.

Rajv Lochan was in school and I knew him fairly well. Much later, in the eighties I heard he was in the Embassy in Washington. I happened to be there and visited him. The fellow was so patronizing. He assumed I was there to ask for a favor. I was quite angry with his attitude.

Another person who was a good friend but died at a young age was Upendra Nath Jha. He was a nice fellow and good friend who went into the army. He developed Hodgkin's disease and died while I was in Medical College.

I will go back to the plays and performances at Colvin. All our performances, lectures and shows were in the library in the Junior Boys hostel. The library was just inside the gate of the hostel. It had a small antechamber where the librarian sat. He was the only person who looked after the library. He did the cataloguing, signing books in and out, and kept discipline in the library. I watched him write the information needed on the catalogue stickers with a very steady hand in a particular, prescribed style. Because I had a problem with my handwriting I noted that.

The plays were regularly done for *Janm Ashtami* in August. It was the only regular dramatic event we had. I participated a few times, once to recite a poem during which I got stage fright and once in 11th class when I played Krishna. A lot of creative energy went into these performances. Mr. L.P. Bharadwaj and Mr. Sheo Raj Singh are the ones I remember as being most involved. I have already talked about Mr. Bharadwaj. Mr. S.R. Singh came a little later. He was a poet, singer and play director. He used to hum during rehearsals, help with music - there was always at least a chorus or two. I once saw him just sitting during rehearsals and writing a poem as he hummed along.

One year there was a piece in English. It was a translation from the *Geeta*, presumably for the benefit of the English principal and his friends. One of the parts of the *Janmastami* play was a shadow play, which was hi-tech to us. Some other shows I remember being in the library include Mr. Kitchlew's talk on art, a magician, a man who taught us to be self reliant, and a talk on the capture of Jhanda Daku.

I already mentioned Mr. Kitchlew's talk on art. We had a Magician who did the usual stuff — hats, hankies, but also a mind control trick. He wrote a number on a board and did not show it to anyone. He chose four boys at random and told them to write down the first number that came to their mind. One of them selected was my friend Anil. Lo and behold, he added up the four numbers that the boys gave him and they equaled the number he had written down previously!! Anil said he felt a funny sensation in his head when he was asked to write down the number that came to his head. As I write this, Anil was supposed to be here but he never showed up.

Another interesting event was a talk by a British police officer who described how he captured the notorious *dacoit* Jhanda Daku. I recall him as a chubby man with a monocle, but not the exploits or the talk.

One time we had an elocution contest held in the library. The theme was on the evils of smoking. Most of the boys said the usual things about how smoking hurt your health. However, one boy, Ratin Nath Sen, spoke on the benefits of smoking. One of his comments was something like, "A wife may fail, but a pipe never." Ratin went on to become a nuclear physicist and settled in Israel.

Another noteworthy event was a recruiting film shown in the school. It was screened in the front hockey field. Why in a school where the oldest students were just 18! I remember it had a story of a young man who joined the army, learnt a lot of good things and came back to visit his village. He was appalled by the poverty and filth and somehow the army training enabled him to reform his village. This film has been on my mind all this time, why I don't know, but I needed to write about it.

At Colvin, we were self-confident, maybe over confident. We were anglicized by the nature of our school and we thought it gave us an extra edge in everything. We did do well in cricket against other schools, but not against La Martiniarre, which had the only other serious cricket team. We seldom played hockey or football against other schools.

One time we competed in a city-wide gymnastic competition, a choreographed exercise drill really. We practiced hard - clapping hands in front, above, left, right, under bent knees etc. We thought we got it when we managed to do the same movement with short whistles from the teacher for each move. When we got to the school where the competition was being held, we found that their teams did the whole routine in quick succession without a break and in unison. We were bad to begin with, and performed really badly - quite an insult for the elite school. In scholastic competitions too we had very few students who got top rankings in state-wide competitions. We had a good number of admissions to colleges, professional colleges, the army, and the administrative services

Digressing from Colvin, I have two memories of my short stay at St. Agnes School. It was there I noticed for the first time that eyeballs move. There was a boy whom I looked at, and his eyeballs moved as he was looking around. I guess I had noticed that before but it came as a surprise. Another was that of a girl who saw a bee and screamed when the bee was near her. I don't know if the bee stung her. But the screaming has stayed in my memory. Those are my earliest sensory memories. The next one was probably my fall at Colvin and my being taken care of by Mrs. Davidson. I also remember a condolence meeting we had when Rabindranath Tagore died. That would be in 1941. The *ghanta* (school bell) rang in the middle of the class; we all marched out to the school playing field near the Imlee tree, which was in the back of the quadrangle where the art class was. We stood in rows, the principal gave a short speech and we stood in silence for some time and returned to our classes. Usha di and Sushma di studied with Tagore in Shantiniketan.

General Sir Claude Auchinleck watching a game of hockey ca. 1945

General Sir Claude Auchinleck visited Colvin when he was a hero of the North African campaign and Commander in Chief of the British Indian Army. I am guessing that he visited because our vice-principal Mr. Brotherton had been in the army. I guess it was a big honor for the school for him to visit us. I recall the event vaguely.

After partition a few refugee students were admitted to Colvin. The one I remember from our class was a chap named Behel. I remember him because he once showed us a knife he carried. It was a good-sized knife built to conceal the blade and to look like a flat piece of plastic. I remember him showing it off and also that Ashhad Hussain was also playing with it. Behel had just been uprooted from a Muslim country but there did not seem to be any hard feelings between the boys.

Ashhad's father was in Government service and lived down the road from us. One day as we were returning from school on our bicycles a new Ford passed us. His father was driving it home from the dealers. Ashad got really excited and took off to enjoy the car at his house. I too was excited because we had also been expecting our new car at the same time; it was being driven from Bombay.

Nikhil Sidhanta was in Neetu's class, son of the professor of English. He was quite smart and tall. I remember him demonstrating the function of lungs at a science fair organized with the Annual Day. Another time he and Nilamber Chatterjee had a heated argument about whether *Brahmo Samajis* were Hindus or not. Nikhil. a *Brahmo*, was adamant that they were part of Hindus. Nilamber insisted they were like Christians. Nilamber's father was a professor of Chemistry. Here we had two Bengalis, both sons of university professors, having an argument about the fine points of their respective religions. It must have struck some cord in me for me to remember the event. But now, with all the debates about what is Hinduism and the push to create a pure Hindu state, this becomes interesting. Was there a Hindutva streak then? Was Dr. A.C. Chatterjee a believer in a conservative Hindu structure? The only thing I remember in reference to him is Papa calling him Fuhrer when he held some executive position in the university.

I had very little to do with university. We visited Rajju Bhal's house a few times and saw occasional cricket and tennis matches. Even in medical college, when I was technically a Lucknow University student, I hardly went there. One interesting visit was when a scaly anteater was caught somewhere in the forests around Lucknow. It was brought to the zoology department and a lot of people went to see it.

As I mentioned, we did have some university professors' children in our school. The Lucknow University did have a few prominent people on its faculty. Professor Radha Kamal Mukerjee in Economics, Professor DP Mukherjee in Sociology, Professor Birbal Sahani in Paleobotany were all well known names in India and in England. Dr. Sahani was a Fellow of the Royal Society. A Coelocanth was caught in the Arabian Sea in the early fifties and sent to Lucknow University's zoology department for study. The Coelocanth is said to be many millions of years older than the current types of fish and has remained unchanged. It was considered to be quite a major find and was a recognition of Lucknow University's reputation that it was sent there for study.

There are some general observations that are worth mentioning. Our teaching method was one of spoon feeding. We got very few chances to have dialogues with our teachers. But we did get solid teaching and Mr. Bharadwaj did engage us in some discussion. Our science laboratories were well equipped and we got a chance to do a lot of hands - on experiments. Discipline was enforced, but physical punishment was rare.

I remember a few funny situations. The Indus civilization of Mohanjodaro was excavated in the early twenties. In the mid forties we were taught about it. We were informed, amongst other things, that they had a system of piped water supply and sewers. I wrote an essay for my homework and said "they knew how to use water." The teacher had a good laugh at that.

In the Hindi and English classes we had some interesting excerpts from major writers. One was the story from Tolstoy about a man who went to settle where one could get as much land as you wanted - as long as you could claim it by covering the perimeter from sunrise to sunset. The man ran all day and as the sun was setting he got greedy and kept covering more and more land even when he was exhausted. He claimed a lot of land but in the end died as the sun set. He was buried in a grave of six feet. How much land does a man need? Six feet! The moral of the story has stayed with me.

One of the senior students who was an older, gentle soul, was Mohammed Mohsin. He was just kind and helpful to all the younger kids. He was like an elder brother whose support was very comforting.

Having done some reading of history and anthropology recently, I was reminded of Mr. H.B. Pande's remark about the man in Africa being the spoiled man of the tropics. His point was that because the people of Africa had plenty of food they were lazy and did not develop as a civilization. It was obviously the attitude put forward by the British Colonial powers.

The most interesting teacher I think was Mr. Abid Ali, somewhat of a rebel himself. He told us about Marx and Engles. He said Marx was a scholar who studied the crimes committed by the rich on the poor. He was so busy working that he had no time to shave or have a haircut. Communists, he said, imitate him by having beards and long hair. Unfortunately, I was too young and too focused on the core subjects to really think about his remarks at that time.

Mr. Bharadwaj taught us to discuss a chapter in one of our books on the "Impeachment of Warren Hastings." He said the impeachment of Warren Hastings, Governor General of India, was carried out by Edmund Burke and went on for months. Rooms were full of the transcripts of the impeachment. It was quite mesmerizing. William Dalrymple has written about Hastings and he depicts a different image.

During my years at Colvin we used a variety of pens. For Hindi we used a reed pen, which had to be shaped a certain way with a knife, cut at the tip at a precise angle, and dipped in ink. For English we had G nibs and Relief nibs. Fountain pens were discouraged, and ball point pens were not allowed.

I have reminisced about my childhood focusing on the place where I had all my schooling. There are many more memories, lots more events, people and things I could describe. But the gist of the story, the place, its people, its values are here. My role as narrator of these is clearly open to alternative reading and interpretation. These are recollections of events from the forties but written about in a new century. They are based on whatever makes a memory stick. Why I remember one thing and not another, why I remember one person and not the next, will always be a question. It would not change however, how a privileged group of young boys got a good education and then went on to various fields with differing degrees of success.

***

Chapter Fourteen
Education as I See It Now

I have described the schooling I had in the private school that I had the privilege of attending. It was a "we-they" phenomenon. I knew there were other schools run by the government or charitable organizations (mostly Christian) that had lower costs and whose students were probably from lower middle class families. I was vaguely aware of them. We had few interactions. I described the gymnastics competition we went to and how we did so poorly. Another time we had a hockey match with one of those schools. I did not witness it because it was held at the other school. During that match their boys attacked Aftab, who was one of our star players (and top student). I remember a few days later that Aftab was running in a race and his bandage from the previous injury came off. He continued to run and won. He was quite a hero.

Those other schools had a reputation for violence and strikes. It was "their" problem. I think students from those school participated in some of the demonstrations during the freedom movement. We never did, if only because we had an English principal. We even may have been supporting the British. I recall no act of protest that we were involved in.

We had a good student-teacher ratio. Our science laboratories were well equipped. Those schools had large classes. In the state run board examinations we had a good number of 1st and 2nd divisions, but it is interesting that the top students in the state never came from our school. We, as a family or a school, never thought about the large number of poor students who got no education at all. That is the way it was; we did not talk or think about it.

The only schools on a par with ours were the schools catering to Christian and Anglo-Indian students, like the La Martinairre schools (boys and girls) and the convent schools for well-to-do girls. Members of our family did go to La Martinairre; Meera went to La Martinairre girls for a short time. Cricket in those days was an upper class sport. La Martinairre boys was the only other school that had cricket and tennis so we were rivals in those areas. We were often compared in other areas as well.

Education in India remains problematic. The expanding middle class, estimated at three hundred million, has led to a demand for large numbers of schools. The government has not been able to meet the need. As a result, the upwardly mobile middle class (many of whose parents did not have good educational opportunities) is seeking private schools for their children. Education has become an industry and produces some good schools but also many private schools that are expensive but deliver poor quality. I know of a hard working taxi owner who works long hours, is constantly working on expanding his fleet, and has hopes for his son's future. He is spending about a quarter of his net income on a private school for his son.

I am lucky I got a good education; it has served me well. I acquired knowledge that qualified me to attend medical college. My confidence to hold my own is partly due to my education. And, with the help of my family, I was able to escape being narrow minded and am able to understand the world I live in.

***

APPENDIX

*Main building of King George's Medical College, Lucknow
Both my father and I trained here*

***

"SEVEN GIFTS OF LIFE"
ADDRESS TO FINAL YEAR STUDENTS
BY
Dr. V. S. MANGALIK

Delivered at the 38th Foundation Day Ceremony
of
King George's Medical College, Lucknow.
16th February, 1950

Sir Homi Mody, Reverend Acharyajee, Ladies and Gentlemen and my young friends—

I do not come as a stranger to this institution. I am like most of those present here today, an "old boy" of the institution, and my associations date back from 1920. For many years I have has the privilege of being associated with you in your academic work, with your athletic activities, and lately with your residence in the hostel. Let me acknowledge today before you all how I have enjoyed this privilege. My contacts with you in various capacities, and the impact of your youthful activities and buoyant outlook on life, have been a source of great inspiration and happiness in my advancing years.

Only the other day, when I mentioned to my daughter that I was to deliver the address this year, her spontaneous remark was "*Papa tum bhi bore karo gay kya?*" During the preceeding years, at the end of the College Day, I have often overheard remarks such as "*Bhai bore ho gay*"; "*Yar bore Kar diya*", and, if I mistake not, these free gratuitouis pieces of advice repeated year after year, have been responsible for the prolific linguistic coinage of expressions such as "*BORYEAT*", "*BORAYALLIS*" and even the creation of a new genus in the Bacterial Kingdom "*BOROCOCCUS*".

I am fully conscious of this honour, the honour that is mine today, in being asked to address you. This honour, however, reminds me of the passage of years. I feel that this honour should usually be reserved for grave and revered persons who have reached an age when "one consoles oneself by giving advice for being no longer able to set a bad example." I do not believe in giving "good advice." But since this tradition of giving addresses to Final Year students has to be honoured, I have thought of a way out. Suppose you were capable of flights of imagination, and I am sure you are. Now suppose I was a good fairy, let me ask you what gifts I should bestow on you on the eve of your setting out on a medical career? By that cunning approach, I hope I may be able to slip in some good advice without your noticing it!

The first gift I would bestow on you would be good luck. Pure luck is one of the chief factors in making for happiness and success in life. Luck in your background, in your home and parents; luck in your choice of a medical college – and if we are not too self-complacent, you have all been lucky in your choice and the privilege of studying in the King George's. I wish you luck in your examinations, and in appointments becoming vacant just when you want them. I wish you luck in the selection of your life's partner – your wife or husband as the case may be. It is no exaggeration to say that most people owe all or nearly all their success in life to luck. As you will soon discover for yourself, "good luck always brings merit, but merit seldom brings good luck."

But even if you be lacking in it in certain respects, let us remember that hard work and patience can make up for that lack of good luck to a large extent. May I also suggest to combine hard work with single-mindedness of purpose? I have had the privilege of being approached by some of you to help you to decide what to do after obtaining your qualifications. My advice always has been to develop a single-mindedness of purpose. Formulate your values of life carefully; think and decide what you want of life – plenty of money and physical comforts or the many other beautiful things of life which can be obtained with lesser amounts of wealth. You have to know your own mind – the sooner the better. Take advice from any one you like – your parents, friends or teachers. But the ultimate decision to join a particular walk of life, to accept a job or service or take to a specialty of your profession, should be yours and yours alone. Once the decision has been made, work for it, stick to it, do not falter. Follow the line without regrets or hesitation. You have no reason to blame others for your failure, and the credit and the satisfaction of success will be all your own.

Health would be my next gift. Remember medicine is a dangerous profession, and therein lies one of its glories. You have before you years of hard and strenuous work. There is nothing so tragic as a sick doctor. I wish you good health, not the athlete's type but that type of constitution which is able to resist fatigue and infection. It would be futile to lay down rules advocated by health cranks, and even if I did, the conditions of your work would not allow your following them. There are, of course, many ways in which health can be ruined – and you know them as well as I do.

Another of my gifts would be equanimity – the power, as Kipling has said, "to turn a keen untroubled face home to the instant need of things." As a doctor, you will often have to face sudden and disconcerting emergencies. No quality of the mind will be more essential for you. It will also do much to preserve you from the corroding effects of those worries from which, as a doctor, there is no escape for you. Some of us are born anxious-minded "born-worriers", if I may say so. Let me comfort you by saying that time and experience tend to produce a degree of equanimity in most of us. But I would not like you to confuse equanimity with indifference.

Having thus bestowed on you, my young friends, good luck and health, coupled with the power to work hard, and an equable temperament, I find that I have still some gifts in reserve for you, gifts of the greatest importance, gifts of character perhaps; and they are: a sense of justice; a sense of human understanding; a sense of humour; and a sense of beauty.

Cultivate a sense of justice to your patient; always give him a fair deal. To do so you must make it your duty to keep abreast of the advances in medical knowledge; for it is unjust that your patient should not have the benefit of the latest and the most recent remedies. A sense of justice to your professional brethren will allow you enter into an honourable competition with them, you will take no unfair advantage and will be slow to believe what you hear to their discredit. Also, be conscious of a sense of what is just to yourself and that you are not being exploited, and a sense of justice to the profession you are going to follow. Remember, your profession has an honourable and hoary background of service and it is up to you to see that the dignity and the honour of medicine is properly respected in your person. A sense of justice is a moral as much as an intellectual quality. Though not a clinician myself, I am sure I am not wrong when I say that the art of diagnosis consists largely in giving due and just weight to each of the signs and symptoms that your patient presents, as well as to the laboratory findings. Diagnosis is an exercise of this judicial faculty, and forms a major part of medicine. A development of this particular sense of justice will help make you a skilled healer of the sick.

Now as to a sense of human-understanding. So far, you have been much segregated from fellow human beings, as a student of your college for a period of five or six years, rarely even meeting fellow students of the other faculties of your University. And even after you have qualified, you will be forced to lead a professional life which shuts you out from your fellow men. Your leisure will not only be restricted, but irregular and uncertain. And thus you will have very limited freedom to make human contacts. It is this regrettable aspect of your life which makes me bestow on you a sense of human understanding. Even for the fulfillment of your professional destiny itself, you require the background of a broad humanising outlook. It seems to me that it is as essential for you to know how people live, in what surroundings they work and what they eat and drink as it is for you to know what they suffer from and how they die. You have to develop an intimate understanding of the patient as a whole, man or woman, with a home and anxieties and economic problems, a past and a future, a job to be lost or held. It is this intimate and humane understanding of your patients, your fellowmen, your comrades in society that I would recommend to you in the largest measure.

I would also bestow on you're a sense of humour. Some of you may regard it as curious that humour should be a valuable gift for a doctor to possess, but I feel that it is so. It will help you to bear with the vagaries of your patients and those of their relatives, and to derive amusement instead of annoyance from the eccentricities of your colleagues. Humour will save you from the sins of your profession – pomposity and "showing off." Humour will prevent you from taking yourself and your work too seriously. It will remind you that besides your work there are many other things also in life worth having. Remember humour is not cultivated alone or in solitude. If you wish to develop it in yourself, you must mix with your fellow beings and take your part in the intellectual, emotional and cultural life of society.

And lastly a sense of beauty. This may appear a rather luxurious gift for a doctor. We often hear you say that you have seen today a "lovely" case of lupus, or rodent ulcer or cancer. I am sure you do not mean to be taken literally. Nor do I mean to bestow this type of sense of beauty on you. Disease is ugly and most of you will be forced to fight it in ugly surroundings – in the dark, dingy, depressing houses of the poor, in the remote, dusty and dirty villages. From all this life, you will find in the appreciation of the many beautiful things of life, a compensation and even a way of escape, if necessary. It will have a sanifying and steadying influence. This sense of beauty will not, and need not, take the same form in all of you. Some will find comfort and refreshment in art, others in music. To some the study of literature, progressive or classics, pieces of prose or verse which are beyond the touch of time, will be a refuge. Your professional readings should not crowd out your reading of general literature. Some of you who the fairy godmother have given no appreciation of art, music or literature will find escape in gardening. Gardening offers a large and varied choice of enjoyments – fresh air, exercise, the contemplation of natural beauty, and the satisfaction of success. It is restful and brings peace of mind which often drives away cares and carries us beyond tiring thoughts and corroding worries. Every one of you will have to find beauty in his or her own way – and this sense will help you to struggle with pains and troubles and out of their mist snatch your joys.

And thus, my dear friends, concludes my list of gifts. You are entering your professional life in times which are truly great – as great as they are critical. A new era has dawned on us. This political freedom is the forerunner of another revolution – the freedom from exploitation of human beings by human beings. And take it from me that we as doctors have great parts to play in there.

After generations of torpor and stagnation, we are beginning to be awake and active again. Human values have changed and are fast changing, and the time is not far distant when you will be free to evolve new cultural values as our ancestors did in the past. These changes in our social, political and economic values of life are not particular to us or our country alone. The world as a whole is being swept by mighty forces. The turmoil and upheaval all round, to my mind, are the birth pangs in the creation of a new social order. We all – each one of us, will have to play a part in the looking after, nursing and welfare of this baby-freedom of ours and of humanity at large.

On the horizon of our own professional world, a new ideal, a new order and a new conception is slowly but steadily rising and has brought about a new orientation in the practice and application of the medical science. Medicine, in the near future, will have to be applied to the service of man as a fellow or comrade. You will have to visualise the practice of medicine as a better understanding and more abiding cure of all the main and contributory troubles of human beings. Medical science is being called upon to study the welfare of human beings in relation to the whole fabric of society. The day is beginning to dawn when medicine will not be sold to the people in the open market, but will be looked upon as a public service to which society is inherently entitled.

Let me hope that armed with some of these gifts you will be able to contribute your share, willingly and happily, in this glorious task of the uplift and betterment of humanity and in shaping of a society of mentally and physically healthy people. Let me hope too that you will be able to face bravely and with equanimity all the weariness and ugliness which your lives as doctors have in store for you.

God bless you.

***

ABOUT THE AUTHOR

Dr. Aroop Mangalik was born and raised in North India in the historic city of Lucknow, site of the state capital and home of one of the oldest universities and medical colleges in India.

After completing his medical training in Lucknow, Delhi, and then in the United States in Chicago and Salt Lake City, Dr. Mangalik served on the faculties of medical schools in Delhi, Denver, and Albuquerque. For many years he was active as a hematologist/oncologist at the University of New Mexico Medical School. Now professor emeritus, he continues to teach students and trainees at UNM.

Dr. Mangalik has also been active in efforts to reduce medically futile treatments, and is a strong advocate for end of life choices and patient comfort.

Made in the USA
San Bernardino, CA
09 July 2013